KULTURWISSENSCHAFTLICHE ZEITSCHRIFT

Herausgegeben von der

Kulturwissenschaftlichen Gesellschatt

Heft 4/2023

FELIX MEINER VERLAG
HAMBURG

Bibliographische Information der Deutschen Nationalbibliothek

Die Deutsche Nationalbibliothek verzeichnet diese Publikation in der Deutschen Nationalbibliographie; detaillierte bibliographische Daten sind im Internet über ‹https://portal.dnb.de› abrufbar.

ISBN 978-3-7873-4894-7 · ISBN eBook 978-3-7873-4896-1
ISSN (Print) 2751-3106 · ISSN (eJournal) 2451-1765

© Felix Meiner Verlag Hamburg 2024
Druck: Books on Demand, Norderstedt
Printed in Germany

Inhalt

Helen Hester

Space Agency

Automation, Autonomy, and Acid Astronautics

ABSTRACT: This essay looks at the figure of the cyborg via its origins in mid-twentieth century American astronautics. It begins by comparing different approaches to the ›space cyborg‹, helping to situate it within the distinctive cultural preoccupations of its times and places. The discussion then proceeds to consider the American cyborg's roots in two discursive regimes: that surrounding military masculinities, and that surrounding the non-human or de-humanized medical test subject. Via an analysis of the 1976 sci-fi novel *Man Plus* by Frederik Pohl, the essay explores how this dual heritage generates tensions in terms of gender, before concluding with an analysis of the ways in which the cyborg's mutable embodiment runs aground on the perceived fixity of human sexuality. How might we use the historical concept of the cyborg to queer the notion of ›participant evolution‹ today?

KEYWORDS: Cyborg; astronautics; TESCREAL; gender and sexuality

1. Introduction

This essay looks at the figure of the cyborg via its origins in mid-twentieth century American astronautics, as part of a wider effort to explore the mutability of the body and ideas around ›participant evolution‹. It will consider the ways in which the human itself is framed as a kind of building material in these discourses, while also exploring the perceived limits to this in terms of gender and sexuality. Over the course of the discussion, we will draw on debates within and around 60s and 70s astronautics to help situate the cyborg (and/as the astronaut) in the context of broader American cultural preoccupations of the era. This will involve reference to discussions from within the field itself, as well as to science fictional texts informed by this discourse. We will use one novel in particular – *Man Plus* by Frederik Pohl (1976) – as a case study via which to explore how ideas about gender, agency, and the (post)humanity of the cyborg are taken up or textually contested.

The opening half of the essay looks for informative comparisons, first in contemporary debates about human enhancement for space travel and exoplanetary living, and then in the Soviet space programme of the 1960s. These comparisons indicate that the cyborg (as we understand it here) is to some extent a product of both its time and its place, thereby providing a rationale for the temporally and spatially delimited discussion that follows. Despite Donna Haraway's famous claim that »the cyborg has no origin story« (1991, 150–151), we can nevertheless admit that it *does* have beginnings. Considering these beginnings might, as I hope to demonstrate in the course of this essay, enrich our appreciation and deepen our understanding of the cyborg's varied afterlives and ongoing cultural influence.

Having undertaken some of this necessary ground-clearing, the second half of our discussion will turn more directly to the relationship between human agency and cyborgian adaptation. In what ways does the figure of the twentieth-century cyborg express, build upon, and ultimately compromise a specific fantasy of the all-American astronaut? Where does the extension of human freedom, via the flexible and trans-formable body, run up against entrenched ideas about essence and the unchangeable, and how should we respond to said ideas? Such questions will be considered in due course. We will start, however, by simply introducing the cyborg and by teasing out some of its connections with both the militarized space programme and the pharma-ceutical research of the period. This dual heritage, as we will see as the essay progresses, places the cyborg in an ambiguous position in terms of its agential capacity – and raises some particularly interesting questions about the immutability (or otherwise) of gender and sexuality.

2. The Cyborg: A Creature of its Time and Place?

The cyborg – »hybrid of machine and organism, a creature of social reality as well as a creature of fiction« (Haraway, 1991: 149) – has long been an animating figure within technofeminist imaginaries as well as within wider culture. The writer Tim Maly points out that our conception of the cyborg revolves largely around the idea of »non-hereditary adaptation. Technological interventions that change the course of biological existence« (2010: n.p.). This is apparent in many of the earliest articulations of the idea of the cybernetic organism. The cyborg emerged in the era of the space race – the word was coined in 1960, just two years after the formation of NASA – and is inexorably entwined with another significant figure of mid-century cultural fantasy: the astronaut.

At this time, there was great interest in meeting the technical challenges of survival in extra-terrestrial environments. As Maly notes, one possible way to respond to the challenges of being off-planet is to think prosthetically or architecturally: »Using the latest construction techniques, you can build a little bubble of earth, and plunk it down on any old alien world. We can send people off to these environments and so long as the walls don't burst and the air doesn't run out, they've got all the comforts of home« (2010, n.p.). Of course, there's a profound degree of vulnerability at play here, just as there is when humans venture into inhospitable *terrestrial* environments – the ocean floors, extreme heat or cold, and so on. From their »departures to the end of their missions, [space envoys] are encased within extensive infrastructures of ground and in-situ support, relying upon intricate arrangements of sophisticated technical apparatus, precise logistics protocols, and pools of expert labour« (Damjanov, 2023: 328). The individual is entirely dependent upon these infrastructures for basic, minute to minute survival.

This vulnerability tends to be somewhat obscured in cultural discourses around astronautics – to the point where, as Haraway notes, the image of man in space has become perversely totemic of »an ultimate self untied at last from all dependency« (1991: 151). The people who popularized the idea of the cyborg, however, were very aware of the exposure of the human in space. In a seminal essay from 1960 – widely viewed as the formative text of cyborg studies – Manfred E. Clynes and Nathan S. Kline write that

> [a]rtificial atmospheres encapsulated in some sort of enclosure constitute only temporizing, and dangerous temporizing at that, since we place ourselves in the same position as a fish taking a small quantity of water along with him to live on land. The bubble all too easily bursts. (1960: 27)

As Benjamin Bratton strikingly puts it, making a wider point about the erosion of »life support systems« here on Earth (2019: 49), the space-walking astronaut is »a pink putty sculpture unable to leave its home without bringing an artificial atmosphere with it as it toddles outward« (2019: 48–49). Hence, Clynes and Kline suggest that, rather than creating an environment-bubble to encapsulate and temporarily support the body, one should instead fit the body of the astronaut to his extra-terrestrial environment.

In the words of their 1961 paper »Drugs, Space, and Cybernetics: Evolution to Cyborgs«, if »man attempts a partial adaptation to the conditions of space instead of being insistent that he carry his entire environment with him, a number of new possibilities appear« (Kline and Clynes, 1961: 347). They propose that man »use his creative intelligence to adapt himself to the space conditions he seeks rather than take as much of earth environment with him as possible. This is to be achieved through the Cyborg, an extension of organic homeostatic controls by means of cybernetic techniques« (1961: 370). So, whilst breathing is »an excellent system for metabolism in an atmosphere with adequate oxygen supply and low carbon dioxide content [...] on other planets atmospheric conditions are all wrong for this purpose« (1961: 356). In this situation, one should not resort to the creation of protective architectural complexes. Rather, »an artificial organ should be provided to replace the lung«, making breathing unnecessary (1961: 356). The cyborg, one might say, is a call for *anthropoforming* over terraforming as a means of extending human agency and mitigating prosthetic-technological dependency.

Here we see the idea of non-hereditary adaptation at play: »In the past evolution brought about the altering of bodily functions to suit different environments«, Clynes and Kline declare (1960: 26). »Starting as of now, it will be possible to achieve this to some degree *without alteration of heredity* by suitable biochemical, physiological, and electronic modifications of man's existing modus vivendi« (1960: 26, original emphasis). They propose a range of potential modifications to adapt the individual human to the rigours of space travel, from artificially induced hibernation to regimens of sensory stimulation, yoga, and hypnosis. Appropriately enough for the 1960s, many of their suggested interventions involve controlled substances or experimental drugs. They toy with the idea of using an »anesthetizing substance of the cocaine series« (Kline and Clynes, 1961: 360) to assist with the sensory disorientation caused by weightlessness, for example, and call for the use of »psychic energizers« such as amphetamines to enhance wakefulness and efficiency on long, monotonous journeys (Kline and Clynes, 1961: 354).

Of the cyborg's two originators, it was Nathan S. Kline who particularly specialized in this area; he was part of the American College of Neuropsychopharmacology, and a member of its Study Group for the Effects of Psychotropic Drugs in Normal Humans.[1] The proceedings of the group's 1967 meeting – which features several contributions attributed to Kline – reveals a keen interest in the intersection of neuropsychopharmacology and astronautics, including a chapter speculating on the future of LSD. A specialist essay on the topic argues that one possible application of »drugs or procedures which alter consciousness may be for individuals who are subjected to prolonged periods of isolation and separation from the usual daily activities of man, such as long space voyages of the future or assignment to remote communications stations« (Kurland et al., 1971: 105–106).

This was the era of ›turn on, tune in, drop out‹, of course, as well as ›better living through chemistry‹, and the cyborg can be seen as representative of a kind of acid astronautics – a figure of speculation grounded in an idea of the prosthetically, pharmaceutically, and otherwise manipulable character of humanity. Indeed, as Alex Dymock's work suggests, this relationship was far from unidirectional. Just as 60s astronautics looked to controlled substances to facilitate non-hereditary adaptations supportive of manned spaceflight, so too did the drugs research and advocacy of the period position psychedelics as specifically evolutionary technologies. Within these discourses, human flourishing is »recast as a kind of striving for evolutionary perfectionism, in which the effects of psychedelics are satisfactorily predictable and measurable enough that they have an evidenced utility that might be used to promote the psychedelic experience to others« (Dymock, 2023: 829).

---

1   I would like to thank Dr Alex Dymock for alerting me to this in the course of our early correspondence about this article.

3. Acid Astronautics, Past and Present

As »radical as these ideas seemed at the time [...], the space-medicine community took them seriously« – at least for a while (Kline, 2009: 342). NASA commissioned an 8-month study, the results of which were published in 1963 as »Engineering Man for Space: The Cyborg Study«. By thorough research into »man's systems and subsystems when subjected to the simulated and actual conditions of extraterrestrial environments«, the report claims, »we will be able to make significant progress toward the better understanding of man as a space voyager« (Driscoll, 1963: 78). The cyborg study concerned itself with the determination of »man's capabilities and limitations under the unpredictable and often hostile conditions of space flight, and the theoretical possibility of incorporating artificial organs, drugs, and/or hypothermia as integral parts of the life support systems in space craft design in the future« (Driscoll, 1963: 76). The influence of Clynes and Kline is palpable throughout – including in the focus on pharmaceutical solutions to a range of issues, including »anxiety, depression, fatigue, [...] metabolism reduction and motion sickness« (Driscoll, 1963: 76–77).

This was a moment when the American counter-culture and military-industrial complex alike were pursuing interests in altered states of consciousness – the CIA, for instance, was looking into possible applications of LSD and hypnosis in psychological torture during the Cold War. Figures such as Clynes (with his ›far out‹ interests in biocybernetics, human creativity, and the communication of emotion) and Kline (with his research into psychopharmacologic drugs) seem in some ways to span these two worlds. Across the ideological spectrum of mid-century America, there was great interest in the utility and untapped potential of controlled substances. To what extent does this interest continue to shape astronautics today, in the face of the »intensification of space activities« characteristic of recent efforts to »commercialise and militarise space« (Salazar and Gorman, 2023: 1)? We can allow ourselves a few brief comments here, as we seek to understand what of the cyborg is unique to its foundational moment and how much of it has endured across time.

Certainly, the broad idea of cyborgian adaptation remains popular in some circles, with thinkers continuing to argue that »our species, *Homo sapiens*, will likely change, through continued evolution, some self-directed, and through human enhancements« (Rappaport and Corbally, 2020: 6). Researchers still point to the necessity of »unnatural selection« in terms of enabling humans (or our successor species) to become multi-planetary (Abood, 2020: 47), with some even suggesting that a »stage of ›directed evolution‹ [...] is an essential step for *life itself* to survive« (Mason, 2021: xii-xiii, original emphasis). We can also detect similarities in terms of the countercultural reference points (and approaches to controlled substance use) coming to inform research agendas within the field, particularly when one looks to the influence of Silicon Valley on contemporary astronautics. Tech companies are very much in the fold of today's space exploration and resource race, with billionaires »pouring millions into ›disrupting‹ space, NASA, and the space programme of yore« (Morozov, 2015: n.p.). As NASA itself puts it, »We will go forward to the Moon, through Silicon Valley – bridging public and private partnerships to capitalize on the innovation and entrepreneurship« of the region (n.d.: n.p.).

That the cyborg remains very much on the table when it comes to the state's new commercial partners is reflected in the tech sector's so-called Tescrealism. The acronym ›TESCREAL‹ has been developed to refer to a bundle of beliefs spanning transhumanism, extropianism, singularitarianism, cosmism, rationalism, effective altruism and longtermism. As a concept, it has some merit; the »various ›-isms‹ overlap in their history and ideology« (Troy, 2023: n.p.), and the acronym allows us to latch on to an apparent taste for the messianic within Silicon Valley communities. However, a Tescrealist framework also risks overemphasising the points of convergence and crossover between its component philosophies, presenting a loose nexus of ideas as a coherent intellectual framework on the basis of sometimes weak associations and the fact that assorted tech industry figures have expressed them. Certain networks of people mapping onto certain networks of ideas is not, to my mind, sufficiently solid ground upon which to construct a critical edifice. As such, I use the acronym somewhat warily (even if I can appreciate its broad explanatory utility).

As Émile P. Torres (who coined the term with computer scientist Timnit Gebru) would have it, the Tescreal bundle equates to

> a techno-utopian vision of the future in which we re-engineer humanity, colonize space, plunder the cosmos, and establish a sprawling intergalactic civilization full of trillions and trillions of ›happy‹ people, nearly all of them ›living‹ inside enormous computer simulations. In the process, all our problems will be solved, and eternal life will become a real possibility. (2023: n.p.)

For Torres, a Tescrealist emphasis on re-engineering humanity for a high-tech, spacefaring future indicates precisely why this worldview might be ethically problematic. He points to the prospect of our replacement by genetically modified posthumans who might »integrate various technologies into their bodies, perhaps connecting their brains to the internet« (2023: n.p.) – cyborgs, in other words. Silicon Valley's lack of repulsion at this prospect then comes to act as one apparently self-evident basis for denouncing Tescreal thinking.

This approach to Tescrealism leaves something to be desired. While we should indeed be highly sceptical of the forms of futures fetishization the acronym attempts to critique, many of the tendencies nested within it have (as Eli Sennesh and James J. Hughes point out) »a progressive political wing that has been ignored. Moreover, the wholesale condemnation of these ideas has cast a pall over all thinking about humanity's future when we desperately need to grapple with the implications of emerging technologies« (2023: n.p.). That being said, it is nevertheless suggestive (for the purposes of this article) that transhumanism and cosmism are included and entangled within the umbrella concept now thought to be defining the bleeding edge of the tech sector. As the influence of such concepts makes clear, the cyborgian preoccupations of the 60s and 70s are continuing to inform ideas around technical development and American space exploration, but under new economic conditions and in an altered cultural context.

The same might be claimed for the »counter-culture libertarianism« of the period (Barbrook and Cameron, 1995: n.p.). A grain of radicalism has always lurked within Silicon Valley, attributable in part to the so-called Californian Ideology (famously characterized as an »eclectic blend of conservative economics and hippie libertarianism« (Barbrook and Cameron, 1995: n.p.). As Richard Barbrook and Andy Cameron put it back in 1995, knowledge workers in the American tech industry are »both a privileged part of the labour force and heirs of the radical ideas of […] community media activists«, with the result that the »cultural divide between the hippie and the organisation man has now become rather fuzzy« (Barbrook and Cameron, 1995: n.p.). Given these commitments and inheritances, it should come as no surprise to find esoteric mid-century research agendas making a partial comeback via an avowed openness to recreational psychedelics and the workplace benefits of mind-expanding drugs (to be found most obviously in the discourses around microdosing).[2] A recent article for the *Wall Street Journal* points to the existence of a Silicon Valley »drug movement that proponents hope will expand minds, enhance lives and produce business breakthroughs« (Grind and Bindley, 2023: n.p.). Acid astronautics rides again – this time for profit!

The role of controlled substances such as LSD in the space programme was always marginal at best, however, and the relationship between government agencies and tech sector cultural disruptors continues to be somewhat uncomfortable. There would appear to be something of a cultural misalignment here, particularly when it comes to attitudes surrounding *recreational* pharmaceuticals. This is reflected in NASA's recent decision to conduct a »cultural assessment study in coordination with [its] commercial partners to ensure the companies are meeting NASA's requirements for workplace safety, including the adherence to a drug-free environment« (quoted in Koren, 2018: n. p.). These reviews followed (and were allegedly prompted by) SpaceX founder Elon Musk's public use of marijuana; one can imagine what NASA might make of his recent favourable comments about ketamine. Thus, we have seen that there are continuities

---

2   »Microdosing – taking small amounts of a substance such as ketamine or LSD – is regularly promoted in Silicon Valley as a way to improve productivity or creativity or treat depression and anxiety« (Titcomb, 2023: n.p.).

between the mid-century rise of the cyborg and twenty-first century astronautics, as evinced by research interests in human enhancement, by the perceived influence of cosmism, transhumanism, and related Tescreal viewpoints, and by a wider work/play drugs movement underpinning the space-facing enterprises of Silicon Valley. Where might we identify *dis*continuities, and how have these changed the tenor of the discourse around cyborgian adaptation today?

Notably, while an engagement with psychoactive substances (from caffeine to ketamine) may now be part and parcel of the corporate culture behind commercial space travel and prospective exoplanetary living – leaving »boards and businesses to wrestle with their responsibilities to a workforce that frequently uses« (Grind and Bindley, 2023: n.p.) – there has been something of a move *away* from such substances within the academic of field astronautics itself. Indeed, there is some obvious discomfort with the idea of the astronaut on drugs, with scholarly commentators often taking particular pains to disavow the idea of participant evolution aiming at increased *pleasure and enjoyment*. NASA researcher Christopher E. Mason's radically optimistic and far-reaching plan for life on other worlds over the next 500 years, for example, sounds an uncustomary note of caution when it comes to recreational enhancement. Noting that epigenetic-editing methods might, at some future point, conceivably enable people to »increase their enjoyment of a drug a hundredfold while taking half the quantity«, he suggests that this could represent an unprecedented and »terrifyingly uncontrolled experiment in cellular disruption and regulatory perturbation« (Mason, 2021: 166).

This would seem to be somewhat out of step with the so-called corporate drugs movement discussed above. Indeed, it may be that such approaches are a reaction not (just) against the spectre of mid-century acid astronautics, but precisely against the Tescrealist currents of contemporary space tech. Some scholarly approaches to space and society seek to explicitly differentiate and distance themselves from a supposedly less reputable transhumanist movement, which is condemned for pursuing changes in human consciousness via »psychoactive drugs« and »physical excess« (Rappaport and Corbally, 2020: 8).[3] An association with Silicon Valley proselytizing may well be seen as something of a liability for those working in less overtly ›disruptive‹ discursive traditions.[4]

---

[3] Indeed, Andrew B. Newburg and David B. Yates explicitly disregard »psychedelic substances« as an approach to managing the »psychological risks of astronaut missions«, and prefer instead to celebrate *wonder* as a »non-pharmacological stimulus for self-transcendence« (2020: 109)!

[4] This would appear to be in accord with Dymock's assertion that psychedelics research more broadly has seen a push to recast controlled substances as principally »medicines or biotechnologies [...]. The framing of their use as purely scientific gives research credibility in the public imaginary, which undoubtedly has had some role to play in the relaxation of laws around possession in some US states« (2023: 820).

Perhaps the more significant factor behind the de-emphasis on drugs in the reframing of the cyborg lies in the shifting biomedical landscape, however. It is important to note that the mechanisms via which non-hereditary adaptations are imagined to be pursued has changed significantly along with the state of scientific and technical knowledge. Whereas once *pharmaco-cybernetic* frameworks dominated discussions about the future of space exploration, today we increasingly find a focus on brain-computer interfaces and (most particularly) gene editing. The University of California recently received a $20 million grant from the US Department of Defense to use CRISPR technologies to »find a genetic alteration that would protect radiation patients, soldiers, and eventually astronauts from exposure to radiation« (Munévar, 2020: 117), for example. Mason's plan, meanwhile, leans into the idea of »resource-saving genetic protocols, such as reducing the amount of required oxygen for cellular function« (2021: 134). Participant evolution is thus imagined to be pursued primarily via new means, with the emphasis on *recoding* the organism rather than pharmaceutically enhancing its consciousness. This is one reason why it makes sense to limit the temporal scope of one's analysis when discussing the image and impact of the biotechnologically enhanced astronaut.

If *mid-twentieth century* America produced one version of the space cyborg, shaped at the interface of experimental drugs, counter-cultural ascendancy and the scientific-military-industrial complex, *early-twenty-first century* America produces another. Today's cyborg emerges instead from the intersection of recreational and productivity-enhancing psychoactives, corporate libertarianism, and space faring via public-private partnership – as well as from the counter-discourses responding to all of these. These two versions of the space cyborg may be sisters, but they are not twins; commonalities and differences abound. The cyborg, then, is a creature both in and across time. Does this also hold when it comes to place?

4. Agential Astronauts and Situated Cyborgs

As we have seen, the cyborg emerged as an attempt to mitigate some of the bodily vulnerability inevitably involved in carbon-based Earthlings attempting to leave their terrestrial home. This vision of overcoming physical precarity via biotechnologies is of course extremely partial. As crip theorists have long argued, living with technologies »does not always mean an effortless integration between bodies and machines that inherently ›fixes‹ bodies; rather, it is continuously labour-intensive and often a source of pain, requiring adaptation, negotiation, and technological maintenance« (Gál and Armstrong, 2023: 164). Nevertheless, however, the cyborg, in its mid-century instantiations, is imagined to represent an approach to counteracting bodily vulnerability and an attempt to technically intervene in the course of biological existence. This framing has notable connections with those media images of the all-American astronaut with which it is contemporary – images that position this figure as the very embodiment of human ingenuity and accomplishment, transcending species limits to make new things possible.

Given that the »space cyborg« is a direct continuation, as well as a speculative extension, of the space*man*, it will come as no surprise that both draw from the same storehouse of cultural imagery (Kline, 2009: 340). They have their roots in icons of skill, courage and derring-do such as the test pilot and the military airman – a fact that can be attributed in large part to the backgrounds of NASA's earliest astronauts, all of whom were »military personnel [with] experience flying jet aircraft« (Deiss, 2022: n.p.). Indeed, according to Saskia Vermeylen, NASA selected such personnel precisely for their »daredevil qualities combined with that element of willingness to be in the service of the wider public and country« – hence the «image of the astronaut as the white, male hero potentially sacrificing his life for the benefit of humanity« (2023: 172).[5] It is via this trope that physical risk can be transformed from a mark of vulnerability into a form of self-overcoming that has implications both individual and collective.

Mid-twentieth century journeys into space could thus be presented to the public as

> monumental accomplishments for ›mankind‹ instead of endeavours that magnified our bodies' limitations and our profound physical dependence on the general hospitality of our planet. This is not how we typically project ourselves as humans into the cosmos, even though dependence is the lived reality of all individual members of humanity. (de Paulis and Haramia, 2023: 132)

But to what extent is the symbolic figure of the astronaut a product of its place as well as its time? Is there such a thing as an all-American cyborg, given that the space race has, by definition, been an international phenomenon since its beginning?

We can certainly see some broad similarities in approach between America and its cold war rivals when it comes to framing space travel and national masculinities. Like the US, Russia also traced a line from airman to spaceman, with »iconic representations« of the new Soviet man shifting »from the heroic aviator in the Stalin period to the cosmonaut in the Khrushchev era« (Gerovitch, 2007: 138). Where there appear to be cultural *differences* between these national space programmes at mid-century, however, is in the role attributed to the spaceman in terms of his direct control of the spacecraft – his ability to act autonomously upon and within the vehicle. In general, Soviet specialists conceptualized the

---

5   As Vermeylen also notes, however, the »whiteness and masculinity of space travel's history in the 1960s« would soon be contested by women and Black people seeking »explicit recognition of the important role they played in the American space programme« (2023: 172).

spacecraft control system as a ‹cybernetic »human-machine« system›. They defined the cosmonaut as a ›living link‹ in this system, and analyzed this living link in cybernetic terms, borrowed from control theory and information theory— the same terms as applied to the other links in this system. (Gerovitch, 2007: 143, quoting Viktor G. Denisov et al. in translation)

Such an approach serves to highlight the ›cy‹ in ›cyborg‹, of course, as well as the inexorable interconnectedness of the embodied human being in space. In contrast to the supposed lack of dependency that Haraway identifies in cultural fantasies of the astronaut, we here find an emphasis on the life-sustaining influence of extra-individual forces.[6] But this is not so much an acknowledgment of the fundamentally ambivalent agency of the spaceman – the fact that he is not a self-determining figure, made autonomous via his skill, but a particularly vulnerable node in a network of inter-reliance. Rather, it is evidence of a distinctive approach to communication and control, in which risk is mitigated beyond (and before) the flight deck.

As Slava Gerovich notes in his groundbreaking work on the topic, »the cybernetic framework underlying this approach fundamentally assigned the human operator a secondary role. Ultimately, the function of the human operator was to enhance the operations of machines, not the other way around« (2007: 144). Cosmonauts were thus assigned a comparatively

limited role on board a spacecraft. Soviet spaceships were fully automated. Although systems of manual control were installed, their functions and use were severely limited. [...] The Soviet engineers' vision of a manned flight was that of a cosmonaut flying on board a spacecraft, rather than flying a spacecraft. (Gerovitch, 2007: 137)

Missions were thus to be planned precisely in advance and run almost entirely from the ground. Despite deliberately seeking out »jet pilots of superior flying ability« for the nation's first cohort of cosmonauts (Burgess, 2022: 37), then, Russia's space programme in fact demanded very little in terms of technical skill from its recruits, and the human in space was considered more of a payload than a pilot.[7]

---

6   This highlights an inevitable facet of human (as well as cyborgian) existence. Indeed, as Ronald Kline notes, »At first thought, ›cybernetic organism‹ seems like a misnomer because all organisms are cybernetic in that they interact with the world through information and feedback control, the key concepts in cybernetics« (2009: 332). This leads him to stress that the cyborg is really a »cybernetically extended organism – an organism extended by means of cybernetic technology« (2009: 332).

7   There was, however, some variation in attitudes on this matter across the Russian space programme. Lieutenant General Nikolai Kamanin, for example – a leading voice in space policy who was in charge of cosmonaut selection and training – is among those who argued that cosmonauts

This approach was arguably less characteristic of the American space programme, where any such perceived decentring of the human in space would have been markedly at odds with the kind of public image being crafted for the astronaut. Indeed, according to Réka Patrícia Gál and Eleanor S. Armstrong, »engineering choices for US spaceflight were themselves heavily influenced by masculinist worldviews«, which could not countenance that space flight might be so heavily automated as to reduce the pilot to a mere passenger (2023: 163). To uphold the idea of the astronaut as a man of action, he had to be granted a certain amount of agency within the cockpit. It is for this reason that Gerovitch positions the figure of the astronaut as a particularly »American ideal, the quintessential American hero« (2007: 156), and that Vermeylen can similarly frame it as »the all-American hero cultivating celebrity status in the media« (2023: 172).

It is perhaps particularly within an American context, then, that the 60s spaceman had associations with not just nerve, valour, and bravery, but also *agency*. The appeal of this cultural framing has endured arguably to this day. In an era in which – according to Donald Goldsmith and Martin Rees – »our robots can outperform astronauts at a far lower cost and without risk to human life« (2022: n.p.), we remain preoccupied with (and invested in) the prospect and practice of human space exploration. It is precisely the »difficulties and dangers«, they argue, that appeal to us (2022: n.p.). Indeed, it is this kind of thinking which prompts the ecofeminist Greta Gaard to argue that »space exploration is advanced within a framework of masculinist ideology that values [...] heroic feats of conquest amid risk-riddled adventure« (2013: 117).

Our discussion so far indicates that any account of ambivalent agency and mid-century cyborgian adaptation might reasonably be restricted to the American space envoy, given the variations in practices and approaches suggested by this brief cross-cultural comparison. In the case of both of the major players of the 60s space race, we find theories of the cybernetic relationship between the spacefaring human and the specialist technologies and machinic infrastructures that keep him alive. Within the culture of American astronautics, however, this interest in adaptation for extraterrestrial environments docks with a particular kind of heroic individualism located within the body of the astronaut himself. In the second half of this essay, we will consider how the positioning of the cyborg both enhances and encroaches upon this figure of the agential astronaut. How does an explicit attempt to extend our collective and individual capacity to act simultaneously work to compromise this same capacity? In what ways can ideas about the cyborg be seen as a culturally specific approach to managing risk and extending control? Where have the limits of this vision of agency been drawn, and where might we seek to redraw them now?

---

should be »assigned a greater role in spacecraft control« (Gerovitch, 2007: 141).

5. Body (Re)Building: Non-, Post- and De-Human Animals

We can see ideas about militarized masculinities and the space race being explored in detail in some of the works of science fiction that emerged in the wake of the cyborg. Martin Caidin's 1972 novel *Cyborg*, for example – upon which the series *The Six Million Dollar Man* is based – centres on the test pilot and astronaut Steve Austin, who is rebuilt with prosthetics after a crash, and subsequently becomes an agent of the state. The protagonist of Frederik Pohl's 1976 novel *Man Plus*, reissued as an ›S.F. Masterwork‹ in 2000, has a similar backstory. Roger Torraway is introduced to the reader as an established astronaut, »[b]right, healthy, smart, personable, technically trained« (2000: 4). He's »good-looking« (2000: 3), deeply in love with his beautiful wife, and something of a celebrity, having once helped rescue a team of stricken Soviet cosmonauts.

Over the course of the novel, we witness his shift from spaceman to space cyborg, as he undergoes processes of non-hereditary adaptation at the hands of the US Exomedicine Project. This demands considerable bravery and self-endangerment on Roger's part, as he is enlisted into a programme of invasive testing, constant monitoring, and transformative medical procedures in preparation for life on Mars. His lungs are replaced by »micro-miniaturized oxygen regeneration cat-cracking systems«, and his organic limbs are replaced with alternatives »served by motors instead of muscles« (2000: 26). As the narrator puts it, »Man is not bound by objective facts. If they inconvenience him, he changes them, or makes an end run around them« (2000: 25). And so, Roger Torraway's body eventually becomes the raw material in an anthropoformational project bent upon overcoming species limits and remaking the human.

This novel, which we will be discussing in more detail below, has clear resonances with Kline and Clynes's account of participant evolution, in which the bodily changes necessary for space survival »have to be created by man himself, using his acquired knowledge of cybernetics and physiology« (1961: 370). As we've seen, these authors thought that becoming a cyborg in this manner would »free humans from their machines, from all the equipment needed to create an earth-like environment in space« (Kline, 2009: 340). The ambition was thus to take the airman-cum-astronaut from his ambivalent position – as part figure »radiating agency«, part vulnerable organism in a bubble – and lead him more decisively to the position of »executive agent incarnate« (Bratton, 2019: 48). But while NASA's cyborg study strives for »a total man-machine complex with man in the control loop as the forcing function« (Driscoll, 1963: 81), a fuller account of cyborgian agency is more complicated than this perspective might allow.

We get a sense of this when we turn our attention to the role of human consciousness in early articulations of the cyborg. In their 1960 paper, Clynes and Kline are particularly interested in homeostatic biological processes – the tendency toward stability and self-regulation within an organism, and the tendency to self-monitor and automatically adjust in response to external conditions (sweating when one gets hot, for example). This plays a prominent role in their characterization of the cyborg; the emphasis on biological feedback has clear links with the central tenets of cybernetics. They are interested in »the devices necessary for creating self-regulating man-machine systems«, noting that this »self-regulation must function without the benefit of consciousness in order to cooperate with the body's own autonomous homeostatic controls« (1960: 27). Cyborgian adaptations – while being the outcome of a deliberate process of participant evolution – are thus understood as functioning without the need for ongoing conscious intervention; they can be set in motion and then largely forgotten about.

The aim is to free the astronaut »from the need of conscious attention to the regulation of his own internal environment« (Kline and Clynes, 1961: 370). After all,

> [i]f man in space, in addition to flying his vehicle, must continuously be checking on things and making adjustments merely in order to keep himself alive, he becomes a slave to the machine. The purpose of the Cyborg, as well as his own homeostatic systems, is to provide an organizational system in which such robot-like problems are taken care of automatically and unconsciously, leaving man free to explore, to create, to think, and to feel. (Clynes and Kline, 1960: 27)

What the body can do, or be made to do, *without the mind's deliberate intervention* becomes the site via which freedom is extended. In Bratton's words, »automation automates autonomy« (2019: 35). As we've seen, some elements of this point of view were in evidence within the Soviet space programme – although in this case, the emphasis was on collective control rather than individual autonomy in the cockpit. What is key for our purposes, however, is the idea that exercising agency might be less a matter of the subject persisting as a forcing function, and more a matter of judicious decision-making about where to *cede* versus where to *seize* direct command.

As we've seen throughout our discussion so far, however, any account of cyborg autonomy also has to reckon with the intensified vulnerability of the body and mind beyond planetary limits.[8] As Daniela de Paulis and Chelsea Haramia note, the astronauts who have so far walked on the moon were also, of necessity, »entirely sealed off

---

8   Colin Burgess reports that the Soviet preference for highly automated space exploration was in fact informed by lingering concerns about just such vulnerability. Of preparations for Yuri Gagarin's historic 1961 launch, for example, he notes that »Some scientists feared that the lack of gravity, combined with disorientation and a strong feeling of isolation, might cause a cosmonaut to become panicky and even deranged. The flight would be fully automatic, controlled from the ground, and there was a reluctance to give Gagarin access to – and possibly allow him to override – the controls in case he became badly disoriented« (2022: 37).

from it. […] They gazed at this world through the medium of their helmets, their fragile, delicate bodies protected by their high-tech suits« (2023: 130–131). And just as, with such a prosthetic approach to survival, the space-walking astronaut is both a figure of Promethean triumph *and* »a fragile animal in a shell« (Bratton, 2019: 48), so, too, is the pharmaceutically enhanced mid-century cyborg both enabled by his biotechnologies and tethered to them.

Thus, while the figure of the cyborg seeks to reduce vulnerability and increase agency by enmeshing the extraordinary measures necessary to support life firmly within the bodily interior, it does not somehow (impossibly) escape dependence. Rather, it shifts this dependence on to other forces, coming to represent a different type of corporeal jeopardy as it does so. Situated at the experimental edge of astronautics, it therefore offers us a differently coded imaginary to that of the heroic military airman – one, I would argue, that brings with it a very different set of race, gender, and even species connotations that then demand to be managed. After all, »fragility and dependence have historically been characterized as feminine and disabled traits« (de Paulis and Haramia, 2023: 131), rather than as the inevitable facets of embodied existence that they are, and the cyborg is at least as much test *subject* as it is test *pilot*.

Let us return to *Man Plus* here. In the novel, both Roger Torraway and his predecessor Will Hartnett are subject to surveillance, monitoring, and invasive medical procedures the precise details of which are sometimes kept from them; we witness Hartnett undergoing the »slow, laborious process« of having the interface between his ruby complex eyes and still-human brain reset: »Like nearly all of the things that had to be done to Willy Hartnett«, we are told, »it was attended with the maximum discomfort for him. The sensitive nerves of the eyelid had long since been dissected out; otherwise he would have been shrieking in pain day and night. But he could feel what was happening« (Pohl, 2000: 48). It is this experimental process of vision resetting that ultimately kills him, making way for Roger as his reluctant replacement, and which also primes the reader to think about the process of becoming cyborg as a form of posthuman vivisection.

It is no coincidence that the pressurized tank in which Roger is kept is described as a »zoo cage« (2000: 30), nor that he is frequently described not only as a cyborg but as a »monster« (2000: 9). As Paul Preciado remarks, many of our understandings of the clinically manipulable workings of the body »were manufactured at the crossroads at which human, the supposedly non-human, and animal meet« (2013: 154). Our biotechnical advances are pursued via the bodies of »rabbits, chickens, bulls, pigs« (Preciado, 2013: 153) – a fact also reflected in the language of ›lab rats‹ and ›guinea pigs‹. This use of non-human animals to pursue human ambitions is common to both medicine and space exploration; Soviet and American scientists alike enlisted »nonhuman animals—mostly monkeys, chimpanzees, and dogs—to test the effects of rapid acceleration, prolonged weightlessness, atmospheric re-entry, and other hazards of space travel« (Gaard, 2013: 118).

Indeed, »one wonders how the space race would have proceeded if non-human animals were not available as ›crash test dummies‹« (Gaard, 2013: 119). Astronaut, cosmonaut, and post-human cyborg alike thus follow in the pawprints of their non-human predecessors.[9] The *humans* who have historically been brought most frequently into the category of test subject, meanwhile, have tended to be those most insistently othered (that is to say, dehumanized) by medical discourses. In the words of Alondra Nelson, »medical experimentation with human subjects has historically involved vulnerable groups, including children, the poor and the institutionalized«, while Black people have »disproportionately borne the burden of the most invasive, inhumane and perilous medical investigations« in the US (2007: n.p.).

In the mid-twentieth century, in particular, the position of controlled and exploited test subject had certain associations with poor, racialized women, thanks in part to some of the large-scale clinical trials underpinning pharmaceutical breakthroughs of the era – the first contraceptive pill, for example, which was approved for use in the US in the very year the word ›cyborg‹ first appeared. According to Preciado, the

> pseudocolonial island of Puerto Rico became the most important clinical site for testing the [contraceptive] Pill outside the national disciplinary institutions of the asylum and the prison and functioned as a parallel, life-sized biopolitical pharmacological laboratory and factory during the late 1950s and 1960s. (2013: 177)

Data collection here involved intrusive monitoring, with social workers moving »daily from house to house collecting fluids, recording information, and encouraging women's cooperation with the pharmacological regimen« – a process later repeated in Haiti and Mexico (Preciado: 2013, 188). The more than 200 women who participated in the trial »received little information about the safety of the product they were given, as there was none to give, and no one thought that it might be necessary to provide such information« (Liao and Dollin, 2012: n.p.). To what extent is the imagined cyborg of American astronautics entangled with this history of the medical test subject, and how might this compromise imaginaries revolving around white military masculinities? Could one argue that the forms of endangerment involved in being a test subject work to trouble the gendering of the hybridized cyborg? In order to address these questions, we will first turn to the later thinking of Manfred E. Clynes.

---

9   For more on this, see Burgess, Colin, and Chris Dubbs, *Animals in Space: From Research Rockets to the Space Shuttle.* Springer: Chichester, 2007.

6. Evolved Beings: Gender, Sexuality, and Non-Hereditary Adaptation

In a 1995 interview with Chris Hables Gray, Clynes argues forcefully *against* the idea
that non-hereditary adaptation might destabilise existing frameworks of sex and
gender. He declares that »the idea of cyborg (sic) in no way implies an it. It's a he or a
she. It is either a male or female cyborg; it's not an it. It's an absurd mistake. The cyborgs
are capable of the same emotional expression and experience as an uncyborg« (Gray,
1995: 48). Later in the interview, he further asserts that:

> the cyborg, per se – talking now of men and women who have altered themselves in
> various cyborgian ways – in no way has that altered their sexuality. In no way has that
> altered their ability to experience emotions, no more than riding a bicycle does. And
> even more importantly, it hasn't altered their essential identity. (Gray, 1995: 49)

These comments strike me as curious, in that they labour to uphold an image of an
immutable, experiencing, embodied self which runs counter to the ideas of acid astronautics and to any process of becoming-cyborg. If the cyborg is a figure against
species boundaries – one engaged in a Promethean refusal to »assume a predetermined
limit to what we can achieve or to the ways in which we can transform ourselves and
our world« (Brassier, 2014: 470) – then this sudden swerve toward an entrenched
stability of identity feels like a move away from the cyborg itself.

While the interview in question took place more than 30 years after the term ›cyborg‹ was first introduced, the perspective on sex and gender it advances is consistent
with certain elements of Clynes' earlier views. A belief in the transcultural and tran-
shistorical character of emotion characterizes his solo-authored 1970 article »Cyborg
II: Sentic Space Travel«, for example. This piece, later printed by Gray in his *Cyborg
Handbook*, asks »How can man be authentic in space?« (Clynes, 1995: 36) – a question
that the author explicitly extends to sexual activity and the satisfaction of erotic needs.
Clynes argues that the »ability of man to express his emotions in accordance with his
nature is indispensable for a prolonged existence in space« (1995: 42) and proposes
several strategies to make this possible. He writes that bodily expressions of emotion –
and, intriguingly, he lists sex *as* an emotion, alongside anger, hate, grief, love, joy, and
reverence (Clynes, 1995: 38) – have »an unconscious origin. They are not wilfully
created by each individual – they represent his heritage. [...] This unconscious heritage travels with us into space« (1995: 42). We see again that sex is assumed to limit
possibilities for participant evolution, serving as an unchangeable fact that we can
aspire to manage or mitigate via enhanced understanding, but which we can never hope
to transform, reprogramme, or overcome.

It is interesting to note, however, that Clyne's account is somewhat at odds with that
of his contemporaries. Other mid-century discourses around space exploration trace

alternative possibilities for the cybernetic organism, as we can see when we look to the work of the cyborg's *other* originator, Nathan S. Kline. In a piece emerging from his 1967 study group on psychotropic drugs, Kline considers how pharmaceuticals might come to alter future life patterns. Several of his suggestions have direct implications for gender and sexuality. By the year 2000, we're told, we may have drugs with the capacity to »*Foster or Terminate Mothering Behavior*« (Kline, 1971: 83, original emphasis). With mothering behaviour »so typical of certain animals«, he suggests, »it appears highly probable that there are ›juices‹ which mediate in the production of this behavior. By enhancing or interfering with their production it is possible that the extent of such behavior could be controlled« (1971: 83).

He speculates too about drugs designed to »*Regulate Sexual Responses*« (1971: 80, original emphasis), »Banking the fires or stoking them biochemically« in an effort to »increase the sum total of pleasure and at the same time allow man to devote more of his time, intelligence and energies to more exclusively human activities« (Kline, 1971: 83) – a sort of intensified libidinal automation. Kline seems to lack his collaborator's squeamishness about gender and sex as territories for technical intervention and challenges the idea that even something as naturalized as maternity might be excluded from Promethean attempts to re-make the given.

Frederick Pohl is similarly interested in exploring ideas around the sexual cyborg. In his work, becoming cyborg means submitting not only to intimate control, monitoring, and surveillance – factors which, even on their own, could feasibly be said to trouble the structures and codes of identity at play – but also to direct interference with the genital organs. The virile astronaut hero of *Man Plus* is castrated, without his prior knowledge or consent, on the basis that (having evolved beyond the elimination of waste) the reproductive organs are now »just a vulnerable spot« (2000: 101). The narrator depicts Roger Torraway's moment of horrified realization thusly:

> There, between his legs, was nothing. Nothing at all of penis, testicles, scrotum; nothing but the gleaming artificial flesh with a transparent bandage over it, concealing the surgery lines. It was as if nothing had ever been there. Of the diagnostic signs of manhood… nothing. The tiny little operation was over, and what was left was nothing at all. (2000: 94)

Reeling from the initial trauma, he experiences »hopeless desolation. He not only had lost Dorrie, he had lost his manhood« (2000: 103). Although Roger's body has been blithely transformed, then, his sense of what it *should* be – his commitment to and identification with a particularly sexed version of his body and himself – remains intact (at least initially).

On the one hand, we could interpret Roger's distress as a fictional demonstration of precisely Clynes's point – that is, as a representation of the idea that essential identity remains steady despite biotechnologically facilitated change. That the character's physical form has been developed in unchosen ways, in profound violation of his bodily autonomy, while his gendered self-understanding persists is shown to be largely the source of his trauma. The »sexual nature of man isn't just the sex organs«, as Clynes puts it, »It is something very much in the identity of the person« (Gray, 1995: 49). Hence, there may be all kinds of cyborg bodies, but their cyborgian qualities do nothing to challenge the fundamental character of the embodied subjects involved. Participant evolution cannot change those ineffable elements of the self where gender and sexuality are situated or from whence they are derived. This reading is perhaps reinforced by the fact that the »monster« of *Man Plus* also receives a »steroid capsule« to ensure he »won't become effeminate« (Pohl, 2000: 101).

Of course, a person's gender is not determined by their genitalia – Clynes is quite right about that. But it's worth stressing that he is not decentring the sexual and reproductive organs here as part of a trans feminist or genderqueer politics of sexual difference. Rather, he's arguing that technological mediation cannot affect the gendered or sexual self because these things are untouchable, stable, and at the very root of human existence. This is a biologically essentialist approach to phenomena which Clynes associates with a necessarily non-cyborgian facet of embodiment. The »genes and chromosomes already determine sex, and the brain circuitry expresses that sexuality«, he argues (1995: 49), meaning that most forms of non-hereditary adaption, no matter how extreme, have little chance of altering it. The flip side of this reading, however, is that the changes that come along with Roger Torraway's becoming cyborg *are* eventually shown to be suggestive of fundamental shifts – that is to say, Pohl seems to be using the novel to explore precisely the possibility that gender and sexuality can in fact be re-engineered.

The reader encounters this most clearly via Roger's evolving attitude to his wife. For much of the book, he is depicted as both besotted and deeply jealous. »In some arcane way«, we're told, »all the processes of his life terminated in Dorrie. [...] The horror of his appearance was that it would offend Dorrie. The tragedy of castration was that he would fail Dorrie« (2000: 138). Roger's »manhood« is to some extent both expressed and constituted by this conjugal connection. The infatuation is so intense that, as he drifts further and further away from the commitments of his previous humanity, the Exomedicine Project starts to use the idea of his wife as a tool via which to manipulate him. It hires a woman called Sulie Carpenter – an aerospace doctor with a passing resemblance to Dorrie – to dye her hair, wear coloured contact lenses, and pose as his nurse so that she can form an exploitable bond with him, thereby extending the project's control over its increasingly unpredictable post-human asset.

As the cyborg's body progressively changes, however, and as his affections start to detach from his wife and transfer to her custom-made replacement, Roger's attitude to sex also changes:

> It's like being told I can't have any caviar […] I don't like caviar. And when you come
> right down to it, I don't want sex right now. […] it finally penetrated my little brain that
> I was just making trouble for myself, worrying about whether I could get along without
> something I really didn't want. It's a reflection of what I think other people think I should
> want. (Pohl, 2000: 152–153)

Even if the changes in Roger are not undertaken with the direct intention of manip-
ulating his sexual and gender identity, then, there is a sense in which the instrumen-
talization of the cyborg shifts perspectives both on what a body can do and on what a
body is for. Over time, the whole suite of changes to which the organism has been made
subject are shown to enact profound shifts in embodied self-understanding.

Towards the end of the novel, while up on Mars alongside the man he knows to be
Dorrie's illicit lover, Roger is himself struck by having undergone an attitudinal shift;
he no longer feels possessive:

> The situation interested him as an abstract problem. Was it because he was a gelding?
> There was testosterone circulating in his system, the steroid implant they had given him
> took care of that. His dreams were sometimes sexual, and sometimes of Dorrie, but the
> hollow despair and anger he had lived with on Earth had attenuated on Mars. (Pohl,
> 2000: 196)

Instead, his affections intensify for Sulie Carpenter. He forgets what sex feels like, and
dwells upon the sensation of touching her fingertips. Of course, rigid adherence to the
heterosexual matrix is maintained here – the stripping away of penis and testicles is
offset via the circulation of testosterone, and the disinvestment from penetrative
marital coitus is transformed into a libidinized investment in a form of touch that,
although non-genital, is nevertheless coded as its straight replacement. But there are at
least hints in the text that cyborgian embodiment might open up queer alternatives –
that non-hereditary adaptation is seen as a possible route to re-engineering the sex/
gender/ sexuality nexus. Sulie, while announcing her intention to stay on Mars and
establish the first colony, is questioned as to how she will cope without sex, given that
her only company will be the monster. She responds that »[t]here are more ways to
orgasm than with a penis in my vagina. And there's more to sex than orgasm« (2000:
190).

Of course, the idea of being assigned to the ranks of an emerging post-orgasmic
species may not be a particularly appealing prospect for still-fleshy readers – particularly for women, who too often experience a pleasure gap under current sociosexual
conditions as it is! And of course, we don't need science fiction to teach us that bodily
transformation without bodily autonomy is the stuff of nightmares – it is a fact made
painfully apparent in the »disproportionately raced occurrences of non-consensual

sterilization in the twentieth century, [...] the exploitation of non-white bodies in medical testing, attempts to impose long-term contraceptives such as Norplant and Depo-Provera upon welfare recipients, and other forms of the racist, classist, and cissexist disciplining of bodies« (Hester, 2018: 121). Nevertheless, however, Sulie's comments *are* suggestive of the potential for new forms of sexual relations – non-teleological, non-reproductive, and non-proprietorial – at just the point at which humanity looks set to become its multi-planetary successor species. Given that, as Clynes puts it, sex and gender are widely assumed to be a part of both a species' and a subject's »essential identity« (Gray, 1995: 49), this suggestion of malleability in the realms of bodily pleasures bespeaks radical transformation. Indeed, it may be as clear an indication of the human transcending itself as the possibility of extra-terrestrial colonies.

7. Conclusion: Everyday Cyborgs

In this essay, we have drawn on mid-century astronautics, a science fictional case study, and two brief cross-cultural comparisons in an effort to better understand what is distinctive (or otherwise) about the all-American cyborg. In the process, we have pointed to the cyborg's roots in two discursive regimes: that surrounding military masculinities, and that surrounding the non-human (or de-humanized) medical test subject. We have considered some of the tensions generated by this dual heritage, particularly in terms of species and gender, touching both on the use of primates and canines in early space flight and on unevenly distributed experiences of clinical suffering and embodied risk more generally. We have discussed some of the problematic ways in which sex and sexuality have been excluded from the perceived mutability of cyborgian embodiment, opposing Manfred E. Clynes's perspective to that of his some-time collaborator Nathan S. Kline and to the visions put forth in Frederik Pohl's *Man Plus.* Throughout the course of our argument, we have discussed a version of the cyborg that emerges distinctively from the astronaut – the ›space cyborg‹ – and as a result, have framed cyborgian adaptation primarily as an extraordinary biotechnical feat.

It is worth remembering, however, that despite its rarefied roots in mid-century astronautics and its speculative representations in science fiction, the cyborg is also a quotidian figure – a fact of life for carbon-based life forms entangled with silicon-based actors. For Haraway, we are all already »chimeras, theorized and fabricated hybrids of machine and organism [...] The cyborg is our ontology« (1991: 150). Today, gendered bodies are a commonplace cyborgian achievement. This is the case whether we define the cyborg broadly, as a biological organism engaged in habitual technological tool use, or more specifically, as the embodiment of non-hereditary adaptations that function without ongoing conscious intervention. After all, some technologies of sex and gender – the IUD and hormonal contraceptive implant, for example – can reasonably be understood as a means of automating autonomy. As Preciado puts it, the »certainty of being a man or a woman is a somato-political bio-fiction produced by a collection of body technologies, pharmacologic and audiovisual techniques that determine and define the scope of our somatic potentialities and function like prostheses of subjectification« (2013: 117).

By this account, becoming cyborg may indeed effect sex, gender, their interconnections and their associated identities, but need not necessarily disrupt or challenge binary gender or compulsory heterosexuality. In fact, one could argue that the prosthetically and pharmaceutically manipulable character of the human subject has, from at least the birth of the term ›cyborg‹, been used to buttress the very regime that it simultaneously appears to dismantle. From the middle of the twentieth century, Preciado notes,

> males are no longer guaranteed to impregnate, females stop menstruating and gestating under the effects of the contraceptive pill, and lactation is provided by food industries instead of female breasts. The heterosexual dimorphic regime of ›sperm and egg cell carriers‹ is going awry. (2013: 105)

We would do well to remember this when tracing out the subterranean emancipatory possibilities of science fiction and acid astronautics.

Contra the comments of Clynes, sex and gender are not facts of pure nature, immune to the influences of technologies and comfortingly immutable (indeed, we need to question for whom this idea of immutability would be comforting in the first place); they are just as much a product of and a territory for participant evolution as any other element of embodiment. The question is thus not *whether* sex and gender can be re-engineered, but rather how they *are already* being re-engineered, by whom, and for what ends. We confront a further, final issue concerning the simultaneous necessity and difficulty of agential intervention here. After all, as today's astronautics discourse attests, »humans are already *accidentally* engineering life and directing evolution«, but are doing so without »volition, direction, and purpose« (Mason, 2021: xiii). If we are to conceive of new possibilities for technology and embodiment, it will be less a matter of *freedom from* cyborgian intrusion, and more an issue of *freedom to* remake – via all means necessary, including the technical – that which we find to be oppressive or unjust about gender and sexuality (and, indeed, the wider social world) as they stand. We can rebuild them. We have the technology.

Bibliography

Abood, Steven (2020): Crossing the Posthuman Rubicon. When do Enhancements Change Our Definition of Human? in: Szocik, Konrad (ed.): *Human Enhancements for Space Missions. Lunar, Martian, and Future Missions to the Outer Planets.* Cham: Springer, pp. 47–70.

Barbrook, Richard/ Cameron, Andy (1995): The Californian Ideology. in: *Mute*, 1/3. https://www.metamute.org/editorial/articles/californian-ideology. 11 September 2023.

Brassier, Ray (2014): Prometheanism and Its Critics. In: Mackay, R./ Avanessian, A. (eds.): *#Accelerate: The Accelerationist Reader.* Falmouth: Urbanomic, pp. 467–487.

Bratton, Benjamin H. (2019): *The Terraforming.* New York: Strelka.

Burgess, Colin (2022): *Soviets in Space. Russia's Cosmonauts and the Space Frontier.* London: Reaktion Books.

Burgess, Colin/ Dubbs, Chris (2007): *Animals in Space. From Research Rockets to the Space Shuttle.* Chichester: Springer.

Caidin, Martin (1972): *Cyborg.* New York: Warner Press.

Clynes, Manfred E. (1995/1970): Cyborg II. Sentic Space Travel. in: in: Gray, Chris Hables/ Figueroa-Sarriera, H.J/ Mentor, S. (eds.): *The Cyborg Handbook.* London: Routledge, pp. 35–43.

Clynes, Manfred E./ Kline, Nathan S. (1960): Cyborgs and space. in: *Astronautics*, 14/9, pp. 26–27 and 74–76.

Damjanov, Katarina (2023): Space Infrastructures and Networks of Control and Care. in: Salazar, Juan Francisco/ Gorman, Alice (eds.): *The Routledge Handbook of Social Studies of Outer Space.* London: Routledge, pp. 328–338.

Deiss, Heather (ed.) (2022): Astronaut Requirements. *NASA.* https://www.nasa.gov/audience/forstudents/postsecondary/features/F_Astronaut_Requirements.html. 11 September 2023.

de Paulis, Daniela/ Haramia, Chelsea (2023): Embodiment in Space Imagery. Beyond the Dominant Narrative. in: Schwartz, James S.J./ Billings, Linda/ Nesvold, Erika (eds.): *Reclaiming Space: Progressive and Multicultural Visions of Space Exploration.* Oxford: Oxford University Press, pp. 127–138.

Driscoll, Robert W. (1963): *Engineering Man for Space. The Cyborg Study. Final Report NASw-512.* Farmington: Corporate Systems Center, United Aircraft.

Dymock, Alex (2023): Acid feminism. Gender, psychonautics and the politics of consciousness. *Sociological Review Monographs*, 71/4, pp. 817–838.

Gál, Réka Patrícia/ Armstrong, Eleanor S. (2023): Feminist Approaches to Outer Space. Engagements with Technology, Labour, and Environment. in: Salazar, Juan Francisco/ Gorman, Alice (eds.): *The Routledge Handbook of Social Studies of Outer Space.* London: Routledge, pp. 158–171.

Gaard, Greta (2013): Animals in (New) Space. Chimponauts, Cosmodogs, and Biosphere II. in: *Feminismo/s*, 22, pp. 113–145.

Gerovitch, Slava (2007): ›New Soviet Man‹ Inside Machine. Human Engineering, Spacecraft Design, and the Construction of Communism. in: *Osiris*, 22/1, pp. 135–157.

Goldsmith, Donald/ Rees, Martin (2022): The End of Astronauts—and the Rise of Robots/ *Wired.* https://www.wired.com/story/end-of-astronauts-robots-space-exploration/. 11 September 2023.

Gray, Chris Hables (1995): An Interview with Manfred Clynes. in: Gray, Chris Hables/ Figueroa-Sarriera, H.J/ Mentor, S. (eds.): *The Cyborg Handbook.* London: Routledge, pp. 43 – 59.

Grind, Kirsten/ Bindley, Katherine (2023): Magic Mushrooms. LSD. Ketamine. The Drugs That Power Silicon Valley. *Wall Street Journal.* https://www.wsj.com/articles/silicon-valley-microdosing-ketamine-lsd-magic-mushrooms-d381e214. 11 September 2023.

Haraway, Donna (1991): A Cyborg Manifesto. Science, Technology, and Socialist-Feminism in the Late Twentieth Century. in: Haraway, Donna: *Simians, Cyborgs, and Women. The Reinvention of Nature.* London: Free Association Books, pp. 149 – 181.

Hester, Helen (2018): *Xenofeminism.* Cambridge: Polity.

Kline, Nathan S. (1971): Manipulation of Life Patterns with Drugs. in: Evans, Wayne O./ Kline, Nathan S. (eds.): *Psychotropic Drugs in the Year 2000. Use by Normal Humans.* Springfield: Charles C Thomas, pp. 69 – 85.

Kline, Nathan S./ Clynes, Manfred E. (1961): Drugs, Space, and Cybernetics. Evolution to Cyborgs. in: Flaherty, Bernard E. (ed.): *Psychophysiological Aspects of Space Flight.* New York: Columbia University Press, pp. 345 – 371.

Kline, Ronald (2009): Where are the Cyborgs in Cybernetics? in: *Social Studies of Science,* 39/3, pp. 331 – 362.

Koren, Marina (2018): Reefer Madness at NASA. in: *The Atlantic.* https://www.theatlantic.com/science/archive/2018/11/nasa-spacex-elon-musk-marijuana-boeing/576490/. 11 September 2023.

Kurland, Albert A./ Pahnke, Walter N./ Unger, Sanford et al. (1971): Psychedelic LSD Research. in: Evans, Wayne O./ Kline, Nathan S. (eds.): *Psychotropic Drugs in the Year 2000. Use by Normal Humans.* Springfield: Charles C Thomas, pp. 86 – 108.

Liao, Pamela Verma/ Dollin, Janet (2012). Half a Century of the Oral Contraceptive Pill. Historical Review and View to the Future. in: *Canadian Family Physician,* 28/12. https://www.ncbi.nlm.nih.gov/pmc/articles/PMC3520685/. 11 September 2023.

Maly, Tim (2010): What's a Cyborg? *Quiet Babylon.* http://quietbabylon.com/2010/whats-a-cyborg/. 29 October 2019.

Mason, Christopher E. (2021): *The Next 500 Years. Engineering Life to Reach New Worlds.* MIT: Cambridge.

Morozov, Evgeny (2015): Silicon Valley exploits time and space to extend the frontiers of capitalism. *Guardian.* https://www.theguardian.com/commentisfree/2015/nov/29/silicon-valley-exploits-space-evgeny-morozov. 11 September 2023.

Munévar, Gonzalo (2020): Science and Ethics in the Human-Enhanced Exploration of Mars. in: Szocik, Konrad (ed.): *Human Enhancements for Space Missions. Lunar, Martian, and Future Missions to the Outer Planets.* Cham: Springer: pp. 113 – 124.

NASA (n.d.): Ames Research Center. NASA's Center in Silicon Valley. *NASA.* https://www.nasa.gov/centers/ames/about/overview.html. 11 September 2023.

Nelson, Alondra (2007): Unequal treatment. *Washington Post.* https://www.washingtonpost.com/wp-dyn/content/article/2007/01/05/AR2007010500180.html. 11 September 2023.

Newburg, Andrew B./ Yates, David B. (2020): Human Enhancement from the Overview Effect in Long-Duration Space Flights. in: Szocik, Konrad (ed.): *Human Enhancements for Space Missions. Lunar, Martian, and Future Missions to the Outer Planets.* Cham: Springer, pp. 105 – 111.

Pohl, Frederik (2000/1976): *Man Plus.* London: Millennium.

Preciado, Paul (2013): *Testo Junkie. Sex, Drugs and Biopolitics in the Pharmacopornographic Era.* Benderson, Bruce (trans.). New York: The Feminist Press.

Rappaport, Margaret Boone/ Corbally, Christopher J. (2020): Normalizing the Paradigm on Human Enhancements for Spaceflight. in: Szocik, Konrad (ed.): *Human Enhancements for Space Missions. Lunar, Martian, and Future Missions to the Outer Planets.* Cham: Springer,: pp. 3–17.

Salazar, Juan Francisco/ Gorman, Alice (2023): Social Studies of Outer Space. Pluriversal Articulations. in: Salazar, Juan Francisco/ Gorman, Alice (eds.): *The Routledge Handbook of Social Studies of Outer Space.* London: Routledge, pp. 1–21.

Sennesh, Eli/ Hughes, James J. (2023): Conspiracy Theories, Left Futurism, and the Attack on TESCREAL. *Medium.* https://medium.com/institute-for-ethics-and-emerging-technologies/conspiracy-theories-left-futurism-and-the-attack-on-tescreal-456972fe02aa. 12 June 2023.

Titcomb, James (2023): Elon Musk ›takes ketamine to manage depression‹. *Telegraph.* https://www.telegraph.co.uk/business/2023/06/27/musk-takes-ketamine-to-manage-depression/. 11 September 2023.

Torres, Émile P. (2023): AI and the threat of ›human extinction‹. What are the tech-bros worried about? It's not you and me. *Salon.* https://www.salon.com/2023/06/11/ai-and-the-of-human-extinction-what-are-the-tech-bros-worried-about-its-not-you-and-me/. 11 September 2023.

Troy, Dave (2023): The Wide Angle: Understanding TESCREAL — the Weird Ideologies Behind Silicon Valley's Rightward Turn. *Washington Spectator.* https://washingtonspectator.org/understanding-tescreal-silicon-valleys-rightward-turn/. 1 May 2023.

Vermeylen, Saskia (2023). The Iconography of the Astronaut as a Critical Enquiry of Space Law. in: Salazar, Juan Francisco/ Gorman, Alice (eds.): The Routledge Handbook of Social Studies of Outer Space. London: Routledge, pp. 172–184.

Nicolas Weisensel

Von getrennter Weltauffassung zu Naturenkulturen

Ludwig Boltzmanns *Reisebericht Reise eines deutschen Professors ins Eldorado* und Franz Kafkas *Der Verschollene*[1]

ABSTRACT: In his America travelogue *Reise eines deutschen Professors ins Eldorado* (1905), the Austrian physicist Ludwig Boltzmann took a surprisingly similar route to that of the protagonist Karl Roßmann in Franz Kafka's novel *Der Verschollene*. So far, however, Boltzmann's report has not been made fruitful for interpretations of Kafka's *Der Verschollene*. This is the aim of this work. In the analysis, both texts are compared against the background of the concept of *entangled naturecultures* (Karen Barad, Donna Haraway). Given the great similarities in the descriptions of different places and topics—this applies, e.g., to the New York harbor, country houses, theaters and landscape descriptions during train journeys through the USA—Boltzmann's travelogue, in which, according to my thesis, a rather separated worldview is represented, serves as a contrasting foil in order to make visible a specific, intertwined worldview in the sense of *naturecultures* in Kafka's *Der Verschollene*. Boltzmann's travel text as a historical parallel text can thus contribute to a better understanding of Kafka's novel.

KEYWORDS: Franz Kafka, Ludwig Boltzmann, Der Verschollene, USA, Naturenkulturen, naturecultures, entanglement, Environmental Humanities, New Materialism, Donna Haraway, Karen Barad, Hafen, Eisenbahn, Landschaft

In seinem Reisebericht *Reise eines deutschen Professors ins Eldorado*, der erstmals 1905 als Kapitel in der Publikation *Populäre Schriften* erschien, beschreibt der österreichische Physiker Ludwig Boltzmann seine Überfahrt von Bremen nach New York, eine daran anschließende Zugreise durch die USA nach San Francisco und den dortigen Aufenthalt an der »Universität Berkeley« [sic].[2] Auch der Protagonist Karl Roßmann in Franz Kafkas Roman *Der Verschollene* beschreitet eine ähnliche Reiseroute von Osten

---

1   Dieser Artikel stellt ein modifiziertes Kapitel der Dissertation »Kafka *entangled.* Das Werk Franz Kafkas aus Perspektive der Environmental Humanities« dar. Die Publikation erfolgt voraussichtlich im Jahr 2025.

2   Ludwig Boltzmann (1905): *Populäre Schriften.* Leipzig: Verlag von Johann Ambrosius Barth, S. 403–435 (=Kapitel: *Reise eines deutschen Professors ins Eldorado*). Fortan zitiert mit der Sigle E und Seitenzahl.

nach Westen, beginnend mit der Ankunft in New York und endend mit der Zugfahrt zum phantastischen »Teater von Oklahama« [sic] (V, 387).[3]

Im vorliegenden Aufsatz sollen beide Texte gegenübergestellt werden, um originäre Merkmale von Kafkas Text herauszuarbeiten und damit eine neue Interpretation vor dem Hintergrund des Naturenkulturen-Konzepts zu ermöglichen. Neben erstaunlichen inhaltlichen Parallelen sprechen für eine vergleichende Untersuchung von Boltzmanns *Eldorado*-Reisebericht und Kafkas *Verschollenem* textgenetische, zeitliche und räumliche Aspekte, darunter: erstens der Zeitpunkt von Boltzmanns Veröffentlichung im Jahr 1905 (die Entstehungszeit des *Verschollenen* liegt zwischen 1911 und 1914);[4] zweitens die Tatsache, dass Boltzmann Professor in Wien war; drittens, dass Boltzmann mit Albert Einstein zu tun hatte, der sich von 1911–1912 in Prag aufhielt und dessen Vorträge Kafka besuchte;[5] viertens, dass sich Kafka intensiv für physikalisch-philosophische Debatten seiner Zeit interessierte;[6] sowie fünftens, dass Boltzmanns Buch explizit populär ausgerichtet war.[7] Kafka hätte Boltzmanns Reisebeschreibung durchaus kennen können.

Methodisch könnte sich die vorliegende Untersuchung damit einerseits an der Einflussphilologie orientieren, jedoch sind die inhaltlichen Ähnlichkeiten zwischen Boltzmanns und Kafkas Text lediglich Indizien, keinesfalls aber als Beweise für ein Rezeptionsverhältnis.[8] Andererseits wäre methodisch eine Untersuchung in Form einer

---

3   Franz Kafka (1983): *Der Verschollene.* Roman in der Fassung der Handschrift. Textband. (Kritische Ausgabe) Hrsg. von Jost Schillemeit. Frankfurt a.M.: S. Fischer. Zitiert mit der Sigle V und Seitenzahl.

4   Vgl. Manfred Engel (2010): Der Verschollene. In: ders. / Bernd Auerochs (Hgg.): *Kafka Handbuch. Leben – Werk – Wirkung.* Stuttgart: Metzler, S. 175–191, hier S. 175f.; Literatur wird in den Fußnoten nach der ersten vollständigen Nennung zitiert mit Nachname und Kurztitel.

5   So besuchte Kafka etwa einen Vortrag Einsteins zur Relativitätstheorie am 24. Mai 1911. Vgl. Ekkehard W. Haring (2010): Leben und Persönlichkeit. In: Manfred Engel / Bernd Auerochs (Hgg.): *Kafka Handbuch. Leben – Werk – Wirkung.* Stuttgart: Metzler, S. 1–27, hier S. 12; Peter-André Alt (2005): *Franz Kafka. Der ewige Sohn. Eine Biographie.* München: Beck, S. 192; zu den Verbindungen zwischen Kafka und Einstein vgl. weiterhin Martin Bartelmus (2022): Kafka-Einstein-Verschränkungen. In: Alexander Kling / Johannes F. Lehmann (Hgg.): *Kafkas Zeiten.* Forschungen der Deutschen Kafka-Gesellschaft Bd. 7. Würzburg: Königshausen & Neumann, S. 159–183.

6   Vgl. etwa Thomas Anz (2009): *Franz Kafka. Leben und Werk.* München: Beck, S. 69.

7   Im Gegensatz zu Boltzmanns wissenschaftlichen Publikationen waren die *Populären Schriften* für eine »breitere Öffentlichkeit« bestimmt. Vgl. Engelbert Broda (1979): Einleitung. In: Ludwig Boltzmann: *Populäre Schriften. Eingeleitet und ausgewählt von Engelbert Broda.* Braunschweig: Vieweg, S. 1–12, hier S. 1. »Die ›Populären Schriften‹, die bei ganz verschiedenartigen Gelegenheiten und für unterschiedliche Zuhörerkreise verfaßt wurden, sind im ungleichen Maß [im Vergleich zu den wissenschaftlichen Publikationen; N.W.] ›populär‹. Zu beachten ist auch die Weite des Feldes, das Boltzmann behandelte, ohne daß man jemals das Gefühl bekäme, es mit einem Dilettanten zu tun zu haben.« Broda: Einleitung, S. 2.

8   Als Kafkas Quellen für den Verschollenen gelten heute – neben Zeitungsartikeln und eventuellen

(historischen) Diskursanalyse denkbar.[9] Ich möchte hier eine dritte Vorgehensweise vorschlagen, nämlich eine vergleichende Analyse vor dem Hintergrund der Environmental Humanities und dem Konzept der *entangled naturecultures*,[10] auf welches ich im Folgenden näher eingehen werde. Bei den großen Ähnlichkeiten kann dabei Boltzmanns Reisebericht, in dem, so meine These, eher eine trennende Weltauffassung vertreten wird, als Kontrastfolie dienen, um in Kafkas *Verschollenem* eine spezifische verflochtene Weltauffassung im Sinne der Naturenkulturen sichtbar zu machen.

Es gibt in der Kafka-Forschung vereinzelte Hinweise darauf, dass Boltzmann als ein Vertreter der atomistischen Physik,[11] die später durch Einsteins Relativitätstheorie und die Quantenphysik – Bohr, Heisenberg, Planck, Schrödinger – abgelöst wurde,[12] eine

---

Berichten von Verwandten aus Amerika – *Der kleine Ahasverus* von Vilhelm Jensen, *Amerika heute und morgen* von Arthur Holitscher, der Reisebericht Amerika *a jeji úřednictvo* von František Soukup sowie *David Copperfield* von Charles Dickens. Vgl. Engel: Der Verschollene, S. 177f.; Hartmut Binder (1983): Erlesenes Amerika: »Der Verschollene«. In: ders.: *Kafka. Der Schaffensprozeß*. Frankfurt a. M.: Suhrkamp, S. 75–135; Alt: *Franz Kafka. Der Ewige Sohn*, S. 354–356; Anthony Northey (1988): Die Entdeckung der Neuen Welt. Kafkas amerikanische Vettern und sein Amerika-Roman. In: ders.: *Kafkas Mischpoche*. Berlin: Wagenbach, S. 47–60; Ritchie Robertson (1988): *Kafka: Judentum, Gesellschaft, Literatur* (Orig. *Kafka. Judaism, politics, and literature*, 1985). Aus dem Englischen übers. v. Josef Billen. Stuttgart: Metzler, S. 56–119; Harald Neumeyer (2013): Raum – Zeit – Macht. Franz Kafkas Der Verschollene und Arthur Holitschers Amerika. In: Harald Neumeyer / Wilko Steffens (Hgg.): *Kafka interkulturell*. Würzburg: Königshausen & Neumann, S. 451–483.

9   Vgl. exemplarisch etwa Harald Neumeyer (2004): »Das Land der Paradoxa« (Robert Heindl). Franz Kafkas In der Strafkolonie und die Deportationsdebatte um 1900. In: Claudia Liebrand / Franziska Schößler (Hgg.): *Textverkehr. Franz Kafka und die Tradition*. Würzburg: Königshausen & Neumann, S. 291–334; zur Diskursanalyse vgl. überblicksweise Harald Neumeyer (2013): Diskurs. In: Roland Borgards / Harald Neumeyer / Nicolas Pethes et. al. (Hgg.): *Literatur und Wissen. Ein interdisziplinäres Handbuch*. Stuttgart: Metzler, S. 32–35; zur historischen Diskursanalyse vgl. auch Clemens Kammler (2005): Historische Diskursanalyse (Michel Foucault). In: Klaus-Michael Bogdal (Hg.): *Neue Literaturtheorien. Eine Einführung*. Göttingen: Vandenhoeck und Ruprecht, S. 32–56.

10   Zu den *entangled naturecultures* vgl. Donna Haraway (2003): *The Companion Species Manifesto: Dogs, People, and Significant Otherness*. Vol. 1. Chicago: Prickly Paradigm Press; Donna Haraway (2008): *When Species Meet*. Minneapolis: University of Minnesota Press; Donna Haraway (2016): *Staying with the Trouble. Making Kin in the Chthulucene*. Durham/London: Duke University Press; Karen Barad (2007): *Meeting the Universe Halfway: Quantum Physics and the Entanglement of Matter and Meaning*. Durham/London: Duke University Press; Friederike Gesing / Michi Knecht / Michael Flitner et al. (Hgg.) (2019): *NaturenKulturen. Denkräume und Werkzeuge für neue politische Ökologien*. Bielefeld: transcript Verlag.

11   Zur Positionierung von Boltzmann zum Atomismus vgl. etwa das Kapitel *Für und gegen Atome (Boltzmann versus Mach)* bei Erhard Scheibe (2007): *Die Philosophie der Physiker*. München: Beck, S. 80–98.

12   Zur Tatsache, wie die Quantenphysik die Weltauffassung veränderte, vgl. etwa Carlo Rovelli (2021): *Helgoland. Wie die Quantentheorie unsere Welt verändert* (Orig. *Helgoland*, 2020). Aus dem

der prägenden intellektuellen Figuren zu Kafkas Zeit war.[13] Bisher hat die Kafka-Forschung Ludwig Boltzmanns *Reise eines deutschen Professors ins Eldorado* jedoch nicht für Interpretationen von Kafkas *Der Verschollene* fruchtbar gemacht. Dies soll mit dieser Arbeit geschehen.

Theoretische Grundlagen: *entangled naturecultures*

Als theoretischen Ausgangspunkt für den vorliegenden Aufsatz möchte ich mich vor allem auf zwei sich nahestehende Konzepte aus dem Bereich der Environmental Humanities beziehen: *naturecultures* (Donna Haraway; dt. »Naturenkulturen«) und *entanglement* (Karen Barad; dt. etwa »Verschränkung«, »Verflechtung«, »Ineinander-Gewebe«), die beide der Strömung des New Materialism (dt. »Neuer Materialismus«) zuzuordnen sind.[14]

Donna Haraway nutzt das Konzept der *naturecultures*, um auf eine »Vermischung« der Dinge hinzuweisen: »Never purely themselves, things are compound.«[15] Der ›Natur‹-Kultur-Dualismus (und damit eine vermeintliche Trennung von ›Natur‹ und Mensch) wurzelt ihrer Sicht nach in einer vielschichtigen Aneignung von ›Natur‹. Sie versteht die Welt als ein »Spiel« von *companion species*, wobei nicht (mehr) der Mensch im Mittelpunkt steht, sondern Intra- und Interaktion, Gegenseitigkeit, Begegnung, Beziehung und »Werden« (»becoming with«). Bei diesem »Spiel« kann alles denkbar Mögliche als »agent« beteiligt sein, etwa Technologien, Organismen, Landschaften, Menschen.[16] In ihrem Werk *Staying with the Trouble. Making Kin in the*

Italienischen übers. v. Enrico Heinemann. Hamburg: Rowohlt Verlag; zwischen der Quantenphysik und den Environmental Humanities besteht indes eine beachtenswerte Verbindung, vgl. dazu insb. Barad: *Meeting the Universe Halfway.*

13   Zur Rolle Boltzmanns zu Kafkas Zeit vgl. etwa Hartmut Binder (1979): *Kafka-Handbuch in zwei Bänden. Bd. 1.: Der Mensch und seine Zeit.* Stuttgart: Kröner, S. 35; Monika Schmitz-Emans (2010): *Franz Kafka: Epoche – Werk – Wirkung.* München: C. H. Beck, S. 33.

14   Einen guten Überblick über den New Materialism und den Material Turn geben etwa Heather I. Sullivan und Christa Grewe-Volpp. Vgl. Heather I. Sullivan (2015): New Materialism. In: Gabriele Dürbeck / Urte Stobbe (Hgg.): *Ecocriticism. Eine Einführung.* Köln/Weimar/Wien: Böhlau Verlag, S. 57–67; Christa Grewe-Volpp (2015): Ökofeminismus und Material Turn. In: Gabriele Dürbeck / Urte Stobbe (Hgg.): *Ecocriticism. Eine Einführung.* Köln/Weimar/Wien: Böhlau Verlag, S. 44–56; Zum Neuen Materialismus, insbesondere auch zu Donna Haraway und Karen Barad, vgl. weiterhin etwa auch Katharina Hoppe / Thomas Lemke (2021): *Neue Materialismen zur Einführung.* Hamburg: Junius.

15   Haraway: *When Species Meet,* S. 250.

16   Vgl. Haraway: *When Species Meet,* S. 3–8, 14–16, 18–20. »For many years I have written from the belly of powerful figures such as cyborgs, monkeys and apes, oncomice, and, more recently, dogs. In every case, the figures are at the same time creatures of imagined possibility and

Chthulucene hält Haraway fest: »Natures, cultures, subjects, and objects do not preexist their intertwined worldings. Companion species are relentlessly becoming-with.«[17] Dabei bezieht sie sich auch auf Karen Barad: »Barad's agential realism and intra-action become common sense, and perhaps a lifeline for Terran wayfarers.«[18]

Haraway untersucht in ihren Studien vor allem auch den materiellen Körper, dem eine andere Bedeutung zukommt als in der humanistischen Philosophie Descartes'scher Prägung. Körper sind keine bloßen, Maschinen ähnliche Objekte, die von rationalen Menschen (meist weißen Männern) definiert werden, sondern sie sind selbst aktiv an der Produktion von Bedeutung beteiligt. […] Das heißt, die Grenzen zwischen Mensch und Tier oder Mensch und Dingen entstehen erst in ihrer materiellen wie sozialen Interaktion, während sie sich gegenseitig bedingen und formen. Natur und Kultur sind in Haraways Konzeption auf komplexe Weise miteinander verwoben, was sie in dem Begriff »Natureculture« zu verdeutlichen sucht.[19]

Der Begriff *entanglement* hat seinen wissenschaftlichen Ursprung in der Quantenphysik und beschreibt dort die Quantenverschränkung.[20] In den letzten Jahren wurde dieser verstärkt in die Geistes-, Kultur- und Sozialwissenschaften übertragen. Maßgeblich für diese Übertragung war das Werk *Meeting the Universe Halfway. Quantum Physics and the Entanglement of Matter and Meaning* von Karen Barad.[21] In ihrer Arbeit bezieht sie sich auf die Quantentheorie Niels Bohrs, der eine atomistische Metaphysik und die kartesische Differenzierung zwischen Subjekt und Objekt in Frage stellt.

---

creatures of fierce and ordinary reality; the dimension tangle and require response. *When Species Meet* is about that kind of doubleness, but it is even more about the cat's cradle games in which those who are to be in the world are constituted in intra- and interaction. The partners do not precede the meeting; species of all kinds, living and not, are consequent on a subject- and object-shaping dance of encounters. Neither the partners nor the meetings in this book are merely literary conceits; rather, they are ordinary beings-in-encounter in the house, lab, field, zoo, park, office, prison, ocean, stadium, barn, or factory. As ordinary knotted beings, they are also always meaning-making figures that gather up those who respond to them into unpredictable kinds of ›we.‹« Ebd., S. 4−5.

17   Haraway: *Staying with the Trouble*, S. 13.

18   Haraway: *Staying with the Trouble*, S. 34.

19   Grewe-Volpp: *Ökofeminismus und Material Turn*, S. 49f.; mit Verweis auf Haraway: *The Companion Species Manifesto*, S. 2.

20   Vgl. etwa Francisco J. Duarte (2019): *Fundamentals of quantum entanglement*. Bristol: IOP Publishing; Jed Brody (2020): *Quantum Entanglement*. Cambridge/London: MIT Press; Rovelli: *Helgoland*, insb. S. 91−100.

21   Vgl. Barad: *Meeting the Universe Halfway*; Zur Bedeutung von Karen Barad für den New Materialism vgl. etwa Grewe-Volpp: *Ökofeminismus und Material Turn*, S. 49; Sullivan: *New Materialism*, S. 59.

Stattdessen schlägt sie als primäre ontologische Einheit *Phänomene* vor. Für Barad gibt es, in Anlehnung an Bohr, keine von vornherein festgelegten Grenzen von Entitäten (»things do not have inherently determinate boundaries or properties«),[22] vielmehr werden diese im Prozess der »intra-action« immer wieder neu erschaffen:

> It is through specific agential intra-actions that the boundaries and properties of the components of phenomena become determinate and that particular concepts (that is, particular material articulations of the world) become meaningful. [...] relata do not preexist relations; rather, relata-within-phenomena emerge through specific intra-actions. [...] The world is a dynamic process of intra-activity and materialization in the enactment of determinate causal structures with determinate boundaries, properties, meanings, and patterns of marks on bodies.[23]

Die Welt wird in diesem Sinne verstanden als ein dynamischer »ongoing flow of agency«, als »open process of mattering« und »ongoing reconfiguring«.[24]

Der New Materialism bietet somit, so Heather I. Sullivan, vor allem zwei Hauptthesen an: »erstens, dass wir nicht von der sonstigen Welt getrennt sind, sondern daran wie alles Wirkende auf der Erde teilhaben; zweitens [...], dass das Ineinander-Gewebe (entanglement) des Materiellen Formen des Kommunizierens und Interpretierens hervorbringt.«[25] Diese ontologische Perspektive möchte ich für meine Interpretation von Franz Kafkas *Der Verschollene* fruchtbar machen, indem ich mittels einer vergleichenden Gegenüberstellung des historischen Paralleltexts *Reise eines deutschen Professors ins Eldorado* von Ludwig Boltzmann, ausgehend von inhaltlichen Ähnlichkeiten, spezifische Eigenheiten von Kafkas Amerika-Roman herausarbeite. Durch dieses theoretisch-methodische Verfahren wird eine neue Interpretation von Kafkas *Der Verschollene* möglich. Meine These dabei lautet: Franz Kafkas *Der Verschollene* ist ein Roman, in dem sich – im Gegensatz zu großen Teilen von Boltzmanns Reisebericht – eine spezifische dynamisch-verflochtene Weltauffassung konstituiert, welche als *entangled naturecultures* beschrieben werden kann.

Inhaltliche Analyse und Interpretation

Bei einem inhaltlichen Vergleich der Texte ist grundsätzlich festzustellen, dass beide Hauptprotagonisten – Ludwig Boltzmann und Karl Roßmann, die einen überraschend

---

22 Barad: *Meeting the Universe Halfway*, S. 138.
23 Barad: *Meeting the Universe Halfway*, S. 140.
24 Barad: *Meeting the Universe Halfway*, S. 140f.
25 Sullivan: *New Materialism*, S. 59.

ähnlichen Familiennamen tragen —[26] nahezu dieselbe Reiseroute beschreiten. Beide überqueren zu Beginn ihrer Reise den atlantischen Ozean von Norddeutschland aus – Boltzmann von Wien kommend über Bremen, Roßmann von einem ungenannten Ort über Hamburg – und treffen schließlich mit dem Schiff in New York ein. Von dort bewegen sie sich Richtung Westen. Boltzmann reist mit der Eisenbahn bis nach San Francisco, Roßmann ist mit dem Automobil (etwa zum »Landhaus bei New York«), zu Fuß (etwa im »Marsch nach Ramses«) und zuletzt ebenfalls mit der Eisenbahn zum »Teater von Oklahama« (V, 387) unterwegs. Potenziell könnte Roßmann bei seiner Zugfahrt, genauso wie Boltzmann, die »Southern Pacific Railroad« (E, 411) genutzt haben. Beachtenswert in diesem Kontext ist außerdem eine Streichung Kafkas: Ursprünglich sollte für das »Teater« von San Francisco aus angeworben werden, worauf Jörg Wolfradt hinweist.[27] Im *Verschollenen* findet die Stadt zudem eine Erwähnung im Landhaus bei New York: Dort übergibt Herr Green Karl Roßmann »eine Karte Dritter nach San Francisko« (V, 124). Als ursprüngliches Reiseziel für die Figur Karl Roßmann war von Kafka im *Verschollenen* also wohl auch – genau wie bei Ludwig Boltzmann – San Francisco angedacht.

Boltzmann beschreibt in seiner Reiseerzählung verschiedene Orte und Themen, die in Kafkas Roman ebenso eine tragende Rolle spielen. Auf einige Beschreibungen möchte ich hier genauer eingehen, darunter das Meer, Wellen, Schiffe, Hafen, New York, Landhaus, Theater, Eisenbahn und Landschaft. Erstaunlich sind dabei einerseits die Parallelen zwischen Boltzmanns und Kafkas Text, exemplarisch zu nennen etwa der Verkehr, welcher durch Beschleunigung und Geschwindigkeit bestimmt wird. Andererseits lassen sich in Kafkas Text systematische und strukturelle Unterschiede erkennen, die sich als eine reflexive Distanz zu historischen Diskursen lesen lassen und eine spezifische naturkulturelle Weltauffassung zum Ausdruck bringen.

Hafen: Meer, Wellen, Schiffe

Der Hafen als Ort der Grenze zwischen Wasser und Land, Schiffe und der Ozean stellen für eine durch die Environmental Humanities gerahmte Untersuchung einen besonders interessanten Gegenstand dar.[28] In seiner Reiseerzählung zeigt sich Boltzmann zu-

---

26   Im Familiennamen findet sich bei beiden an zweiter Stelle der Buchstabe »o« sowie die Endung »mann«.

27   Vgl. Jörg Wolfradt (1996): *Der Roman bin ich. Schreiben und Schrift in Kafkas »Der Verschollene«.* Würzburg: Königshausen & Neumann, S. 154; mit Verweis auf Franz Kafka (1983): *Der Verschollene. Apparatband. (Kritische Ausgabe)* Hrsg. v. Jost Schillemeit. Frankfurt a.M.: S. Fischer, S. 255.

28   Vgl. etwa Stacy Alaimo (2012): States of Suspension: Trans-corporeality at Sea. In: *Interdisciplinary Studies in Literature and Environment* 19/3, S. 476–493; Astrida Neimanis (2017): *Bodies*

nächst auffällig begeistert und emotional ergriffen vom »großen Ozean« und seinem »Wellenspiel«, insbesondere während seiner Überfahrt mit dem Schiff »Kronprinz Wilhelm« nach Amerika (und der Rückfahrt mit der »Kaiser Wilhelm II«) (E, 408f., 425). So schreibt er relativ zu Beginn seines Berichts:

Lieber Leser! Meine Eile ist groß, aber die Meerfahrt von Bremen bis New York mit diesem banalen Witz ganz abzutun, bin ich doch nicht imstande. Die großen Ozeandampfer gehören zu dem Bewunderungswürdigsten, was der Mensch geschaffen hat und die Fahrt damit findet man bei jeder Wiederholung wiederum schöner. Das wundervoll brausende Meer jeden Tag wieder anders und jeden Tag wieder staunenswürdiger! Heute weißschäumend, wild stürmend. Siehe das Schiff dort! Nun ist es von den Wellen verschlungen! Nein! Schon taucht der Kiel wieder siegend empor.

Morgen ist das Wetter ruhig, das Meer glatt aber nebelgrau; nebelgrau auch der Himmel, wie man die Melancholie malt. Dann bricht die Sonne aus dem Nebel, und gelbe und rote Funken tanzen auf den Wellen zwischen den tiefschwarzen Flächen der Wolkenschatten, das goldige Licht vermählt sich der Finsternis. Und dann ist wiederum der ganze Himmel blau, und das Meer, azur in weiß, strahlt von so überwältigendem Glanze, daß man die Augen schließen muß. Nur an auserwählten Tagen schmückt es sich mit dem schönsten, dem ultramarinblauem Kleide, eine Farbe so dunkel und doch so leuchtend, mit milchweißem Schaume wie mit Spitzen eingefaßt! Ich lachte einmal, als ich las, daß ein Maler nach einer einzigen Farbe Tage und Nächte suchte; jetzt lache ich nicht mehr darüber. Ich habe beim Anblick dieser Farbe des Meeres geweint; wie kann uns eine bloße Farbe weinen machen? Dann wieder Mondesglanz oder Meerleuchten in pechschwarzer Nacht! Um von allen diesen Herrlichkeiten einen Begriff geben zu können, müßte man Maler sein und dann könnte man es erst recht nicht. (E, 408f.)

Im weiteren Verlauf schildert Boltzmann eindringlich die Einfahrt in den New Yorker Hafen:

---

of Water. Posthuman Feminist Phenomenology. London/New York: Bloomsbury Publishing; Nils Markwardt (2020): *Meer denken.* Philosophie Magazin 24.10.2020. https://www.philomag.de/ artikel/meer-denken (28.03.2023); Gunter Scholtz (2016): *Philosophie des Meeres.* Hamburg: Mare Verlag; Ralf Konersmann (2003): Die Philosophen und das Meer. In: *Akzente. Zeitschrift für Literatur* 50/3, S. 218–233; Rudolf Holbach / Dietmar von Reeken (2014): Das Meer als Geschichtsraum, oder: Warum eine historische Erweiterung der Meeresforschung unabdingbar ist. In: Dies. (Hgg.): *»Das ungeheure Wellen-Reich«. Bedeutungen, Wahrnehmungen und Projektionen des Meeres in der Geschichte.* Oldenburg: BIS-Verl. der Carl-von-Ossietzky-Univ., S. 7–22.

Wenn ich dann im Hafen von New York einfahre, so erfaßt mich immer eine Art Rausch. Diese turmhohen Häuser und die alles überragende Statue der Freiheit mit der Fackel! Dabei dieses Pfeifen und Singen der Schiffe durcheinander; das eine schroff warnend, das andere erschreckt aufschreiend, das eine munter pfeifend, das andere in Quarten melancholisch jammernd; dort erschallen gar die unnachahmlichen Töne der Sirenen! Wenn ich ein Musiker wäre, ich würde eine Symphonie komponieren: Der Hafen von New York.

Doch damals hatte ich keine Zeit zur Sentimentalität. (E, 410)

Auch in Franz Kafkas *Verschollenem* nehmen Wellen, Schiffe und der New Yorker Hafen eine besondere Rolle ein, so etwa zu Beginn des Romans im *Heizer*-Kapitel während der Überfahrt Karl Roßmanns mit der »Hamburg Amerika Linie« (V, 13). Dort schreibt Kafka:

Der Heizer klopfte respektvoll an der Türe an und forderte, als man »herein« rief, Karl mit einer Handbewegung auf, ohne Furcht einzutreten. Er trat auch ein, aber blieb an der Türe stehn. Vor den drei Fenstern des Zimmers sah er die Wellen des Meeres, und bei Betrachtung ihrer fröhlichen Bewegung schlug ihm das Herz, als hätte er nicht fünf lange Tage das Meer ununterbrochen gesehen.[29] Große Schiffe kreuzten gegenseitig ihre Wege und gaben dem Wellenschlag nur soweit nach, als es ihre Schwere erlaubte. Wenn man die Augen kleinmachte, schienen diese Schiffe vor lauter Schwere zu schwanken. Auf ihren Masten trugen sie schmale aber lange Flaggen, die zwar durch die Fahrt gestrafft wurden, trotzdem aber noch hin und her zappelten. Wahrscheinlich von den Kriegsschiffen her erklangen Salutschüsse, die Kanonenrohre eines solchen nicht all-zuweit vorüberfahrenden Schiffes, strahlend mit dem Reflex ihres Stahlmantels, waren wie gehätschelt von der sichern, glatten und doch nicht wagrechten [sic] Fahrt. Die kleinen Schiffchen und Boote konnte man wenigstens von der Tür aus nur in der Ferne beobachten, wie sie in Mengen in die Öffnungen zwischen den großen Schiffen ein-liefen. Hinter alledem aber stand Newyork und sah Karl mit den hunderttausend Fenstern seiner Wolkenkratzer an. Ja in diesem Zimmer wußte man, wo man war. (V, 19f.)

---

[29]　Laut Birgit Ottmüller-Wetzel dauerten die Überfahrten mit der H.A.P.A.G. von Hamburg nach New York auf den 1889 in Betrieb genommenen Doppelschrauber-Schnelldampfern etwa sieben Tage, auf den Auswandererschiffen, die vor allem Passagiere im Zwischendeck und Frachtgut transportierten, etwa neun Tage. Vgl. Birgit Ottmüller-Wetzel (1986): *Auswanderung über Hamburg. Die H.A.P.A.G. und die Auswanderung nach Nordamerika. 1870– 1914.* (Diss.) Berlin/ Hamburg: Freie Univ. Berlin, S. 65.

Wenig später heißt es:

> Inzwischen gieng vor den Fenstern das Hafenleben weiter, ein flaches Lastschiff mit einem Berg von Fässern […] zog vorüber und erzeugte in dem Zimmer fast Dunkelheit, kleine Motorboote […] rauschten nach den Zuckungen der Hände eines am Steuer aufrecht stehenden Mannes schnurgerade dahin, eigentümliche Schwimmkörper tauchten hie und da selbstständig aus dem ruhelosen Wasser, wurden gleich wieder überschwemmt und versanken vor dem erstaunten Blick, Boote der Ozeandampfer wurden von heiß arbeitenden Matrosen vorwärtsgerudert und waren voll von Passagieren, […] wenn es auch manche nicht unterlassen konnten, die Köpfe nach den wechselnden Scenerien zu drehn. Eine Bewegung ohne Ende, eine Unruhe, übertragen von dem unruhigen Element auf die hilflosen Menschen und ihre Werke. (V, 26f.)

Vor allem drei Dinge treten bei Boltzmanns und Kafkas Beschreibungen auffällig und gleichermaßen in Erscheinung, wenn auch unterschiedlich ausgeprägt und gewichtet: erstens eine emotionale Ergriffenheit der Protagonisten, zweitens konstante Bewegung und Transformation, sowie, drittens Wechselwirkung.[30]

Sowohl bei Boltzmann als auch bei Kafka ist zu beobachten, dass das Meer mit seinem »Wellenspiel« und der Hafen eine starke emotionale Reaktion der Hauptfiguren verursachen. So berichtet Boltzmann von einem »wundervoll brausende[n; N. W.] Meer«, das »jeden Tag wieder anders und jeden Tag wieder staunenswürdiger« ist. Das Spiel der Farben und des Lichts ist für Boltzmann »überwältigend« und beim Anblick einer bestimmten »Farbe des Meeres« ist Boltzmann so ergriffen, dass er weint. Auch bei der Einfahrt in den New Yorker Hafen erfasst Boltzmann »immer eine Art Rausch«. In Kafkas Roman bewirkt der Anblick der »Wellen des Meeres« mit ihrer »fröhlichen Bewegung« bei der Figur Karl Roßmann in Form des gesteigerten Herzschlages ebenfalls eine intensive emotionale Reaktion.

Das Meer und die Wellen sind sowohl bei Boltzmann als auch bei Kafka weiterhin durch eine umfassende Dynamik und regelmäßige Veränderung gekennzeichnet. Das betrifft bei Boltzmann einerseits die Gestalt des Wassers und der Wellen – diese schwankt von »weißschäumend, wild stürmend« bis hin zu »glatt«–, andererseits und noch vielmehr das Licht und die Farben des Wassers sowie des Himmels. So reicht das Farbspektrum des Meeres von »tiefschwarz« »vermählt« mit tanzenden »gelben und roten Funken«, über »nebelgrau«, »azur in weiß« bis hin zu »ultramarinblau[] […] mit milchweißem Schaume«. In Kafkas Hafenszene ist ebenso eine allumfassende

---

30   Meer und Wellen repräsentieren nicht nur bei Kafka und Boltzmann Mannigfaltigkeit, Bewegung, Wechselwirkung, Transformation und rufen emotionale Reaktionen hervor. Vgl. hierzu überblicksweise etwa Scholtz: *Philosophie des Meeres*; Alaimo: *States of Suspension: Trans-corporeality at Sea*; Konersmann: *Die Philosophen und das Meer*.

Bewegung und Transformation zu erkennen, doch um einen entscheidenden verflochtenen Faktor erweitert. So »kreuzten« dort Schiffe »gegenseitig ihre Wege«. Bei Boltzmann »strahlt« das Meer, bei Kafka hingegen strahlt der »Reflex« des »Stahlmantels« der Schiffe. Während man bei Boltzmann die Augen »schließen muß«, muss man sie bei Kafka »klein« machen, um das »schwanken« der Schiffe zu erkennen. Nicht nur das Meer, die Wellen und der Himmel (Boltzmann) sind bei Kafka in Bewegung, sondern und vor allem auch die sich darin befindlichen und konstant bewegenden Schiffe und Menschen – und alles damit Verbundene – in Wechselwirkung mit den Elementen. Beispiele für diese naturkulturelle Verflechtung mit dem Wasser und dem Wind sind etwa die Flaggen, Schwimmkörper, Motorboote und Schiffe.

Doch auch bei Boltzmann kommen Schiffe vor. Deren Vielzahl, Gewirr und Omnipräsenz insbesondere im New Yorker Hafen stellt eine auffällige Gemeinsamkeit dar, die sich im Modus der synästhetischen Wahrnehmung allerdings im Detail unterscheiden. Boltzmann betont im Hafen vornehmlich akustische Eindrücke, er spricht von einem im »Rausch« wahrgenommenen »Pfeifen und Singen der Schiffe durcheinander«, was er als »Symphonie« des New Yorker Hafens versteht. Kafka wiederum schildert neben zahlreichen optischen Eindrücken *gleichzeitig* auch »Salutschüsse« von den »Kriegsschiffen«. Dies führt an dieser Stelle zu einem der entscheidenden Unterschiede zwischen Kafka und Boltzmann: Bei Boltzmann existieren die Eindrücke nur getrennt voneinander – hier die vermeintlich rein ›natürliche‹ Welt (Meer, Himmel, Licht), dort die vermeintlich rein ›menschliche‹ Welt (New York, Häuser, Freiheitsstatue, Schiffe). Boltzmanns Programm – eine getrennte, atomistische Welt mit dem Menschen an der Spitze – wird in diesem Kontext durch zwei Punkte bekräftigt: die Konjunktivkonstruktionen im Rahmen der Beschreibungen (»müßte man Maler sein«; »Wenn ich ein Musiker wäre«) und den finalen Ausspruch »Doch damals hatte ich keine Zeit zur Sentimentalität.« Kafkas Beschreibungen lassen sich hingegen, so meine These, vielmehr mit dem Konzept nonbinärer *entangled naturecultures* fassen, in der der Mensch untrennbar in Naturkultur verflochten ist und darin sympoietisch intra-agiert.[31] Kafkas Kontrast-Programm in Form einer neuen Weltauffassung bringt damit eher folgender Satz auf den Punkt: »Eine Bewegung ohne Ende, eine Unruhe, übertragen von dem unruhigen Element auf die hilflosen Menschen und ihre Werke.«

Genauso wie ›Natur‹ und ›Kultur‹ bei Boltzmann grundsätzlich getrennt sind, sind es bei ihm äquivalent die Arten der sinnlichen Eindrücke: entweder existieren diese rein optisch oder rein akustisch. Bei Kafka hingegen vermischen sich die Eindrücke in der Hafenszene als synästhetisches Gesamtbild zu einem buchstäblichen – um Kafkas

---

31   Vgl. Haraway: *The Companion Species Manifesto*; dies.: *When Species meet*; dies.: *Staying with the Trouble*; Barad: *Meeting the Universe Halfway*; Gesing et al.: *NaturenKulturen*.

Begriff zu nutzen – »Hafen*leben*« [eigene Hervorh.]: optisch, akustisch, räumlich, emotional.

Zuletzt ist sowohl bei Boltzmann als auch bei Kafka Interaktion zu erkennen, jedoch unterschiedlicher Art. Bei Boltzmann findet die Interaktion in getrennten Sphären statt. So beschränkt sie sich einerseits visuell auf die vermeintlich rein ›natürliche‹ Sphäre, also auf Interaktionen zwischen Meer, Himmel, Sonne und Mond, was zu regelmäßigen Farbveränderungen führt. So sind der Himmel und gleichermaßen das Meer »nebelgrau«. Plötzlich aber »bricht die Sonne aus dem Nebel, und gelbe und rote Funken tanzen auf den Wellen zwischen den tiefschwarzen Flächen der Wolkenschatten«. Analog erkennt der Physiker offensichtlich Spiegelungen des Himmels im Ozean, wenn er diese in ihren blauen und weißen Farbtönen direkt nacheinander stellt. Andererseits existiert bei Boltzmann eine davon getrennte auditive Aktivität der Schiffe des Hafens, also einer vermeintlich rein ›menschlichen‹ Sphäre. Explizit kann in diesem Punkt nicht von einer Wechselwirkung gesprochen werden, da jedes Schiff »durcheinander« unabhängig für sich tönt. Entscheidend ist dabei die mehrfach von Boltzmann unterstrichene Begeisterung für die menschlichen Errungenschaften und deren ›Sieg‹ über die Natur. So gehören für ihn »die großen Ozeandampfer […] zu dem Bewunderungswürdigsten, was der Mensch geschaffen hat«. Wenn auch die Schiffe regelmäßig »von den Wellen verschlungen« werden, tauchen sie doch stets »wieder siegend empor.« Noch bewunderungswürdiger als die »Naturschönheit« ist für Boltzmann nur die »Kunst des Menschen«, der die Natur in Boltzmanns Augen bezwungen hat. So schreibt er wenig später:

> Wenn eines unserer Bewunderung noch mehr wert sein kann als diese Naturschönheit, so ist es die Kunst des Menschen, welcher in dem seit den Zeiten der Phönizier und noch viel länger geführten Kampf mit diesem unendlichem [sic] Meere so vollständig siegte. Wie unbarmherzig der Kiel die Flut durchschneidet, wie der Meergott wild aufschäumt unter der bohrenden Schraube! Fürwahr, das höchste Wunder der Natur, das ist der kunstfertige Geist des Menschen! (E, 409)

Auch bei Kafka werden Schiffe »in Mengen« verschlungen, doch nicht wie bei Boltzmann vom Meer, um daraus wie aus einem Kampf siegreich hervorzugehen, sondern von anderen Schiffen. Die Schiffe selbst indes »gaben dem Wellenschlag nur soweit nach, als es ihre Schwere erlaubte«, was man folglich mehr als ein dynamisches Wechselspiel (Kafka) statt einen Wettkampf (Boltzmann) verstehen kann. Siegt bei Boltzmann der omnipotente Mensch über die Natur, sind die Menschen bei Kafka »hilflos«. Was im *Verschollenen* in dieser Szene entwickelt wird, lässt sich vor diesem Hintergrund als eine Welt beschreiben, in der der Mensch untrennbarer, partiell auch machtloser, Bestandteil von Naturkultur ist.

Das Schauspiel im New Yorker Hafen betrachtet die Figur Roßmann genau an der Türschwelle – im Zwischenraum – durch »drei Fenster« des Zimmers, also durch ein trennendes, doch zugleich transparentes, durchlässiges und damit auch verbindendes Medium.[32] Ein neuer produktiver Möglichkeits- und Wirklichkeitsraum entsteht, in dem die Wechselwirkung verschiedener Aktanten – Menschen, Boote, Wellen, Luft – und eine Mannigfaltigkeit an Bewegungen im Mittelpunkt stehen. Roßmann, räumlich eigentlich getrennt von den Wellen und dem Meer, wird durch sein Innehalten und empathisches Betrachten selbst Teil des Hafen-Spektakels, das sich vor seinen Augen abspielt. Er ist einerseits mit dem Schiff gemeinsam in Bewegung, bleibt jedoch an der Türschwelle »stehn«, um durch sein Sehen und Fühlen wiederum Teil einer fließenden Dynamik des New Yorker Hafens zu werden. Roßmann ist dabei emotional hochgradig bewegt, sein subjektives Ich löst sich für einen Moment auf und er wird Eins mit der Atmosphäre des Hafenschauspiels, was sich mit Stacy Alaimo als »trans-corporeality« fassen lässt.[33]

Auch für Boltzmanns auffällige Beschreibung der Freiheitstatue und der New Yorker Hochhäuser findet sich bei Kafka eine Entsprechung, wobei sich Kafkas Beschreibung in einem entscheidenden Detail unterscheidet. Bei Kafka heißt es in Bezug auf die Freiheitsstatue im ersten Satz des Romans:

Als der siebzehnjährige Karl Roßmann, der von seinen armen Eltern nach Amerika geschickt worden war, [...] in dem langsam gewordenen Schiff in den Hafen von

---

[32] Jörg Wolfradt etwa spricht von einem sich wiederholenden Motiv der »höheren Beobachtung« im *Verschollenen* im Zusammenhang mit Fenstern, Balkonen oder Galerien. Vgl. Wolfradt: *Der Roman bin ich*, S. 148f.

[33] Vgl. Stacy Alaimo (2010): *Bodily Natures: Science, Environment and the Material Self.* Indianapolis: Indiana University Press; Alaimo: *States of Suspension: Trans-corporeality at Sea*; vgl. auch Timothy Mortons »ambient poetics«, Timothy Morton (2009): *Ecology Without Nature. Rethinking Environmental Aesthetics.* Cambridge/London: Harvard University Press, S. 34; vgl. in diesem Kontext etwa auch Ursula K. Heise (2008): *Sense of Place and Sense of Planet. The Environmental Imagination of the Global.* New York: Oxford University Press, S. 15–115 (=Teil 1: *World Wide Webs: Imagining the Planet*). In ihrem Aufsatz *States of Suspension: Trans-corporeality at Sea* bemerkt Alaimo, dass der Ozean mit den Grenzen des terrestrisch-menschlichen Verstehens konfrontiert. Vgl. Alaimo: *States of Suspension: Trans-corporeality at Sea*, S. 477. Das Erkennen dieser Grenzen »may be an epistemological-ethical moment that debars us from humanist privilege and keeps us ›fixed or lost as in wonder or contemplation.‹« Ebd.; für Alaimo ist die suspension, also eine Unterbrechung oder Aufschub in Form einer »receptiveness«, dasjenige, wodurch die Intra-Aktion materieller Agenzien in der Welt erkannt werden kann. Vgl. ebd.; Alaimo arbeitet in ihrem Konzept von trans-corporeality dezidiert mit den Theorien von Donna Haraway und Karen Barad. Vgl. ebd., S. 479; sie sieht in der suspension eine Lebenskraft (»buoyancy«), »a sense that the human is held, but not held up, by invisible genealogies and a maelstrom of often imperceptible substances that disclose connections between humans and the sea.« Ebd., S. 478.

Newyork einfuhr, erblickte er die schon längst beobachtete Statue der Freiheitsgöttin wie in einem plötzlich stärker gewordenen Sonnenlicht. Ihr Arm mit dem Schwert ragte wie neuerdings empor und um ihre Gestalt wehten die freien Lüfte.

»So hoch«, sagte er sich (V, 7)

So wird die Fackel der Statue bei Kafka bekanntermaßen zum Schwert, während sie bei Boltzmann, der Realität entsprechend, eine Fackel ist – eine geringfügige, jedoch beachtenswerte Änderung.[34] Übereinstimmung zwischen Boltzmann und Kafka besteht indes in der imponierenden Höhe und Größe der Gebäude.

Verkehr: Geschwindigkeit, Züge, Automobile

Mobilität, Verkehr und das Reisen erfahren in den umweltorientierten Geistes- und Sozialwissenschaften hohe Beachtung.[35] Aus Perspektive der Environmental Humanities und in dieser Arbeit ist dabei vor allem die Tatsache interessant, dass Mensch-Natur-Beziehungen beim Reisen besonders klar zutage treten.[36] In seinem *Eldorado*-Reisebericht zeigt sich Boltzmann etwa besonders begeistert von der Verkehrsgeschwindigkeit in den USA. Eine »Tramwayfahrt« in New York – »welch reichen Stoff der Unterhaltung und Beobachtung bietet nur eine einfache Tramwayfahrt!« (E, 411) – kommentiert er mit: »wie rasend schnell eine freie Strecke durchmessen wird« (E, 411). Die Zugfahrt mit der »Southern Pacific Railroad« wiederum schildert er wie folgt: »In

---

[34] Über das Schwert wurde in der Kafka-Forschung vielfach diskutiert. Vgl. etwa eine Übersicht bei Neumeyer: *Raum – Zeit – Macht*, S. 458f. oder Karlheinz Fingerhut (1997): Auswandern – Schreiben. Kafkas Der Verschollene als doppeltes Erzählspiel und als Experiment einer doppelten Lektüre. In: Maurice Godé / Michel Vanoosthuyse (Hgg.): *Entre critique et rire. Le Disparu de Franz Kafka.* Montpellier: Groupe de Recherche Etudes Germaniques et Centre-Européennes de l'Université Paul-Valéry, S. 117–143, hier S. 118.

[35] Vgl. etwa Michael Cronin (2022): *Eco-Travel. Journeying in the Age of the Anthropocene.* Cambridge: Cambridge University Press; Peter Adey (2017): *Mobility. Second Edition.* Oxon/New York: Routledge; Peter Merriman / Lynn Pearce (Hgg.) (2018): *Mobility and the Humanities.* Oxon/New York: Routledge; Julie Cidell / David Prytherch (Hgg.) (2015): *Transport, Mobility, and the Production of Urban Space.* New York/Oxon: Routledge; Thomas Zeller (2022): *Consuming Landscapes. What We See When We Drive and Why It Matters.* Baltimore: Johns Hopkins University Press; Sigurd Bergmann / Thomas Hoff / Tore Sager (Hgg.) (2014): *Spaces of Mobility. The Planning, Ethics, Engineering and Religion of Human Motion.* Oxon/New York: Routledge.

[36] Vgl. etwa Michael Cronin: »Human encounters with the natural world are inseparable from the history of travel.«; »The natural world is profoundly shaped by human agency and human agency is, in turn, deeply influenced by the constructs it uses to interpret or understand that world. These constructs are both revealed by and elaborated through the medium of writing about travel.« Cronin: *Eco-Travel,* Abstract, S. 3.

vier Tagen und vier Nächten kam ich von New York nach San Franzisko [sic]. Man wird einfach fortgeschleudert, gewissermaßen fortgeschossen.« (ebd.) Die Zuggleise beschreibt er bei seiner Fahrt als »endloses Band, das mit rasender Geschwindigkeit unter dem Wagen hervorgezogen wird.« (E, 411f.)

Auch in Kafkas Amerika spielt die Geschwindigkeit – vor allem auch in Verbindung mit dem Verkehr – eine auffällige Rolle, worauf die Kafka-Forschung vielfach hingewiesen hat:[37] »Alle Entwicklungen gehn hier so schnell vor sich« (V, 68). Wird man als Passagier bei Boltzmann im Zug »einfach fortgeschleudert, gewissermaßen fortgeschossen«, schreibt Kafka über eine Fahrt Roßmanns mit der »Untergrundbahn« vom Hotel occidental in die Stadt Ramses: »die Fahrt vergieng im Nu, als werde der Zug ohne jeden Widerstand nur hingerissen« (V, 194). In beiden Fällen findet sich eine Passiv-Formulierungen, jedoch mit einem kleinen Unterschied: Bei Boltzmann betreffen die Verben die individuellen menschlichen Passagiere, bei Kafka hingegen das ganze ontologische Geflecht »Zug«. Das Verb ›schießen‹ im Verkehrskontext findet sich bei Kafka außerdem in Bezug auf Automobile, so »schoß« im *Verschollenen* etwa »hie und da […] ein Automobil aus dem Nebel« (V, 139f.). »Kolonnen von Fuhrwerken«, die sich »so ununterbrochen dahinzogen, daß niemand die Straße hätte überqueren können« (V, 140) werden im Roman darüber hinaus beschrieben – und ein Verkehr, der »blitzschnell vorbeijagte« (V, 141), Automobile, die »vorübereilten« (V, 151) oder »Eisenbahnzüge«, die »auf den hoch sich schwingenden Viadukten donnern.« (V, 151)

In Kafkas *Verschollenem* spielt – stets verflochten mit Dynamik und Geschwindigkeit – allerdings noch ein weiterer Aspekt eine Rolle, der in diesem Kontext eine essentielle Unterscheidung zu Boltzmann darstellt: Konstante Transformation und Vermischung. Über New York schreibt Kafka:

Und morgen wie abend und in den Träumen der Nacht vollzog sich auf dieser Straße ein immer drängender Verkehr, der von oben gesehn sich als eine aus immer neuen Anfängen ineinandergestreute Mischung von verzerrten menschlichen Figuren und von Dächern der Fuhrwerke aller Art darstellte, von der aus sich noch eine neue vervielfältigte wildere Mischung von Lärm, Staub und Gerüchen erhob (V, 55)

Kafkas Amerika zeichnet sich also nicht alleine durch Geschwindigkeit und neue Technologien wie Automobile, »sprühende[s; N.W.] elektrische[s; N.W.] Licht« (V, 66), Züge und »elektrische[] Straßenbahn[en; N.W.]« (V, 74) aus, sondern diese befinden sich zudem in einer »unaufhörlichen« Veränderung, Verflechtung, Vermischung. Ganze 36 Mal kommt im Roman etwa der Begriff »immerfort« vor, »unun-

---

37　Vgl. etwa Manfred Engel (2010): Kafka und die moderne Welt. In: ders. / Bernd Auerochs (Hgg.): *Kafka Handbuch. Leben – Werk – Wirkung.* Stuttgart: Metzler, S. 498–515.

terbrochen« immerhin zehn Mal und »unaufhörlich« sieben Mal. So ist im »riesenhaften« (V, 66) Betrieb des Onkels, für dessen »Durchsicht man viele Tage verwenden mußte, selbst wenn man jede Abteilung gerade nur gesehen haben wollte« (V, 67), besonders die telefonische Abteilung paradigmatisch, welche »unaufhörliche telephonische und telegraphische Verbindungen mit den Klienten unterhalten mußte.« (V, 66) In diesem ›Verbindungssaal‹, in dem ein »beständiger Verkehr« (V, 67) herrscht, diesem Ineinander-Gewebe, welches man mit Timothy Morton als *mesh* fassen könnte,[38] werden »unaufhörlich« Verbindungen gelöst und neu erschaffen. Ob nun der »alles umfassende Verkehr« (V, 270), die Stadt New York als »ineinandergestreute Mischung [...], von der sich noch eine neue vervielfältigte wildere Mischung [...] erhob«, oder die »unaufhörlichen« Verbindungen im Betrieb des Onkels: Ich möchte diese Form der Darstellung mit Karen Barad als *entanglement* fassen – Kafkas Welt im *Verschollenen* lässt sich als eine Welt verstehen, die sich im Prozess der intraaction immer wieder neu erschafft, als ein »ongoing flow of agency«, als »open process of mattering«, als »ongoing reconfiguring«.[39] Genau in diesem Punkt geht Kafka einen Schritt weiter als Boltzmann. Während bei Boltzmann, dem atomistischen Physiker, die Weltauffassung getrennt ist – dezidiert in Form einer binären Trennung der Sphären ›Kultur‹ und ›Natur‹ – ist die Welt in Kafkas Verschollenem vielmehr eine »aus immer neuen Anfängen ineinandergestreute Mischung«: Naturkultur.

Landhaus: Luxus, Dinner, Klavierspiel

Neben dem Verkehr und der Geschwindigkeit finden sich zwischen Boltzmann und Kafka weitere Parallelen. Eine erste ist das amerikanische Landhaus, das sowohl bei Boltzmann als auch bei Kafka eine essentielle Rolle spielt und als Grenzort zwischen Stadt und Land aus Perspektive der Environmental Humanities beachtenswert ist.[40] Während seiner Zeit in Berkeley wird Boltzmann auf den »prachtvollen Landsitz in der Nähe von Livermore« von »Mrs. Hearst« eingeladen, die die Universität Berkeley mit ihrem Privatvermögen finanziert:[41]

---

38 *Mesh* versteht Morton als »interconnectedness of all living and non-living things«. Vgl. Timothy Morton (2010): *The Ecological Thought*. Cambridge/London: Harvard University Press, S. 28.

39 Vgl. Barad: *Meeting the Universe Halfway*, S. 140f.

40 Zum amerikanischen Landhaus vgl. etwa Clive Aslet (2004): *The American Country House*. New Haven/London: Yale University Press; historisch vgl. etwa Charles Edward Hooper (1905): *The Country House. A Practical Manual of the Planning and Construction of the American Country Home and its Surroundings*. New York: Doubleday, Page & Company; im größeren Kontext vgl. etwa Thomas F. Gieryn (2002): What buildings do. In: *Theory and Society* 31/1, S. 35–74.

41 Phoebe Hearst (1842–1919), Witwe des Multimillionärs, Bergbauunternehmers und Politikers George Hearst (1820–1891). Vgl. Phoebe A. Hearst Museum: *Our Founder: Phoebe Apperson*

Am nächsten würde man der Wahrheit kommen, wenn man sagte, sie ist die Universität Berkeley. In Europa ist die alma mater eine antike Idealgestalt, in Amerika ist es eine wirkliche Dame und, was am wichtigsten ist, mit wirklichen Millionen, von denen sie alljährlich so etliche zur Erweiterung der Universität hergibt; auch meine Amerikareise wurde natürlich aus ihrem Gelde bezahlt. Der Präsident der Universität [...] ist nur das ausführende Organ der Trustees, an deren Spitze Mrs. Hearst steht. (E, 417)

Über das Landhaus von Mrs. Hearst schreibt Boltzmann weiter:

Sie hatte mich, wie schon erwähnt, mit einer Reihe anderer an der Sommerschule lehrenden [sic] Professoren nach ihrem Landsitze in der Nähe von Livermore geladen, einem Juwel, wie es Luxus, Reichtum und guter Geschmack nur in so verschwenderisch ausgestatteter Natur zu schaffen vermögen. Auf der Bahnstation empfingen uns die Kutschen und bald ging es durch ein stark phantastisches aber nicht unschönes Eingangstor nach einem Parke von fabelhafter Baumpracht und Blumenschönheit. Der Reichtum setzt sich hier in Wasser um, und wo dieses nicht gespart wird, ersteht in Kalifornien ein Blumenflor, der Sommer und Winter gleichmäßig fortblüht. Lange, doch für mich noch zu kurz, durchquerten wir den Park, der auch die schönsten Aussichtspunkte nach dem Mount Diable und Mount Hamilton bietet. Endlich erreichten wir das Wohnhaus. Es ist in portugiesisch-mexikanischem Stile erbaut, ein Kranz von Gebäuden rund um einen durch schwere eiserne Tore verschlossenen Hof; offenbar eine Art Festung. Den Mittelpunkt des Hofes bildet ein antiker Marmorbrunnen, den die Besitzerin selbst in Verona kaufte und bis ans stille Meer hatte transferieren lassen. Nach ihm heißt der ganze Landsitz »Hazienda del pozzo di Verona«. (E, 419f.)

In Franz Kafkas *Verschollenem* nimmt Pollunders »Landhaus bei New York« indes bekanntlich gar ein ganzes Kapitel ein (V, 76–127). Genauso wie Boltzmann beschreibt Kafka das Landhaus als riesenhaft, pompös und verschwenderisch:

»Wir sind angekommen«, sagte Herr Pollunder gerade in einem von Karls verlorenen Momenten. Das Automobil stand vor einem Landhaus, das, nach der Art von Landhäusern reicher Leute in der Umgebung Newyorks, umfangreicher und höher war, als es sonst für ein Landhaus nötig ist, das bloß einer Familie dienen soll. Da nur der untere Teil des Hauses beleuchtet war, konnte man gar nicht bemessen, wie weit es in die Höhe reichte. Vorne rauschten Kastanienbäume, zwischen denen – das Gitter war schon geöffnet – ein kurzer Weg zur Freitreppe des Hauses führte. (V, 76)

Hearst. https://hearstmuseum.berkeley.edu/phoebe-heast/ (28.03.2023) sowie Matthew Bernstein (2021): *George Hearst. Silver King of the Gilded Age.* Norman: University of Oklahoma Press.

Eine auffällige Parallele zwischen Boltzmanns Reisebericht und Kafkas Roman ist die Tatsache, dass beide den Begriff »Festung« für das Landhaus verwenden. Daneben gibt es weitere Gemeinsamkeiten.

Sowohl bei Boltzmann als auch bei Kafka finden sich in den Landhaus-Beschreibungen, erstens, Luxus und Reichtum in verschwenderischem Ausmaß.

Zweitens verfügen beide Landhäuser über einen großen Garten mit parkähnlicher Struktur, in denen Pflanzen eine zentrale Rolle einnehmen. Bei Boltzmann findet sich dort eine »fabelhafte Blumenpracht«, bei Kafka sind es »Kastanienbäume« und eine »Kastanienallee« (V, 76). Die Blumen wiederum finden sich bei Kafka dann wenig später im Speisezimmer des Landhauses: »schob Karl und Klara vor sich in das Speisezimmer, das besonders infolge der Blumen auf dem Tische, die sich aus Streifen frischen Laubes halb aufrichteten, sehr festlich aussah« (V, 79). Das Speisezimmer verfügt darüber hinaus über eine »große Glastüre zum Garten hin«, durch die »ein starker Duft [...] herein[wehte; N.W.] wie in eine Gartenlaube«. (V, 80). Erneut sind hier bei Kafka starke Vermischungen festzustellen, in diesem Fall zwischen Kultur und Pflanzenwelt.

Drittens sticht bei beiden Beschreibungen das Tor bzw. Gitter heraus. Boltzmann beschreibt »einen durch schwere eiserne Tore verschlossenen Hof«, Kafka ein geöffnetes »Gitter«. Auch an einer anderen Stelle in Kafkas Amerika-Roman finden sich darüber hinaus relativ prägnant Gitter bzw. Gittertore, und zwar auf dem »Marsch nach Ramses«, ebenfalls in Verbindung mit luxuriösen Landhäusern und Gärten:

> Gegen Abend kamen sie in eine mehr ländliche fruchtbare Gegend. Ringsherum sah man ungeteilte Felder die sich in ihrem ersten Grün über sanfte Hügel legten, reiche Landsitze umgrenzten die Straße und stundenlang gieng man zwischen den vergoldeten Gittern der Gärten, mehrmals kreuzten sie den gleichen langsam fließenden Strom und viele mal [sic] hörten sie über sich die Eisenbahnzüge auf den hoch sich schwingenden Viadukten donnern. (V, 151)

Kafka spricht hier im *Verschollenen* – möglicherweise als Hinweis auf San Francisco, das ursprünglich angedachte Reiseziel Roßmanns – von »vergoldeten Gittern der Gärten«, Boltzmann an anderer Stelle vom »goldene[n; N.W.] Tor« als Synonym für die »Bai von San Franzisko« [sic] (E, 416).[42] Boltzmann artikuliert in diesem Zusam-

---

42   Den Namen »Golden Gate« erhielt die die Meerenge bereits 1846 von John C. Frémont, der damals die Unabhängigkeit Kaliforniens von Mexiko erklärte und die Meerenge als *Chrysopylae* bezeichnete (griech. für »Golden Gate«, wohl auch in Anspielung an das Goldene Horn am Bosporus, griech. *Chrysokeras*, welches gewissermaßen die ›Grenze‹ zwischen Europa und Asien darstellt). Vgl. Golden Gate Bridge, Highway and Transportation District: *Key Dates in Bridge District History*. https://www.goldengate.org/bridge/history-research/moments-events/key-dates/ (28.03.2022); »The name given by John C. Frémont in 1846 to the entrance of San

menhang seinen offenbar unmöglichen »Wunsch, malen zu können«, den er »wie schon oft auf der Amerikareise« (E, 416) hat, Kafka an anderer Stelle freilich den berühmten unmöglichen *Wunsch, Indianer zu werden.*[43]

Entscheidender Unterschied zwischen Boltzmann und Kafka ist in Bezug auf das Landhaus erneut die Art der Weltbeschreibung: bei Boltzmann eher trennend, bei Kafka eher vermischend. So ist das Wohnhaus bei Boltzmann vom Park mit seinen zahlreichen Pflanzen streng getrennt. Die Grenze zwischen ›Natur‹ und ›Kultur‹ stellt für Boltzmann hier »ein Kranz von Gebäuden« und ein durch »schwere eiserne Tore« verschlossener Hof dar. In Kafkas Beschreibung hingegen ist das Gitter »geöffnet«, genauso wie die (zumindest bis zur Schließung durch Herrn Green) geöffnete »große Glastüre zum Garten hin«, durch die »ein starker Duft« hereinweht und das Speisezimmer für Roßmann wie »eine Gartenlaube« erscheinen lässt. Auch ist das Landhaus bei Kafka nur teilweise und nicht vollständig elektrisch beleuchtet – »Die neue elektrische Leitung ist bisher nur im Speisezimmer eingeführt« (V, 88) –, weshalb das Haus gleichzeitig durch »Armleuchter« von Dienern beleuchtet wird. In Boltzmanns Wohnung in Berkeley ist hingegen dezidiert »alles elektrisch beleuchtet« (E, 414). Auch Karls Schlafzimmer ist durch das Fenster zum Garten durch eine Offenheit und verbindende Eigenschaften geprägt. Mit anderen Worten: Die ›kulturelle‹ und die ›natürliche‹ Sphäre sind in Kafkas Landhaus nicht getrennt, sondern stets »streng zusammengehörig[]« (V, 108) – *entangled naturecultures.*

> Ein überraschendes Dunkel vor dem Fenster erklärte sich durch einen Baumwipfel, der sich dort in seinem vollen Umfang wiegte. Man hörte Vögelgesang. Im Zimmer selbst, das vom Mondlicht noch nicht erreicht war, konnte man allerdings fast gar nichts unterscheiden. [...] Er setzte sich aufs Fensterbrett und sah und horchte hinaus: Ein aufgestörter Vogel schien sich durch das Laubwerk des alten Baumes zu drängen. Die Pfeife eines Newyorker Vorortzuges erklang irgendwo im Land. Sonst war es still. (V, 89)

Trotz der zahlreichen inhaltlichen Parallelen in den Landhaus-Beschreibungen zeigt sich hier also die maßgebliche Differenz zwischen Kafka und Boltzmann: So ist im *Verschollenen* alles – egal ob organisch oder anorganisch, mechanisch oder biologisch (exemplarisch hier etwa die analoge Nennung von »Vögelgesang« und der »Pfeife

---

Francisco Bay, in anticipation not of the Gold Rush, but of the riches of Asia that would enter the port.« William Bright (1998): *1500 California Place Names. Their Origin and Meaning. A revised version of 1000 California Place Names, by Erwin G. Gudde, third edition.* Berkeley/Los Angeles/London: University of California Press, S. 37.

43 Franz Kafka (2010): Wunsch, Indianer zu werden. In: ders.: *Die Erzählungen und andere ausgewählte Prosa.* Hrsg. v. Roger Hermes. Frankfurt a.M.: S. Fischer, S. 7.

eines Newyorker Vorortzuges«) – untrennbar verflochten. Selbst die Grenze zwischen innen und außen scheint sich hier aufzulösen, wenn das Speisezimmer zur »Gartenlaube« wird oder »Baumwipfel« ins Schlafzimmer dringen, sodass »man allerdings fast gar nichts unterscheiden« kann. Verdeutlicht wird diese Verflochtenheit nochmals eindringlich an anderer Stelle in Kafkas Landhaus-Kapitel. Der gesamte Weg vom Landhaus bis zum Haus des Onkels in New York – Gebäude, Gärten, Alleen, Straßen, ländliche und urbane Landschaften einschließend – erscheint Roßmann in dieser Szene »als etwas streng zusammengehöriges«:

> Der Weg zum Onkel durch die Glastüre, über die Treppe, durch die Allee, über die Landstraßen, durch die Vorstädte zur großen Verkehrsstraße, einmündend in des Onkels Haus, erschien ihm als etwas streng zusammengehöriges, das leer, glatt und für ihn vorbereitet dalag und mit einer starken Stimme nach ihm verlangte. (V, 108)

Sowohl bei Boltzmann als auch bei Kafka nimmt außerdem eine umfangreiche Essensszene im Landhaus Raum ein, wobei beide Protagonisten – Ludwig Boltzmann und Karl Roßmann – in diesem Moment über keinen Appetit verfügen und sich darüber, vor allem in Bezug auf Ihre Gastgeber:innen, Sorgen machen. Boltzmann schreibt:

> Bei Tisch saß ich, als einziger anwesender Europäer zur Rechten der Mrs. Hearst. Das erste Gericht waren Brombeeren. Ich dankte. Dann kam eine Melone, welche die Hausfrau eigenhändig für mich recht appetitlich gesalzen hatte. Ich dankte wieder. Dann kam oat-meal, ein unbeschreiblicher Kleister aus Hafermehl, mit dem man in Wien vielleicht die Gänse mästen könnte; ich glaube aber eher nicht, denn Wiener Gänse würden das kaum fressen. Ich hatte aber schon beim Abweisen der Melone einen etwas ungnädigen Blick der alma mater bemerkt. Auf ihre Küche ist ja auch eine alma mater stolz. Ich würgte also mit abgewandtem Gesicht und danke Gott, daß mir nichts Menschliches [sic] dabei passierte. […] Glücklicherweise kam dann noch Geflügel, Kompott und manches, womit ich den Geschmack wieder decken konnte. (E, 420f.)

Auch bei Kafkas Essensszene im Landhaus ist Karl Roßmann der »einzige[] anwesende[] Europäer«. Kafka schreibt:

> Das Essen zog sich besonders durch die Genauigkeit in die Länge, mit der Herr Green jeden Gang behandelte, wenn er auch immer bereit war, jeden neuen Gang ohne Ermüdung zu empfangen […]. Hin und wieder lobte er Fräulein Klaras Kunst in der Führung des Hauswesens, was ihr sichtlich schmeichelte, während Karl versucht war ihn abzuwehren, als greife er sie an. Aber Herr Green begnügte sich nicht einmal mit ihr, sondern bedauerte öfters, ohne vom Teller aufzusehen, die auffallende Appetitlosigkeit Karls. Herr Pollunder nahm Karls Appetit in Schutz, trotzdem er als Gastgeber Karl auch

zum Essen hätte aufmuntern sollen. [...] »Ich werde schon morgen dem Herrn Senator erzählen, wie Sie das Fräulein Klara durch Ihr Nichtessen gekränkt haben«, sagte Herr Green [...]. »Sehen Sie nur das Mädchen an, wie traurig es ist«, fuhr er fort und griff Klara unters Kinn. (V, 82–84)

Bei einer Gegenüberstellung der Essensszenen im Landhaus ist erstens festzustellen, dass bei beiden eine sehr lange Essensdauer thematisiert wird, bei Boltzmann sichtbar durch die zahlreichen quälenden und für ihn unappetitlichen Gänge, bei Kafka noch expliziter die Dauer: »Das Essen vergieng langsam wie eine Plage« (V, 80). Zweitens nimmt bei beiden eine potenzielle Kränkung der Gastgeber:innen eine zentrale Rolle ein. Bei Kafka wird die Kränkung der Gastgeberin durch das Nichtessen allerdings noch expliziter formuliert – inklusive drohender negativer sozialer Konsequenzen –, jedoch nicht (wie bei Boltzmann) durch den Hauptprotagonisten selbst, sondern durch den Mitanwesenden Green. Die Rollen sind bei Kafka also anders gelagert: Während bei Boltzmann die Gastgeberin und die gekränkte Person auf eine Person fallen, die wohlhabende »alma mater« Mrs. Hearst, spalten sich die Rollen und Zuschreibungen im *Verschollenen* auf: Gastgeber ist (eigentlich) Herr Pollunder, in dessen Landhaus sich die Anwesenden befinden. Die Rolle des Gastgebers und Wortführers übernimmt allerdings immer mehr der als abstoßend (»ihm wurde fast übel«; V, 82) beschriebene Herr Green. Die Kränkung wiederum soll vor allem bei der Figur Klara erfolgen, der Tochter des eigentlichen Gastgebers Pollunder. Ob Klara tatsächlich gekränkt ist, ist jedoch fragwürdig, so wird dies im Text nie explizit artikuliert, die Attribution der vermeintlichen Kränkung erfolgt vielmehr durch den vermeintlichen Gastgeber Green. Der tatsächliche Gastgeber Pollunder verteidigt indes sogar noch Karls Appetitlosigkeit.

Es lässt sich diesbezüglich folgendes Zwischenfazit ziehen: In beiden Essens-Szenen werden mögliche Kränkungen der Gastgeber:innen thematisiert, jedoch unterschiedlich eingebettet und akzentuiert. Die gekränkte reiche Witwe und Gastgeberin Mrs. Hearst unterscheidet sich von der vermeintlich gekränkten Gastgeber-Tochter Klara. In Kafkas *Verschollenem* existiert jedoch an anderer Stelle ebenfalls eine reiche Witwe, die im Roman als ›Gastgeberin‹ fungiert und Diener beschäftigt, von denen Roßmann stellenweise sogar selbst einer ist: Brunelda.

Der größte Unterschied zwischen den Landhaus-Essensszenen ist freilich deren Ausgang. Bei Boltzmann ist dieser ›positiv‹, so berichtet er am Ende von Speisen, mit denen er »den Geschmack wieder decken konnte.« Man könnte vor diesem Hintergrund also sagen, dass sich Boltzmann am Ende ›zusammenreißt‹ und damit das worst case scenario – eine ernsthafte Kränkung der Gastgeberin Mrs. Hearst – verhindert. Die Figur Roßmann hingegen reißt sich nicht zusammen und verhindert damit auch keine Kränkung, die potenziell eigentlich vielmehr Herrn Green zugeschrieben werden könnte. Das Landhaus-Kapitel endet bei Kafka mit dem worst case scenario: dem folgenreichen Brief des Onkels, den Roßmann nachts – passenderweise von Green – übergeben bekommt: »muß ich Dich nach dem heutigen Vorfall unbedingt von mir fortschicken [...]. Du hast Dich gegen meinen Willen dafür entschieden, heute Abend von mir fortzugehen, dann bleibe auch bei diesem Entschluß Dein Leben lang« (V, 122f.).

Zuletzt finden sich im Landhaus sowohl bei Ludwig Boltzmann als auch bei Franz Kafka prägnante Klavierszenen, bei Kafka sogar noch eine zusätzliche im Haus des Onkels.[44] Boltzmann schreibt über sein Klavier-Erlebnis im Landhaus bei Mrs. Hearst:

Nach Tisch ging man in das Musikzimmer, ein Raum, wenn ich recht schätze, ungefähr so groß, wie der Bösendorfer Saal, aber welche phantastisch-barocke Ausschmückung! An Schönheit wüßte ich ihm keinen der kleineren Wiener Konzertsäle zu vergleichen. Die Kunde von meinem armseligen Klavierspiel war bis in die Hazienda gedrungen. Ich wurde aufgefordert, das Konzert zu eröffnen. Nach einigem Sträuben setzte ich mich an den Flügel, einen Steinway von der allerhöchsten Preislage. Ahnungslos griff ich in die Tasten; einen Flügel von solcher Klangschönheit hatte mein Ohr vielleicht schon in einem Konzerte gehört, nie mein [sic] Finger berührt. Wenn mich je die Strapazen meiner kalifornischen Reise gereut hätten, von jetzt an nicht mehr. Ich spielte eine Sonate von Schubert, anfangs freilich war mir die Mechanik etwas fremd, aber wie leicht gewöhnt man sich an das Gute! Schon der zweite Teil des ersten Satzes ging gut und im zweiten Satze, einem Andante, vergaß ich mich selbst; nicht ich spielte die Melodie, sondern diese lenkte meine Finger. Ich mußte mich mit Gewalt zurückhalten, nicht auch noch das Allegro zu spielen und das war gut, denn dort wäre meine Technik abgefallen. Nach mir spielte eine Schülerin Barths in Berlin mit ebensoviel Technik als Musikverständnis. Unter den Anwesenden war auch ein Professor der Musik in Milwaukee, eine martialisch männliche Gestalt, sicher ein vortrefflicher Bärenjäger; aber auch musikalisch gründlich gebildet. Er hatte ebenfalls bei Barth Klavierspiel betrieben, man kann nicht sagen, gelernt. Er wußte, daß Beethoven neun Symphonien geschrieben hat und daß die neunte davon die letzte ist. Mir tat er unverdiente Ehre an; denn gelegentlich einer Debatte, ob Musik auch humoristisch sein könne, ersuchte er mich, das Scherzo aus der neunten vorzuspielen. Sollte ich sagen, ich kann es nicht, einem Professor in Milwaukee gegenüber? Da ward auch ich humoristisch und sagte: »Gerne, nur bäte ich ihn, die Pauke zu spielen, es nimmt sich besser aus, wenn die ein zweiter hineinspielt.« Darauf wurde er mit seiner Bitte still. (E, 421f.)

Genau wie bei Boltzmann existiert bei Kafka im Landhaus nach dem Essen eine Klavierszene:

44　Zur Musik im Werk von Franz Kafka vgl. weiterführend etwa Steffen Höhne / Alice Stašková (Hgg.) (2018): *Franz Kafka und die Musik.* Köln/Weimar/Wien: Böhlau.

»Nach dem Nachtmahl«, so sagte sie, »werden wir wenn es Ihnen recht ist gleich in meine Zimmer gehen, damit wir wenigstens diesen Herrn Green los sind [...]. Und sie werden dann so freundlich sein mir Klavier vorzuspielen, denn Papa hat schon erzählt, wie gut Sie das treffen, ich aber bin leider ganz unfähig Musik auszuüben und rühre mein Klavier nicht an, so sehr ich die Musik eigentlich liebe.« (V, 79)

Bereits im Kapitel zuvor, beim Onkel Jakob in New York, nimmt das Piano einen gewissen Raum ein. Auf einen Hinweis Karls – »In den ersten Tagen [...] hatte Karl auch erzählt, daß er zu hause [sic] wenig zwar, aber gern Klavier gespielt habe« (V, 59) – schafft der Onkel tatsächlich ein »prachtvolles Piano« (V, 116) für Roßmann an: »etwa acht Tage später sagte der Onkel fast in der Form eines widerwilligen Einge-ständnisses, das Klavier sei eben angelangt« (ebd.).

Als er es in seinem Zimmer hatte und die ersten Töne anschlug, bekam er eine so närrische Freude, daß er statt weiterzuspielen aufsprang und aus einiger Entfernung die Hände in den Hüften das Klavier lieber anstaunte. Auch die Akustik des Zimmers war ausgezeichnet und sie trug dazu bei sein anfängliches kleines Unbehagen, in einem Eisenhause zu wohnen, gänzlich verschwinden zu lassen. (V, 60)

Das Klavierspiel Karls beschränkt sich beim Onkel allerdings – mehr offenbart der Text nicht – vor allem auf »ein altes Soldatenlied seiner Heimat«, sowie »amerikanische[] Märsche« und die »Nationalhymne« (V, 60f.). Im Landhaus wiederum spielt Roßmann schließlich auch, mit einiger Verzögerung, Klavier, nicht ohne zuvor Klara einzuge-stehen »ich kann noch gar nichts, Sie würden staunen, wie wenig ich kann« (V, 116f.), und auf seine limitierten Liedkenntnisse hinzuweisen: »es sind leider nicht viele, und sie passen auch gar nicht zu so einem großen Instrument, auf dem nur Virtuosen sich hören lassen sollten.« (V, 116) Das Musikspiel selbst gestaltet sich dann ernüchternd und für Roßmann emotional niederschmetternd:

»Wollen Sie Noten haben?« fragte Klara. »Danke, ich kann ja Noten nicht einmal vollkommen lesen«, antwortete Karl und spielte schon. Es war ein kleines Lied, das wie Karl wohl wußte ziemlich langsam hätte gespielt werden müssen, um besonders für Fremde auch nur verständlich zu sein, aber er hudelte es im ärgsten Marschtempo hinunter. Nach der Beendigung fuhr die gestörte Stille des Hauses wie in großem Gedränge wieder an ihren Platz. »Ganz schön«, sagte Klara, aber es gab keine Höf-lichkeitsformel, die Karl nach diesem Spiel hätte schmeicheln können. [...] »Entweder oder. Ich muß ja nicht alle zehn Lieder spielen, die ich kann, aber eines kann ich nach Möglichkeit gut spielen.« Und er fieng sein geliebtes Soldatenlied an. So langsam, daß das aufgestörte Verlangen des Zuhörers sich nach der nächsten Note streckte, die Karl zurückhielt und nur schwer hergab. Er mußte ja tatsächlich wie bei jedem Lied die nötigen Tasten mit den Augen erst zusammensuchen, aber außerdem fühlte er in sich ein Leid entstehn, das über das Ende des Liedes hinaus, [sic] ein anderes Ende suchte und es nicht finden konnte. »Ich kann ja nichts«, sagte Karl nach Schluß des Liedes und sah Klara mit Tränen in den Augen an. (V, 118f.)

Damit kann an dieser Stelle zunächst festgehalten werden: Beide Protagonisten – sowohl Ludwig Boltzmann als auch Karl Roßmann – spielen Klavier im Landhaus. Beide werden von ihren Gastgeber:innen zum Vorspielen aufgefordert und sind dabei von ihren geringen Fähigkeiten überzeugt. In beiden Texten wird außerdem die hohe Qualität der Instrumente und der Akustik betont.

Neben diesen auffälligen Gemeinsamkeiten gibt es allerdings erneut entscheidende Abweichungen, insbesondere in der musikalischen Ausführung, den musikalischen Inhalten des Klavierspiels und zuletzt dessen Bewertung. Boltzmann gelingt es nach einigen Anfangsschwierigkeiten, gut und erfolgreich zu spielen. Bei Kafka hingegen gelingt es der Figur Karl Roßmann durchgehend bis zum Ende nicht, angemessen und zufriedenstellend zu spielen, was für ihn letztendlich in einer emotionalen Katastrophe endet. Diesen Eindrücken entspricht – dies unterstreichend – auch die externe Bewertung durch die (nicht-)anwesenden Figuren. Stößt Boltzmann mit seinem Klavierspiel in der Abendgesellschaft im Haus von Mrs. Hearst sogar bei einem Musikprofessor auf Wohlgefallen, wird Roßmanns schlechtes Klavierspiel wenig später von Mack, der im Nebenzimmer heimlich zugehört hat, bestätigt: »Es ist ja reichlich anfängerhaft und selbst in diesen Liedern, die Sie doch eingeübt hatten und die sehr primitiv gesetzt sind, haben Sie einige Fehler gemacht« (V, 120). Vereinfacht könnte man sagen: Das Klavierspiel endet bei Boltzmann in »Schönheit«, bei Roßmann in »Leid«. Ein entscheidender Unterschied findet sich darüber hinaus auch in den musikalischen Inhalten des Klavierspiels. So spielt Boltzmann mit einer »Sonate von Schubert« Hochkultur, Roßmann im Gegensatz dazu ein primitives »Soldatenlied«. Auch hier zeigt sich Boltzmanns – im Kontrast zu Kafka stehende – überschwängliche Begeisterung für die kulturellen Errungenschaften des Menschen und dessen herausragende Stellung in der Welt, was sich im Folgenden anhand des Theaters noch weiter veranschaulichen lässt.

Landschaft: Theater, Eisenbahn, Gebirge

Neben der Eisenbahn, die einerseits als Technik der Weltbeherrschung,[45] andererseits als lebendiges Werkzeug für eine durch Verbindung und Wechselwirkung geprägte

---

45   Vgl. hierzu exemplarisch der österreichische Nationalökonom Emanuel Herrmann in seinem Werk *Cultur und Natur. Studien im Gebiete der Wirthschaft* (1887): »Der Planet Erde ist eine

Weltauffassung verstanden werden kann, stellt auch das Theater einen besonderen transmedialen Ort der Reflexion über das Verhältnis von ›Natur‹ und ›Kultur‹ dar.[46] Ein Theater wird bei Boltzmann im Rahmen seines Aufenthaltes in Berkeley erwähnt. Er schreibt:

> Dafür hörte ich Sonntag den 2. Juli die half hour of music, die wie jeden Sonntag im griechischen Theater gratis zum besten gegeben wurde. Dieses Theater ist eine getreue Kopie des Sophokleischen Theaters in Athen, nur, wie mir schien, noch vergrößert. Da es in Berkeley im Sommer nie regnet und doch auch wegen des häufigen Nebels die Sonne wenig scheint, so tut das vollständig unbedeckte Theater gute Dienste. Nur die Musik war in dem architektonisch wunderschönen, rings von Eukalyptus und lifeoaks umrahmten Raume unendlich dünn. Da hätte Mahler mit den Philharmonikern hingehört, die dritte Symphonie spielend, so daß die Bäume vor Wonne gezittert hätten und der stille Ozean aufhorchend noch stiller geworden wäre; die Menschen dort hätten es ja doch nicht verstanden. (E, 416)

Bei Kafka hingegen ist das »Teater von Oklahama« selbst nur sehr bruchstückhaft auf einer Fotografie beschrieben (vgl. V, 412f.), dafür jedoch sehr umfangreich der phantastische Aufnahmeprozess für das nach Aussage Fannys »größte Teater der Welt« (V, 394) auf dem »Rennplatz in Clayton« (V, 387). Kafka schreibt:

> Als er in Clayton ausstieg, hörte er gleich den Lärm vieler Trompeten. Es war ein wirrer Lärm, die Trompeten waren nicht gegeneinander abgestimmt, es wurde rücksichtslos geblasen. Aber das störte Karl nicht, es bestätigte ihm vielmehr daß das Teater von Oklahama ein großes Unternehmen war. Aber als er aus dem Stationsgebäude trat und die ganze Anlage vor sich überblickte, sah er, daß alles noch größer war, als er nur irgendwie hätte denken können, und er begriff nicht wie ein Unternehmen nur zu dem Zweck um Personal zu erhalten derartige Aufwendungen machen konnte. Vor dem Eingang zum Rennplatz war ein langes niedriges Podium aufgebaut, auf dem hunderte Frauen als Engel gekleidet in weißen Tüchern mit großen Flügeln am Rücken auf langen goldglänzenden Trompeten bliesen. Sie waren aber nicht unmittelbar auf dem Podium,

---

Maschine, welche dem Druck des Menschengeschlechts so gehorchen sollte, wie die Locomotive dem Hebeldrucke ihres Führers.« Emanuel Herrmann (1887): *Cultur und Natur. Studien im Gebiete der Wirthschaft.* Berlin: Allgemeiner Verein für Deutsche Literatur, S. 23.

46　Zum Theater vgl. exemplarisch die *Critical Theatre Ecologies*, einführend etwa bei Martin Middeke / Martin Riedelsheimer (2022): Co-Mutability, Nodes, and the Mesh: Critical Theatre Ecologies – An Introduction. In: *Journal of Contemporary Drama in English* 10/1, S. 2–25; zum Theater als Raum vgl. auch Erika Fischer-Lichte / Benjamin Wihstutz (Hgg.) (2013): *Performance and the Politics of Space. Theatre and Topology.* New York/Oxon: Routledge.

sondern jede stand auf einem Postament, das aber nicht zu sehen war, denn die langen wehenden Tücher der Engelskleidung hüllten es vollständig ein. Da nun die Postamente sehr hoch, wohl bis zwei Meter hoch waren, sahen die Gestalten der Frauen riesenhaft aus [...]. Damit keine Einförmigkeit entstehe, hatte man Postamente in der [sic] verschiedensten Größen verwendet, es gab ganz niedrige Frauen, nicht weit über Lebensgröße, aber neben ihnen schwangen sich andere Frauen in solche Höhe hinauf, daß man sie beim leichtesten Windstoß in Gefahr glaubte. Und nun bliesen alle diese Frauen. (V, 389f.)

Sowohl Boltzmann als auch Kafka präsentieren in ihrem Text ein Theater und beide betonen dabei, erstens, dessen Größe. Zweitens wird in beiden Beschreibungen die Architektur der Theater als besonders ästhetisch und prachtvoll hervorgehoben. Boltzmann spricht einerseits von einem »architektonisch wunderschönen [...] Raume«, Roßmann sagt andererseits später zu Fanny: »Es ist ja schön« (V, 392) – und Fanny betont: »Es ist sehr schön, wie überhaupt die ganze Ausstattung sehr kostbar ist.« (V, 393) Drittens spielt bei beiden Theater-Beschreibungen die Musik eine herausragende Rolle, die allerdings bei beiden als qualitativ minderwertig empfunden wird. Bei Kafka ist schon gar nicht mehr von Musik die Rede, sondern von einem wirren »Lärm« der Trompeten. Feiner Unterschied zwischen Boltzmann und Roßmann ist hier, dass Boltzmann die »dünne« Musik offensichtlich stört, wobei er in diesem Zusammenhang auch den Musikgeschmack der Menschen vor Ort kritisiert, der »Lärm« im *Verschollenen* hingegen »störte Karl nicht«. Später heißt es in diesem Kontext bei Kafka weiter:

> Er hatte gedacht, es sei eine grob gearbeitete Trompete, nur zum Lärmmachen bestimmt, aber nun zeigte sich daß es ein Instrument war, das fast jede Feinheit ausführen konnte. Waren alle Instrumente von gleicher Beschaffenheit, so wurde ein großer Mißbrauch mit ihnen getrieben. (V, 393)

Boltzmann hört die Musik nur (und empfindet sie als minderwertig), Roßmann hört die Musik und spielt sie zugleich: »Karl blies, ohne sich vom Lärm der andern stören zu lassen mit voller Brust ein Lied das er irgendwo in einer Kneipe einmal gehört hatte« (V, 393). Das, was Boltzmann in seinem *Eldorado*-Reisebericht immer wieder als nie erreichten Wunsch artikuliert (»müßte man Maler sein«; »Wenn ich ein Musiker wäre«), erreicht Roßmann überraschend am Ende des Romans durch sein Musikspielen, was ihm Fanny bestätigt: »Du bist ein Künstler« (V, 393).

Weiterhin beachtenswert ist, dass bei Boltzmann Bäume und der Ozean im Rahmen der Theaterbeschreibung eine Rolle spielen. Sie sind für Boltzmann in dieser Situation bessere Zuhörer als die Menschen, vorausgesetzt ein Meisterwerk von Gustav Mahler würde dort statt der »unendlich dünn[en; N.W.]« Musik gespielt. Dies ist eines der

Beispiele, in denen Boltzmann seine eher trennende Weltsicht – exemplarisch hierfür in der *Eldorado*-Reiseerzählung das Meer, welches durch die Schiffe und die vom Menschen und dessen Leistungen übertroffen und beherrscht wird – partiell für einen Moment verlässt. Hier sind plötzlich die Bäume und der Ozean die besseren Zuhörer, »die Menschen dort hätten es ja doch nicht verstanden«: »so daß die Bäume vor Wonne gezittert hätten und der stille Ozean aufhorchend noch stiller geworden wäre«. Durch das meisterhafte Wirken des Menschen, bei Boltzmann versinnbildlicht in Form der dritten Symphonie von Mahler, wird ›Natur‹, die hier von Boltzmann zugleich eine *agency* zugeschrieben bekommt, mit ›Kultur‹ verflochten und verfeinert. Boltzmann imaginiert demzufolge buchstäblich ein ›Naturtheater‹ mit einer immer anwesenden, mithörenden und wechselwirkenden ›Natur‹.

Auch bei Kafka finden sich beim ›Ersatz-Theater‹ am Rennfeld in Clayton Bäume: »Er blieb sogar stehn und überblickte das große Rennfeld das auf allen Seiten bis an ferne Wälder reichte. Ihn erfaßte Lust einmal ein Pferderennen zu sehn« (V, 404). Es kann dabei als Ironie angesehen werden, dass gerade *Roß*mann, dessen Name sich aus einem Tier und einem Menschen zusammensetzt, »einmal ein *Pferde*rennen« sehen möchte [eigene Hervorh.]. Über das tatsächliche »Teater von Oklahama« ist im *Verschollenen* wie gesagt nur relativ wenig zu lesen. Es ist ausschließlich auf Fotografien zu sehen, die beim gemeinsamen Essen »von Hand zu Hand gehen sollten. Doch kümmerte man sich nicht viel um die Bilder und so geschah es daß bei Karl, der der Letzte war nur ein Bild ankam.« (V, 412) Über das Bild schreibt Kafka:

Dieses Bild stellte die Loge des Präsidenten der Vereinigten Staaten dar. Beim ersten Anblick konnte man denken, es sei nicht eine Loge, sondern die Bühne, so weit geschwungen ragte die Brüstung in den freien Raum. Diese Brüstung war ganz aus Gold in allen ihren Teilen. Zwischen den wie mit der feinsten Scheere ausgeschnittenen Säulchen waren nebeneinander Medaillons früherer Präsidenten angebracht [...]. Rings um die Loge, von den Seiten und von der Höhe kamen Strahlen von Licht; weißes und doch mildes Licht enthüllte förmlich den Vordergrund der Loge, während ihre Tiefe hinter rotem, unter vielen Tönungen sich faltenden Sammt [sic] der an der ganzen Umrandung niederfiel und durch Schnüre gelenkt wurde, als eine dunkle rötlich schimmernde Leere erschien.[47] Man konnte sich in dieser Loge kaum Menschen vorstellen, so selbstherrlich sah alles aus. (V, 412f.)

---

[47] Vgl. parallel dazu Boltzmanns Schilderungen insbesondere in Hinblick auf die Beschaffenheit des Lichts: »Dieses Theater ist eine getreue Kopie des Sophokleischen Theaters in Athen, nur, wie mir schien, noch vergrößert. Da es in Berkeley im Sommer nie regnet und doch auch wegen des häufigen Nebels die Sonne wenig scheint, so tut das vollständig unbedeckte Theater gute Dienste.« (E, 416) Auf Kafkas Formulierung »als eine dunkle rötlich schimmernde Leere« hat etwa Dietmar Voss hingewiesen. Vgl. Dietmar Voss (2001): *Dialektik der Grenze. Aufsätze zu Literatur und Ästhetik einer unverantwortlichen Moderne.* Würzburg: Königshausen & Neumann,

Eine Parallele zu Boltzmanns »Kopie des Sophokleischen Theaters in Athen« zeigt sich hier bei Kafka an den »mit der feinsten Scheere ausgeschnittenen Säulchen« als Bezug auf das antike Griechenland. Während bei Boltzmann allerdings die Größe betont wird, wird dies bei Kafka – sichtbar am Diminutiv »Säulchen« – partiell und temporär in ein geradezu belustigendes Gegenteil verkehrt.

Über seine Zugfahrt wiederum schreibt Boltzmann an zwei Stellen in seinem Reisebericht. Über die Hinfahrt von New York nach Berkeley:

> Die Püffe [sic], die man beim Gehen durch den endlos langen Zug nach dem Speisewagen, Aussichtswagen usw. erhält, sind nicht gerade angenehm. Die Aussichtswagen sind rückwärts ganz offen, man kann sich auf das Abschlußgitter setzen oder darüber hinausbeugen und hat dann einfach acht zu geben, daß man nicht bei einem jähen Stoße hinunterfällt.

> Die Landschaft war freilich meist einförmig, doch ist schon die direkte Beobachtung der Schnelligkeit der Fahrt interessant. Wenn man vom Aussichtswagen aus nach rückwärts blickt, so erscheinen die Eisenbahnschienen wie ein endloses Band, das mit rasender Geschwindigkeit unter dem Wagen hervorgezogen wird. Interessant war auch die Fahrt auf dem riesigen Holzdamm mitten durch den Salzsee und die ausgedehnten von Salzkristallen wie mit Schnee bedeckten Felder vor und nach demselben. Gegen das Ende der Fahrt [sic] ist der Übergang über die Sierra-Nevada wunderschön. Er erinnert an den Semmering, freilich nicht ganz so malerisch, aber noch viel großartiger an Länge der Strecke und Höhe der Berge. (E, 411f.)

Und über die Rückfahrt von Berkeley nach New York:

> Die Fahrt war wunderschön, wenn es nur immer Tag gewesen wäre! Das Herrlichste ist der Mount Shasta mit seinem hohen schneebedeckten Haupte in der subtropischen Vegetation. An manchem See fuhr ich vorüber, bergumragt, waldumkränzt, gegen den der Gmundner- und Attersee unbedeutend erscheinen. Hier sieht man kein Haus an dessen Ufer, ich weiß nicht einmal, ob alle schon Namen haben. Über den Yellowstonepark sage ich nichts. Er ist ein Wunder, wie es schwerlich in der Welt noch irgendwo existiert. Man lese das im Baedeker nach oder betrachte gute Bilder davon oder am besten, man sehe es sich in der Natur an, wenn man ausreichend Zeit, Geld und guten Humor hat. Aber man mache es nicht so wie ich. Man gehe anfangs [sic] Juni hin, wo die Hitze noch nicht so groß ist, und widme dazu 14 Tage oder besser einen Monat,

---

S. 96. »Kafkas Schreiben ist auch der fortgesetzte Versuch, eine spezifische Leere, ein immanentes ›Nichts‹ in der Sprache selbst zu erzeugen.« Voss: *Dialektik der Grenze*, S. 98.

daß man alles mit Muße ansehen kann und vom Staunen auch zum Genießen kommt.
[…] Dazu die fürchterliche Hitze. Ich hatte immer ein Handtuch in der Hand, die man
glücklicherweise in den amerikanischen Bahnen in beliebiger Menge bekommt, um mir
den Schweiß abzuwischen. Ich begreife jetzt, was ein Schweißtuch ist. Zudem lieben es
die Amerikaner, ihre Eisenbahnwagen hermetisch zu verschließen, nicht aus Furcht vor
dem Luftzug, die sie nicht kennen, sondern vor dem Ruß. Die schönen Aussichtswagen
ganz hinten, wo weniger Ruß ist, gibt es auf dieser Strecke nicht. Ich ließ einmal in
meinem Abteil, das mehr vorne war, längere Zeit das Fenster offen, wurde aber dann so
schwarz (E, 430f.)

Bei Kafka wird am Ende des Romans die Zugfahrt zum »Teater von Oklahama« im
Vergleich dazu wie folgt beschrieben:

Sie fuhren zwei Tage und zwei Nächte. Jetzt erst begriff Karl die Größe Amerikas.
Unermüdlich sah er aus dem Fenster […]. Alles was sich in dem kleinen, selbst bei
offenem Fenster von Rauch erfüllten Coupee ereignete vergieng vor dem was draußen
zu sehen war. Am ersten Tag fuhren sie durch ein hohes Gebirge. Bläulichschwarze
Steinmassen giengen in spitzen Keilen bis an den Zug heran, man beugte sich aus dem
Fenster und suchte vergebens ihre Gipfel, dunkle schmale zerrissene Täler öffneten sich,
man beschrieb mit dem Finger die Richtung, in der sie sich verloren, breite Bergströme
kamen eilend als große Wellen auf dem hügeligen Untergrund und in sich tausend
kleine Schaumwellen treibend, sie stürzten sich unter die Brücken über die der Zug fuhr
und sie waren so nah daß der Hauch ihrer Kühle das Gesicht erschauern machte.
(V, 418f.)

Bei einer gegenüberstellenden Analyse von Boltzmanns und Kafkas Eisenbahnszenen
sind die Übereinstimmungen zunächst abermals beachtlich. So spricht Boltzmann von
einem Aussichtswagen, der »rückwärts ganz offen« ist, Kafka von einem Fenster, das
»geöffnet« ist. Boltzmann beschreibt ein »Rauchkoupé« (E, 415), Kafka ein »von
Rauch erfüllte[][s; N.W.] Coupee«. In Bezug auf die amerikanische Landschaft erwähnt
Boltzmann die »Höhe der Berge« sowie den »hohen« Mount Shasta, Kafka ein »hohes
Gebirge«. Boltzmann beschreibt ein »Abschlußgitter« des Zuges, über das man sich
»hinausbeugen« kann, Kafka schreibt schlicht »man beugte sich aus dem Fenster«. Ein
zusätzlicher interessanter Aspekt in diesem Kontext ist eine Formulierung Kafkas, die
zunächst unlogisch scheint: »Alles was sich in dem kleinen, selbst bei offenem Fenster
von Rauch erfüllten Coupee ereignete« – warum sollte das Coupee selbst bei geöffnetem Fenster »von Rauch erfüllt« sein?[48] Ludwig Boltzmann liefert die Antwort,

---

48   Mein Gedanke ist hier, dass wenn das Fenster geöffnet ist, der Rauch aus dem Coupee entwei-
      chen müsste, und dieses somit nicht »von Rauch erfüllt« sein kann. Andererseits könnte ent-

Abb.: Von Ludwig Boltzmann erwähnte Semmeringbahn mit Viadukten an der Krauselklause in Niederösterreich (ca. zwischen 1890 und 1900). Auf dem Photochromdruck finden sich auch die von Kafka erwähnten »spitzen Keile[]« aus Stein, die an den Zug heranreichen: »Bläulichschwarze Steinmassen giengen in spitzen Keilen bis an den Zug heran« (V, 418f.). Bildquelle: Library of Congress Prints and Photographs Division Washington, D.C., USA. Reproduction number LC-DIG-ppmsc-09590. https://www. loc.gov/pictures/item/2002710979/ (28.03.2023)

indem er darauf verweist, dass »die Amerikaner« es lieben, »ihre Eisenbahnwagen hermetisch zu verschließen«, um sich vor dem Ruß der Lokomotive zu schützen. Weiterhin schildert Boltzmann »die Fahrt auf dem riesigen Holzdamm«, Kafka wiederum beschreibt »Brücken über die der Zug fuhr«. In diesem Kontext ist auch die von Boltzmann erwähnte, 1854 eröffnete Semmeringbahn beachtenswert, eine zu Kafkas Zeit berühmte österreichische Gebirgs-Bahnstrecke, die über zahlreiche Viadukte führt. Potenziell kannte Kafka die Semmeringbahn, etwa durch Fotografien oder Postkarten.

---

gegengesetzt argumentiert werden, dass das Coupee gerade bei geöffnetem Fenster von Rauch erfüllt sein müsste, da das Fenster explizit aufgrund des Rauchens innerhalb des Coupees geöffnet wird.

Viadukte, die so zahlreich bei der österreichischen Semmeringbahn vorkommen, finden sich indes an anderer Stelle in Kafkas Amerika-Roman – im Kapitel »Marsch nach Ramses«:

> Gegen Abend kamen sie in eine mehr ländliche fruchtbare Gegend. Ringsherum sah man ungeteilte Felder die sich in ihrem ersten Grün über sanfte Hügel legten, reiche Landsitze umgrenzten die Straße und stundenlang gieng man zwischen den vergoldeten Gittern der Gärten, mehrmals kreuzten sie den gleichen langsam fließenden Strom und viele mal [sic] hörten sie über sich die Eisenbahnzüge auf den hoch sich schwingenden Viadukten donnern. (V, 151)

Interessant in diesem landschaftlichen Kontext sind auch die Formulierungen Boltzmanns. Er spricht von Seen, die »bergumragt, waldumkränzt« sind, wobei er feststellt: »Hier sieht man kein Haus an dessen Ufer«. Kafka spricht im Vergleich dazu in dieser Szene von »ungeteilte[n; N.W.] Felder[n; N.W.]«, die sich »ringsherum« befinden und sich »über sanfte Hügel legten« – und zugleich, das ist wichtig, von »reiche[n; N. W.] Landsitze[n; N.W.]«, die die Straße »umgrenzten«. Bei Boltzmann umgrenzen Berge und Wälder die Seen, bei Kafka umgrenzen »Landsitze« und »Gärten« die Straße. Mein Fazit an dieser Stelle: Bei Boltzmann existiert ›echte Natur‹ nur ohne Menschen, bei Kafka nur Naturkultur.

Neben einer eher getrennten, atomistischen Weltauffassung bei Boltzmann und einer untrennbar vermischten bei Kafka, ist der größte Unterschied in den Eisenbahn-Szenen freilich die Landschaftsbeschreibung selbst, insbesondere in Hinblick auf Boltzmanns Hinfahrt von New York nach Berkeley. So schreibt er dort: »Die Landschaft war freilich meist einförmig, doch ist schon die direkte Beobachtung der Schnelligkeit der Fahrt interessant.« Wenig begeistert zeigt sich Boltzmann demzufolge von der Landschaft, vielmehr ist er fasziniert von der Geschwindigkeit des Zuges. Die Figur Karl Roßmann in Kafkas Roman dagegen ist von der Landschaft vollkommen eingenommen und scheint geradezu mit ihr zu verschmelzen – paradigmatisch für ein landschaftliches *embodiment*.[49] Deutlich wird eine große emotionale Bewegtheit des Protagonisten Karl Roßmann, der »unermüdlich« aus dem Fenster sieht und von der Landschaft, wie in der Hafen-Szene zu Beginn des Romans, vollständig in Anspruch genommen ist. Die Nähe der »Bergströme« während der Zugfahrt ruft bei Roßmann eine körperliche Reaktion hervor und lässt ihn »erschauern«. Die amerikanische Landschaft dringt, wie im Landhaus, in den Zugwaggon ein und die Grenze zwischen innen und außen verschwindet.[50] Der Roman gipfelt in einer finalen Grenzauflösung,

---

49　Vgl. exemplarisch Nancy K. Dess (2021): *A Multidisciplinary Approach to Embodiment. Understanding Human Being*. New York/Oxon: Routledge.

50　Vgl. dazu das Konzept *trans-corporeality*. Alaimo: *Bodily Natures*.

nämlich derjenigen zwischen Subjekt und Objekt: Das ganze Coupee, in dem sich Roßmann befindet, löst sich gemeinsam mit ihm auf und alles »vergieng vor dem was draußen zu sehen war.«

Durch eine vergleichende Analyse konnte veranschaulicht werden, dass zwischen Ludwig Boltzmanns *Reise eines deutschen Professors ins Eldorado* und Franz Kafkas Roman *Der Verschollene* einerseits erstaunliche inhaltliche Parallelen bestehen. Dies betrifft etwa Beschreibungen des New Yorker Hafens, von Landhäusern, Theatern und Landschaften bei Zugfahrten durch die USA. Andererseits konnten entscheidende Differenzen aufgezeigt werden, die vor allem das Verhältnis von ›Natur‹ und ›Kultur‹ betreffen. Während der atomistische Physiker Ludwig Boltzmann in seiner Reiseerzählung zum Großteil eine Weltauffassung vertritt, in der der Mensch als externe Entität außerhalb von ›Natur‹ steht und diese durch Wissenschaft ›objektiv‹ beobachten und beherrschen kann, entwickelt Kafka in seinem Amerikaroman verflochtene Naturenkulturen, in denen der Mensch einen »hilflosen« und untrennbaren konstitutiven Bestandteil einer »immerfort« wechselwirkenden Welt darstellt. Vor diesem Hintergrund kann Boltzmanns Reisetext als historischer Paralleltext zu einem besseren Verständnis von Kafkas *Der Verschollene* beitragen.

Literaturverzeichnis

1. Primärliteratur

Boltzmann, Ludwig (1905): *Populäre Schriften.* Leipzig: Verlag von Johann Ambrosius Barth. (Kapitel: *Reise eines deutschen Professors ins Eldorado* = S. 403–435) [Sigle E]

Kafka, Franz (1983): *Der Verschollene.* Roman in der Fassung der Handschrift. Textband. (Kritische Ausgabe) Hrsg. von Jost Schillemeit. Frankfurt a.M.: S. Fischer. [Sigle V]

— (2010) Wunsch, Indianer zu werden. In: Franz Kafka: *Die Erzählungen und andere ausgewählte Prosa.* Hrsg. v. Roger Hermes. Frankfurt a.M.: S. Fischer, S. 7. (Textgrundlage dieser Ausgabe ist die Kritische Ausgabe bei S. Fischer)

2. Forschungsliteratur

Adey, Peter (2017): *Mobility. Second Edition.* Oxon/New York: Routledge.

Alaimo, Stacy (2010): *Bodily Natures: Science, Environment and the Material Self.* Indianapolis: Indiana University Press.

— (2012): States of Suspension: Trans-corporeality at Sea. In: *Interdisciplinary Studies in Literature and Environment* 19/3, S. 476–493.

Alt, Peter-André (2005): *Franz Kafka. Der ewige Sohn. Eine Biographie.* München: Beck.

Anz, Thomas (2009): *Franz Kafka. Leben und Werk.* München: Beck.

Aslet, Clive (2004): *The American Country House.* New Haven/London: Yale University Press.

Barad, Karen (2007): *Meeting the Universe Halfway: Quantum Physics and the Entanglement of Matter and Meaning.* Durham/London: Duke University Press.

Bartelmus, Martin (2022): Kafka-Einstein-Verschränkungen. In: Kling, Alexander / Lehmann, Johannes F. (Hgg.): *Kafkas Zeiten.* Forschungen der Deutschen Kafka-Gesellschaft Bd. 7. Würzburg: Königshausen & Neumann, S. 159–183.

Bergmann, Sigurd / Hoff, Thomas / Sager, Tore (Hgg.) (2014): *Spaces of Mobility. The Planning, Ethics, Engineering and Religion of Human Motion.* Oxon/New York: Routledge.

Bernstein, Matthew (2021): *George Hearst. Silver King of the Gilded Age.* Norman: University of Oklahoma Press.

Binder, Hartmut (1983): Erlesenes Amerika: »Der Verschollene«. In: Ders.: *Kafka. Der Schaffensprozeß.* Frankfurt a.M.: Suhrkamp, S. 75–135.

— (1979): *Kafka-Handbuch in zwei Bänden. Bd. 1.: Der Mensch und seine Zeit.* Stuttgart: Kröner.

Bright, William (1998): *1500 California Place Names. Their Origin and Meaning. A revised version of 1000 California Place Names, by Erwin G. Gudde, third edition.* Berkeley/Los Angeles/London: University of California Press.

Broda, Engelbert (1979): Einleitung. In: Ludwig Boltzmann: *Populäre Schriften. Eingeleitet und ausgewählt von Engelbert Broda.* Braunschweig: Vieweg, S. 1–12.

Brody, Jed (2020): *Quantum Entanglement.* Cambridge/London: MIT Press.

Cidell, Julie / Prytherch, David (Hgg.) (2015): *Transport, Mobility, and the Production of Urban Space.* New York/Oxon: Routledge.

Cronin, Michael (2022): *Eco-Travel. Journeying in the Age of the Anthropocene.* Cambridge: Cambridge University Press.

Dess, Nancy K. (2021): *A Multidisciplinary Approach to Embodiment. Understanding Human Being.* New York/Oxon: Routledge.

Duarte, Francisco J. (2019): *Fundamentals of quantum entanglement.* Bristol: IOP Publishing.

Engel, Manfred (2010): Der Verschollene. In: Ders. / Auerochs, Bernd (Hgg.): *Kafka Handbuch. Leben – Werk – Wirkung.* Stuttgart: Metzler, S. 175–191.

— (2010): Kafka und die moderne Welt. In: Ders. / Auerochs, Bernd (Hgg.): *Kafka Handbuch. Leben – Werk – Wirkung.* Stuttgart: Metzler, S. 498–515.

Fingerhut, Karlheinz (1997): Auswandern – Schreiben. Kafkas Der Verschollene als doppeltes Erzählspiel und als Experiment einer doppelten Lektüre. In: Godé, Maurice / Vanoosthuyse, Michel (Hgg.): *Entre critique et rire. Le Disparu de Franz Kafka.* Montpellier: Groupe de Recherche Etudes Germaniques et Centre-Européennes de l'Université Paul-Valéry.

Fischer-Lichte, Erika / Wihstutz, Benjamin (Hgg.) (2013): *Performance and the Politics of Space. Theatre and Topology.* New York/Oxon: Routledge.

Gesing, Friederike / Knecht, Michi / Flitner, Michael et al. (Hgg.) (2019): *NaturenKulturen. Denkräume und Werkzeuge für neue politische Ökologien.* Bielefeld: transcript Verlag.

Gieryn, Thomas F. (2002): What buildings do. In: *Theory and Society* 31/1, S. 35–74.

Grewe-Volpp, Christa (2015): Ökofeminismus und Material Turn. In: Dürbeck, Gabriele / Stobbe, Urte (Hgg.): *Ecocriticism. Eine Einführung.* Köln/Weimar/Wien: Böhlau Verlag, S. 44–56.

Haraway, Donna (2016): *Staying with the Trouble. Making Kin in the Chthulucene.* Durham/London: Duke University Press.

— (2003): *The Companion Species Manifesto: Dogs, People, and Significant Otherness.* Vol. 1. Chicago: Prickly Paradigm Press

— (2008): *When Species Meet.* Minneapolis: University of Minnesota Press.

Haring, Ekkehard W. (2010): Leben und Persönlichkeit. In: Engel, Manfred / Auerochs, Bernd (Hgg.): *Kafka Handbuch. Leben – Werk – Wirkung.* Stuttgart: Metzler, S. 1–27.

Heise, Ursula K. (2008): *Sense of Place and Sense of Planet. The Environmental Imagination of the Global.* New York: Oxford University Press.

Herrmann, Emanuel (1887): *Cultur und Natur. Studien im Gebiete der Wirthschaft.* Berlin: Allgemeiner Verein für Deutsche Literatur.

Höhne, Steffen / Stašková, Alice (Hgg.) (2018): *Franz Kafka und die Musik.* Köln/Weimar/Wien: Böhlau.

Holbach, Rudolf / Reeken, Dietmar von (2014): Das Meer als Geschichtsraum, oder: Warum eine historische Erweiterung der Meeresforschung unabdingbar ist. In: Dies. (Hgg.): *»Das ungeheure Wellen-Reich«. Bedeutungen, Wahrnehmungen und Projektionen des Meeres in der Geschichte.* Oldenburg: BIS-Verl. der Carl-von-Ossietzky-Univ., S. 7–22.

Hoppe, Katharina / Lemke, Thomas (2021): *Neue Materialismen zur Einführung.* Hamburg: Junius.

Kafka, Franz (1983): *Der Verschollene.* Apparatband. (Kritische Ausgabe) Hrsg. v. Jost Schillemeit. Frankfurt a.M.: S. Fischer.

Kammler, Clemens (2005): Historische Diskursanalyse (Michel Foucault). In: Klaus-Michael Bogdal (Hg.): *Neue Literaturtheorien. Eine Einführung.* Göttingen: Vandenhoeck und Ruprecht, S. 32–56.

Konersmann, Ralf (2003): Die Philosophen und das Meer. In: *Akzente. Zeitschrift für Literatur* 50/3, S. 218–233.

Merriman, Peter / Pearce, Lynn (Hgg.) (2018): *Mobility and the Humanities.* Oxon/New York: Routledge.

Middeke, Martin / Riedelsheimer, Martin (2022): Co-Mutability, Nodes, and the Mesh: Critical Theatre Ecologies – An Introduction. In: *Journal of Contemporary Drama in English* 10/1, S. 2–25.

Morton, Timothy (2009): *Ecology Without Nature. Rethinking Environmental Aesthetics.* Cambridge/London: Harvard University Press.

— (2010): *The Ecological Thought.* Cambridge/London: Harvard University Press.

Neimanis, Astrida (2017): *Bodies of Water. Posthuman Feminist Phenomenology.* London/New York: Bloomsbury Publishing.

Neumeyer, Harald (2004): »Das Land der Paradoxa« (Robert Heindl). Franz Kafkas In der Strafkolonie und die Deportationsdebatte um 1900. In: Liebrand, Claudia / Schößler, Franziska (Hgg.): *Textverkehr. Franz Kafka und die Tradition.* Würzburg: Königshausen & Neumann, S. 291–334.

— (2013): Diskurs. In: Borgards, Roland / Neumeyer, Harald / Pethes, Nicolas et. al. (Hgg.): *Literatur und Wissen. Ein interdisziplinäres Handbuch.* Stuttgart: Metzler, S. 32–35.

— (2013): Raum – Zeit – Macht. Franz Kafkas Der Verschollene und Arthur Holitschers Amerika. In: Ders. / Steffens, Wilko (Hgg.): *Kafka interkulturell.* Würzburg: Königshausen & Neumann, S. 451–483.

Northey, Anthony (1988): Die Entdeckung der Neuen Welt. Kafkas amerikanische Vettern und sein Amerika-Roman. In: Ders.: *Kafkas Mischpoche.* Berlin: Wagenbach, S. 47–60.

Ottmüller-Wetzel, Birgit (1986): *Auswanderung über Hamburg. Die H.A.P.A.G. und die Auswanderung nach Nordamerika. 1870–1914.* (Diss.) Berlin/Hamburg: Freie Univ. Berlin.

Robertson, Ritchie (1988): *Kafka: Judentum, Gesellschaft, Literatur* (Orig. *Kafka. Judaism, politics, and literature,* 1985). Aus dem Englischen übers. v. Josef Billen. Stuttgart: Metzler.

Rovelli, Carlo (2021): *Helgoland. Wie die Quantentheorie unsere Welt verändert* (Orig. *Helgoland,* 2020). Aus dem Italienischen übers. v. Enrico Heinemann. Hamburg: Rowohlt Verlag.

Scheibe, Erhard (2007): *Die Philosophie der Physiker.* München: Beck.

Schmitz-Emans, Monika (2010): *Franz Kafka: Epoche – Werk – Wirkung.* München: C. H. Beck.

Scholtz, Gunter (2016): *Philosophie des Meeres.* Hamburg: Mare Verlag.

Sullivan, Heather I. (2015): New Materialism. In: Dürbeck, Gabriele / Stobbe, Urte (Hgg.): *Ecocriticism. Eine Einführung.* Köln/Weimar/Wien: Böhlau Verlag, S. 57–67.

Voss, Dietmar (2001): *Dialektik der Grenze. Aufsätze zu Literatur und Ästhetik einer unverantwortlichen Moderne.* Würzburg: Königshausen & Neumann.

Wolfradt, Jörg (1996): *Der Roman bin ich. Schreiben und Schrift in Kafkas »Der Verschollene«.* Würzburg: Königshausen & Neumann.

Zeller, Thomas (2022): *Consuming Landscapes. What We See When We Drive and Why It Matters.* Baltimore: Johns Hopkins University Press.

3. Weitere Literatur

Golden Gate Bridge, Highway and Transportation District: *Key Dates in Bridge District History.* https://www.goldengate.org/bridge/history-research/moments-events/key-dates/ (28.03. 2023)

Hooper, Charles Edward (1905): *The Country House. A Practical Manual of the Planning and Construction of the American Country Home and its Surroundings.* New York: Doubleday, Page & Company.

Markwardt, Nils (2020): *Meer denken.* Philosophie Magazin 24.10.2020. https://www.philomag. de/artikel/meer-denken (28.03.2023)

Phoebe A. Hearst Museum: *Our Founder: Phoebe Apperson Hearst.* https://hearstmuseum.berkeley.edu/phoebe-heast/ (28.03.2023)

Florian Scherübl

Das Bild in der Stimme

Giorgio Agamben als Leser von Averroes

ABSTRACT: Giorgio Agamben's philosophy has contributed a great number of concepts to the Humanities. Terminology like homo sacer, state of exception and the like are frequently used in cultural studies. Agamben's theoretical triangle of image, writing and voice is known to a far less extent. The following paper argues that this linkage provides an important foundation for Agamben's philosophy and needs to be understood before the backdrop of intellect theory. In drawing notions from Averroes, the medieval Arabic commentator of Aristotle, Agamben develops a theory of intellect, which allows to establish a link between language and phantasm, i.e. word and image as different medial forms, connected by the human voice. This emphasis on the voice is meant to provide an alternative to the structuralist model of the linguistic sign. The paper seeks to explore Averroes' traces in Agamben's thought discussing possible consequences for cultural studies.

KEYWORDS: Form of Life, Intentional Species, New Materialism, Italian Theory, Speculative Thought

D er mittelalterliche arabische Philosoph Ibn Rushd alias Averroes stellt eine wiederkehrende Referenz für das Denken Giorgio Agambens dar. In dem von Adam Kotsko und Carlo Salzani besorgten Kompendium *Agamben's philosophical Lineage* taucht er nicht auf.[1] Für Averroes' Aufnahme hätte nicht wenig gesprochen. *Forma di Vita*, das Exposé des *Homo-Sacer*-Projektes ebenso wie dessen letzter Band *L'uso dei corpi* weisen dem Kordubenser keine geringere Rolle zu, als den Anfangspunkt des modernen politischen Denkens zu markieren.[2] Vor diesem Zusammenhang scheint es nicht unerheblich, dass das Vorwort zu Emanuele Coccias bahnbrechender Averroes-Studie *La Trasparenza dell'immagini. Averroé e l'Averroismo* von Agamben stammt.[3] Coccia legt darin eine der ausführlichsten Rekonstruktionen von Averroes' Denken und seiner Rezeption seit dem 13. Jahrhundert vor. Erst kürzlich hat Agamben in dem persönlich gehaltenen Text *Quel che ho visto, udito, appreso…* von 2022 die Bedeutung des Averroes für seine eigene Philosophie klar zuerkannt:

---

1   Kotsko, Adam/Salzani, Carlo Salzani (Eds.) (2017): Agamben's Philosophical Lineage, Edinburgh: Edinburgh UP.

2   Agamben, Giorgio (2000): Lebensform, in: ders.: Mittel ohne Zweck, Zürich/Berlin: Diaphanes, S. 13–20, hier S. 19; Agamben, Giorgio (2021): Der Gebrauch der Körper, Frankfurt am Main: S. Fischer, S. 358.

3   Coccia, Emanuele (2005): La trasparenza delle immagini. Averroè e l'averroismo, Milano: Bruno Mondadori.

Dall'andaluso Averroè ho appreso che l'intelleto è unico e che questo non significa che tutti pensano la stessa cosa, ma che, quando pensiamo il vero, allora la molteplicità delle opinioni si spegne e finalmente a pensare non sono piú io. E, tuttavia, »non piú io« significa non soltanto che io c'ero, ma che in qualche modo ancora ci sono, perché, dice l'andaluso, mi congiungo con l'unico non attraverso il pensiero – che è suo e non mi appartiene – ma attraverso i fantasmi e i desideri dell'immaginazione, che è soltanto mia. E questo è anche il senso dell'architettura araba: le immaginazioni dei singoli sono come le ceramiche variegate che incrostano le pareti della moschea o come gli schizzi di luce che, filtrando all'interno attraverso minuscoli spiragli, trascrivono un solo, complicato rabesco. [4]

Hier wird Averroes als Denker jenes einen, gemeinschaftlichen und geteilten Intellekts benannt, an dem die Einzelnen vermittels einer Konjunktion im Sinne der mittelalterlichen Philosophie teilhaben: durch eine Verbindung mit diesem Intellekt, die sie selbst im Denken aktiv herstellen. Diese Verbindung bedarf ihrerseits der Phantasie oder Imagination und sie verbindet, wie es genauer zu sehen gilt, den Einzelnen mit einer Gemeinschaft über die Praxis des Denkens.

Schon in Agambens ausführlichster Beschäftigung mit Averroes (1977 in *Stanzen*) zeichnet sich dessen Denken als Grundlage einer weiterführenden, von Agamben immer wieder aufgenommenen Konzeption ab: Das Bild, mit dem die Phantasie als Einbildungskraft arbeitet, verbindet sich im Sprechen des Einzelnen mit der Stimme; hierin greift es nicht nur die allgemein als Schrift und Grammatik niedergelegten Elemente der Sprache auf, sondern vermag sie gleichsam um weitere zu bereichern; darüber hinaus verbindet es sich im Akt des Sprechens mit einem Intellekt, an dem eine Vielheit oder *multitudo* von Denkenden teilhat.

Die Averroes-Lektüre instruiert so letztlich Agambens Konzept der Lebensform. Dieses ist nicht auf eine Variation von Heideggers Begriff des Daseins einzuschränken. Der averroistische Intellekt überschreitet das bei Heidegger noch zu solipsistisch gedachte Dasein hin auf die *multitudo*. Ausgehend von einem solchen Intellekt-Ver-

---

4   Agamben, Giorgio (2022): Quel che ho visto, udito, appreso…, Torino: Einaudi, S. 36. »Vom Andalusier Averroes habe ich gelernt, dass der Intellekt Einer ist und dass dies nicht bedeutet, dass alle das Gleiche denken, sondern dass, wenn wir das Wahre denken, die Vielheit der Meinungen verglüht und letztlich nicht mehr nur ich denke. Und dennoch bedeutet »nicht mehr ich« nicht einfach, dass ich da war, sondern dass ich es noch auf gewisse Weise bin, da ich mich, wie der Andalusier sagt, mit dem Einen nicht über das Denken verbinde – welches das seine ist und woran ich nicht teilhabe – sondern über die Phantasmen und die Begierden über die Phantasmen und die Begierden aus der Einbildung, die nur meine ist. Und das ist auch der Sinn der arabischen Architektur: die Einbildungen der Einzelnen sind wie die gestreiften Keramiken, welche die Mauern der Moscheen verfliesen oder wie die Lichtstrahlen, die durch die winzigen Ritzen ins Innere gelangen und dabei eine einzige, komplizierte Arabeske niederschreiben«.

ständnis rücken für Agamben immer wieder zwei Probleme in den Fokus: 1.) Schrift und Schreiben: Der Intellekt wird schon von Aristoteles in *De Anima* mit einer Schreibtafel verglichen, auf der noch nichts geschrieben steht. Ausgehend von dieser Problematisierung der Schrift setzt Agamben dem kulturwissenschaftlichen Schrift-Paradigma, wie es im Zuge der Dekonstruktion an Bedeutung gewann, einen Begriff der Stimme entgegen. Während die Schrift auf die materielle, grammatische und ko-difizierte Seite der Sprache konzentriert ist, eröffnet die Stimme einen Raum der Variation und der poetischen Produktivität, mithin der Spracheränzung und Veränderung, die sich aus der Phantasie speist. Dies sehen schon averroistisch inspirierte Dichter und Sänger des *dolce stil nuovo* wie Guido Cavalcanti, bei deren Averroismus Agamben Anleihen macht. Dabei wird die Stimme zum Titel für sprachliche Bedeutungsproduktion überhaupt, die auf der Grundlage von Averroes' Intellekt-Begriff eine kollektive, politische und lebensweltliche Dimension erhält. 2.) Mit seiner Differenzierung verschiedener Phasen des Intellekts und insbesondere derjenigen eines *intellectus materialis* unterhält der averroistische Intellekt ein besonderes Verhältnis zur Materie. Agambens Interesse für Averroes lässt sich daher auch als heimlicher und als solcher noch nicht gewürdigter Beitrag zu Debatten um einen *New Materialism* auffassen. Hierbei erweisen sich heutige Auffassungen einer aktiven Materie bereits vom arabischen Aristotelismus des Mittelalters vorweggenommen – wobei der Averroismus den Menschen als ausführenden Aktivator von Möglichkeiten in einen von der Materie vorkonfigurierten Möglichkeitsraum einzurücken erlaubt.

Averroes liest Aristoteles

Die Kommentare des arabischen Arztes Ibn Ruschd alias Averroes (1126–1198) gelten als Höhepunkt in der arabischen Auseinandersetzung mit dem Werk des Aristoteles, welche die mittelalterliche Philosophie bis in die Scholastik hinein geprägt hat. Die hierzu zählenden Kommentare wie jene des Alfarabi (870–950) und Avicenna (980–1037) sind ihrerseits informiert von den antiken Kommentatoren Alexander von Aphrodisias und Themistios. Anders als seine arabischen Vorläufer ist es Averroes, der dabei am deutlichsten eine eigene Philosophie und Schülerschaft ausgebildet hat.[5] Die Rede vom Averroismus, der mittelalterliche Denker wie Siger von Brabant oder Dichter und Intellektuelle wie Guido Cavalcanti und Dante beeinflusste, ist philosophiege-

---

5 Davidson, Herbert A. (1992): Alfarabi, Avicenna and Averroes, on Intellect. Their Cosmologies, Theories of the active Intellect, and Theories of Human Intellect, New York: Oxford University Press, insbes. S. 259–265. Eine ausführliche Rekonstruktion des Averroismus bei Coccia, Emanuele (2005): La trasparenza delle immagini. Averroè e l'averroismo, Milano: Bruno Mondadori.

schichtlich etabliert.[6] Der später zum zentralen Streitpunkt und Skandal avancierte Kern der averroistischen Philosophie – wenn man denn von ihr als *einer* sprechen mag und sie nicht vielmehr als Denkbewegung begreift – besteht sicher in der Lehre von den Intellekten.[7] Diese wird an verschiedenen Stellen bei Averroes entfaltet, so etwa in den kleineren Texten, die als die drei Abhandlungen über die Konjunktion bekannt geworden sind[8]; der zentrale Text, auf den die Forschung immer wieder zurückkommt, ist hier aber der große Kommentar zu Aristoteles' *De Anima*.[9] Jahrhundertelang war Averroes dafür als der Philosoph verschrien, der eine Theorie des einen, für alle Menschen ungeteilten Intellekts vertreten habe, einen oft polemisch so genannten Monopsychismus. Demzufolge gäbe es nur einen, mit dem einzelnen Menschen unvermischten und von außen hinzutretenden Intellekt, der unzerstörbar und ewig sei.[10] Thomas von Aquins Streitschrift *De unitate intellectus contra Averroistas* von 1270 bereitete den Weg zur Ächtung der averroistischen Philosophie durch die Scholastik, indem sie dieses Denken verwarf. Ein ungeteilter Intellekt? Das stellt offensichtlich eine Leugnung der Ewigkeit und Unzerstörbarkeit der Einzelseele dar, erwies sich daher neben anderen Aspekten des averroistischen Denkens als unannehmbar für die kirchlichen Autoritäten und die sie legitimierende Philosophie.

Averroes' Lehre von den Intellekten gestaltet sich indes weit komplexer. So sprechen die lateinischen Kommentatoren des Aristoteles zunächst nicht einfach von *dem* Intellekt. Im großen Kommentar des Averroes zu *De Anima* ist unter anderem von *intellectus speculativus, intellectus agens, intellectus seperatus, intellectus possibilis, intellectus materialis* die Rede. Überhaupt scheinen uns bei den Aristoteles-Kommentatoren des Mittelalters eine Vielzahl von Intellekten zu begegnen, die sich oft durch die

---

6   Alain de Libera geht so weit, auch wegen des Averroismus ein spezifisches Konzept des Intellektuellen ins Mittelalter vorzudatieren: vgl. de Libera, Alain (1991): Penser au Moyen Âge, Paris: Editions de Seuil.

7   Zum Aufgehen von Averroes' Denken in einer Strömung des Averroismus vgl. Coccia, Emanuele (2005): La trasparenza delle immagini. Averroè e l'averroismo, Milano: Bruno Mondadori, S. 20–53.

8   Deutsch als Averroes (1869): Drei Abhandlungen über die Conjunction des separaten Intellects mit dem Menschen, herausgegeben, übersetzt und erläutert von J. Herz, Berlin: H.G. Herman.

9   Dieser Text ist nicht im arabischen Original überliefert, das verloren ging. Erhalten ist lediglich die lateinische Abschrift, aus der sich die Averroes-Rezeption bis heute speist. Siehe dazu Winkelmann-Liebert, Holger (2005): Die Intellektlehre des Averroës, in: Der Islam. Zeitschrift für Geschichte und Kultur des islamischen Orients 82, S.273–290, hier S. 276.

10   Der abschätzige Begriff Monopsychismus geht auf die *Theodizee* von Leibniz zurück und unterstellt die Unmöglichkeit für den Einzelnen, zu denken. Vgl. Coccia, Emanuele (2005): La trasparenza delle immagini. Averroè e l'averroismo, Milano: Bruno Mondadori, S. 22–24. Die Verbindung der Lehre des Averroes mit einem Monopsychismus wirkt bis in die Schwelle zur Gegenwart nach. Siehe etwa Blumenberg, Hans (2018): Husserl – ein Averroist?, in: ders., Phänomenologische Schriften 1981–1988, ed. von Nicola Zambon, Berlin: Suhrkamp 2018.

schwierige Überlieferung mittels verschiedener Übersetzungen ergeben.[11] Seit Alfarabi geht die arabische Linie der Aristoteles-Kommentatoren von wenigstens vier Intellekten aus. Die diversen Intellekte sind dabei als »verschiedene Grade der Aktualisierung des menschlichen Intellekts« aufzufassen.[12] Indes handelt es sich stets um ein- und denselben Intellekt in verschiedenen Phasen. Erhält der Intellekt gemäß seinem Tun und Lassen verschiedene Bezeichnungen, besteht der kritische Punkt des Averroismus im Verhältnis zwischen *intellectus agens* und *intellectus materialis*, zwischen *aktivem/ tätigem Intellekt* und *materialem/möglichem Intellekt*.[13]

Die Weichenstellung findet schon bei den antiken Kommentatoren Alexander und Themistios statt. Materialer und möglicher Intellekt können miteinander identifiziert werden, da Aristoteles in *De Anima* die These vertritt, der materiale Intellekt sei alles Denkbare oder Denkmögliche, er könne alle Formen der Natur aufnehmen. Der Intellekt sei die Form aller Formen.[14] Daraus folgert Alexander, dass es sich um einen Intellekt handeln müsse, der reine Potenzialität sei, da etwas, das alle Formen aufzunehmen fähig sei, selbst keine bestimmte Form besitzen könne. Während Alexander den materialen Intellekt noch als Fähigkeit der Einzelseele (*psyché*) disponiert, geht Themistios einen Schritt weiter und behauptet die Abgetrenntheit des materialen Intellekts, der von außen hinzutrete und sich nicht mit dem zerstörbaren, sterblichen Körper des Einzelnen vermische. Denn nur etwas Körperloses, folglich Unsterbliches könne auch reine Form sein, die alle Formen aufzunehmen vermag. Holger Winkelmann-Liebert, dessen Darstellung der beiden Kommentatoren ich in diesem Absatz folge, konstatiert bei Averroes von den drei Abhandlungen über die Konjunktion bis zum großen *De-Anima*-Kommentar eine Bewegung von der Position Alexanders hin zu

---

11 Ein ausführliches Verzeichnis, welche Intellekt-Begriffe sich bei welchem Kommentator finden, bietet Hasse, Dag Nikolaus (1999): Das Lehrstück von den vier Intellekten in der Scholastik: Von den arabischen Quellen bis zu Albertus Magnus, in: Récherches des théologie et philosophie mediévale 66.2, S. 21–77, hier S. 22–28.

12 Ebd., S. 29.

13 Daneben kennt Averroes weitere Intellekt-Arten, die allerdings hier nicht ins Gewicht fallen. Vgl. Esposito, Roberto (2018): Zwei. Die Maschine der politischen Theologie und der Ort des Denkens, Zürich: diaphanes, S. 212: »Obgleich sich Averroes auf fünf Arten von Intellekt bezieht – den ›tätigen‹, den ›materiellen‹, den ›erworbenen‹, denjenigen ›in habitu‹ sowie den ›spekulativen‹ –, kommt es vor allem auf das wechselseitige Verhältnis der ersten beiden an, insofern sich die anderen von der Form ableiten lassen, die diese jeweils annehmen. Beide sind voneinander getrennt, aber während der tätige Intellekt die Funktion besitzt, die intelligiblen Formen im materiellen Intellekt zu aktualisieren, ist dieser als eine reine Potenzialität zu verstehen, die an sich keine andere Natur besitzt als diejenige der reinen Rezeptivität«.

14 Infrage steht hier die Auslegung des vierten Abschnitts des dritten Buches von *De Anima* (429a – 430a). Siehe Aristoteles (2011): Über die Seele, übersetzt und herausgegeben von Gernot Krapinger, Stuttgart: Reclam, S. 148–153.

jener des Themistios.[15] Averroes wird zum Parteigänger eines vom Einzelnen abtrennbaren, unsterblichen Intellekts, an dem die Einzelnen temporär teilhaben, wenn sie denken.

Wie äußert sich diese Positionsänderung in Averroes' großem Kommentar zu *De Anima*? Averroes beharrt mit Themistios darauf, dass der materiale Intellekt immer ein Intellekt ist, der seine Möglichkeit, alles zu sein, durch seine reine Passivität besitzt.[16] In dieser rein kontemplativen Phase vermag er die Form von allem Möglichen anzunehmen.

Nun besitzen allerdings die vom materialen Intellekt aufgenommenen Gegenstände durchaus bereits eine Form. In der aristotelischen Tradition ist der Übergang von der Wahrnehmung zum Erkennen einer von der Materie zur Form. Die Wahrnehmung nimmt die Materie als Bilder auf, wobei deren Form vom Intellekt aus der Materie extrahiert wird, der auf diese Weise die intelligiblen Formen herstellt. Diese Extraktion der Formen, die in der aristotelischen Tradition, etwa auch bei Averroes' Vorgänger Alfarabi dem Prozess der Digestion nachmodelliert ist, wird vom tätigen oder aktiven Intellekt (*intellectus agens*) aktiv betrieben.[17] Um Formen auf Wahrnehmungen anwendbar zu machen, ist zudem ein phantastisches Vermögen vonnöten, das die Verbindung der Form mit dem Sinneseindruck vermittels der im Einzelnen gespeicherten Phantasmen ermöglicht. Die Wahrheit intelligibler Formen wird nur durch die Korrespondenz mit Bildern aus der Phantasie erreicht.[18] Das einzelne wahrgenommene

---

15   Vgl. Winkelmann-Liebert, Holger (2005): Die Intellektlehre des Averroës, in: Der Islam. Zeitschrift für Geschichte und Kultur des islamischen Orients 82, S. 273–290, hier 277–278. Eine ausführlichere Übersicht, als sie hier möglich ist, welche die verschiedenen Entwicklungsstadien von Averroes' Position zum materiellen Intellekt darstellt, angefangen von den Abhandlungen über die Konjunktion und den mittleren Kommentar zu *De Anima* bis zu der hier thematisierten Position aus dem Großen Kommentar, bietet Davidson, Herbert A. (1992): Alfarabi, Avicenna and Averroes, on Intellect. Their Cosmologies, Theories of the active Intellect, and Theories of Human Intellect, New York: Oxford University Press, S. 265–314.

16   Vgl. Averroes (1953): Commentarium magnum, in: Aristotelis De anima libros (1953), herausgegeben von F. Stuart Crawford, Cambridge/Massachusetts: Cambridge UP, S. 583. Im Kommentar zu der Passage 429 b 29 bis 439 a 2 von *De Anima* heißt es: »Deinde exposuit« – die Rede ist vom Verfasser von *De Anima*, dessen Originalpassagen im Zitat kursiviert wiedergegeben werden – »quid significat hoc nomen *passio in intellectu. Et dixit: quod intellectus est in potentia,* etc. Idest, et ista intentio universalis de passione in intellectu nichil aliud est nisi quod est in potentia in intellectu, non in actu, quousque intelligat. Et dicere etiam ipsum esse in potentia est alio modo ab eis secundum quos dicitur quod res materiales sunt in potentia.« Ebd., S. 428–429.

17   Dieses digestive Modell wird von Alfarabi in die Tradition der arabischen Kommentatoren eingebracht. Vgl. hierzu Illuminati, Augusto (2002) L'intelligentia di Averroè, in: Belfagor, 57.1, S. 103–108, hier S. 105.

18   Davidson, Herbert A. (1992): Alfarabi, Avicenna and Averroes, on Intellect. Their Cosmologies, Theories of the active Intellect, an Theories of Human Intellect, New York: Oxford University Press, S. 289–290.

Sinnesbild wird mittels der vom tätigen Intellekt gebrauchten Form identifiziert; die Korrespondenz von intelligibler Form und singulärem Gegenstand wird sichergestellt, indem diese Form mit den bekannten Phantasiebildern auf Ähnlichkeit mit dem besonderen Eindruck abgeglichen wird. Hierfür stellt der materiale Intellekt ein Reservoir bereit, welches das Intelligible empfängt und in denen die einmal aus der Welt extrahierten Formen gespeichert werden, derer sich ein aktiver Intellekt denkend und mithilfe der Phantasie bedienen kann. Wie schon Ernst Bloch gesehen hat, wird die bereits bei Aristoteles mit dem Möglichen verbundene Materie somit bei Averroes auch zum Schoß von Möglichkeiten, die nicht einfach als Aktualisierung eines inaktuellen, mentalen Modells anzusehen sind. Anders als bei Kant, wenn er auf dem Unterschied zwischen 50 möglichen und 50 wirklichen Talern besteht, aber je schon den Begriff von 50 Talern voraussetzt, ist jenes Mögliche, das aus den Formen der Welt extrahiert wird, weder schon als Begriff besessen noch ein diesem gegenüber vollkommen formlos Unbestimmtes. Das Mögliche findet daran seine Grenze, was sich aus einer konkreten Materiekonfiguration verwirklichen lässt und wozu diese Denkanlass sein kann. Für Bloch impliziert der mögliche Intellekt, den die arabische Tradition nach Avicenna auszubilden beginnt, daher auch eine Aktivität der Materie: denn das Mögliche wird von den Menschen nicht frei erfunden, sondern lediglich aus der jeweils schon vorausliegenden Konfiguriertheit der Materie entfaltet.[19] Der materiale Intellekt stellt dabei selbst ein seinerseits materiales Reservoir aufgenommener, fortentwickelter, kultivierter Formen bereit, die ursprünglich aus der Natur stammen.

Was hier außerdem noch von einer Aktivität der Materie sprechen lässt, ist, dass dieses Verhältnis, demzufolge sich der aktive Intellekt den im potenziellen und materialen Intellekt gespeicherten Formen aktualisierend bedient, nicht als bewusste Aktion

---

[19] Bloch, Ernst (1963): Avicenna und die Aristotelische Linke, Frankfurt am Main: Suhrkamp, S. 94–95: »Das Hinüberführen des Möglichen zum Wirklichen beginnt schon im Möglichen, indem es als solches ein Schoß ist. In der Materie reifen die Formen selber als dispositionelle, latente heran, und der Aktus [...] kann keine einzige neue hervorbringen, er verwirklicht nur. [...] Folglich sind auch die Seelen und Gedanken als Formen in der Materie schon angelegt, und zwar derart, daß dieses wie alles Angelegtsein eine nicht bloß passive, sondern suo genere aktive Möglichkeit einschließt. Die damit bedeutete Fähigkeit: Formen bis zu ihrer Aktualisierung, das heißt bis zum Sprung des Wirklichwerdens auszureifen, erweitert den Begriff des Möglichen sehr stark; Möglichkeit als aktive Disposition wird Inkubation, wird Schoß einer natura naturans«. Dies mache die »dynamis-Materie zum Schwangerschaftsort der ungewordenen, doch heranreifenden Formgestalten« (ebd., S. 95). Wie Bloch weiter ausführt, lässt sich Averroes so lesen, dass nicht alles zu jeder Zeit möglich ist, jedoch unter verschiedenen materiellen Bedingungen Verschiedenes möglich ist. Die Materie kann sich gewissermaßen entwickeln und Konstellationen hervorbringen, in denen etwas qualitativ Neues zunächst als dem Modell nach Mögliches zuerst denkbar wird und dann von den Menschen – als ausführender Kraft – zur Realisation gebracht werden kann. Diese Ausführung lässt sich als eine dynamische Fortentwicklung des *intellectus materialis* auffassen.

vorgestellt werden darf. Aristoteles vergleicht die Relation in *De Anima* selbst mit dem Verhältnis zwischen dem Licht, das die Farben erzeugt und der Luft als durchscheinendem (diaphanem) Medium: »Et quemaddmodum lux facit colorem in potentia esse in actu ita quod possit movere diaffonum, ita intellectus agens facit intentiones in potentia intellectuas in actu ita recipit eas intellectus materialis.«[20] Das »Licht der Dinge« geht vom tätigen *intellectus agens* aus, der sich auf den rezeptiven *intellectus materialis* stützt. Die Lichtmetapher des Aristoteles wird schon von Averroes' Vorläufer Alfarabi gebraucht und tradiert sich dann bei den arabischen Kommentatoren, wobei Averroes-Exegeten wie Herbert A. Davidson keine genauere Bestimmung der Lichtquelle durch Averroes erkennen können.[21] Dass auf die Lichtquelle selbst so wenig Licht geworfen wird, veranlasst Coccia etwa dazu, von einem »Licht [...] außerhalb unserer selbst« zu sprechen, wobei die Formen, die gespeichert und aktualisiert werden, selbst nichts anderes sind als mittels der Einbildungskraft erinnerte, die aus der bisherigen »Entzündungen« des Intellekts an den singulären und akzidentiellen Dingen der Welt stammen, vom aktiven Intellekt extrahierte Bilder.[22]

Der *intellectus materialis*, der alles Mögliche werden kann, indem er alle möglichen Formen aufzunehmen vermag, fungiert als Speicher dieser bildhaften Formen; der *intellectus agens* realisiert sie beim Erkennen. Dieses Verhältnis erscheint übermäßig komplex. Abgesehen davon, dass es der hylemorphistischen Tradition im Aristotelismus Rechenschaft trägt, erhält es bei Averroes seinen weiteren Sinn dadurch, dass der aktive Intellekt individuell ist, während der materiale Intellekt als kollektiv bestimmt wird. Das Denken, dass sich aktiv der intelligiblen Formen bedient, ist das meinige; diese Formen, mittels derer etwas gedacht werden kann, sind selbst allerdings nicht auf mich beschränkt. Der aktive Intellekt kann vor diesem Hintergrund als Denken begriffen werden, das im Einzelnen in den Akt übergeht und aufhört, wenn der Einzelne nicht mehr ist. Der materiale Intellekt ist demgegenüber die Schreibfläche, in der die vom menschlichen Denken individuierten Formen sich über das Leben der Einzelnen hinweg bewahren, von anderen und späteren neu aktiviert werden können. Die In-

---

20   Averroes (1953): Commentarium magnum in Aristotelis De anima libros (1953), herausgegeben von F. Stuart Crawford, Cambridge/Massachusetts: Cambridge UP, S. 411.

21   Davidson, Herbert A. (1992): Alfarabi, Avicenna and Averroes, on Intellect. Their Cosmologies, Theories of the active Intellect, and Theories of Human Intellect, New York: Oxford University Press, S. 316. Davidson verweist zudem darauf, dass die Intelligibilia hinter den wahrgenommenen Formen Konzepte oder Universalien darstellen. Vgl. ebd.: »By illuminating both the material intellect and the intelligible thoughts latent in images, the active intellect enables the material intellect to behold the intelligible thoughts and think them. The intelligible thoughts spoken of here are presumably concepts, rather than propositions, since they are compared to colors and not to judgments about colors".

22   So Coccia, Emanuele (2020): Sinnenleben. Eine Philosophie, München: Hanser 2020, S. 23; siehe auch Coccia, Emanuele (2005): La trasparenza delle immagini. Averroè e l'averroismo, Milano: Bruno Mondadori, S. 108–114.

telligibilia sind »unvergänglich unter dem Gesichtspunkt des materiellen Intellekts und vergänglich in Bezug auf jedes einzelne Individuum«.[23] Dieser Intellekt, der die Formen bewahrt, ist unsterblich und vom Einzelnen abtrennbar – er stellt als zweite Natur, der ihrerseits ganz wie der Materie eine Entwicklungsoffenheit inhäriert, das Formen- als Wissensreservoir einer Kultur und in letzter Konsequenz der ganzen Menschheit dar. So lässt sich in Averroes' materialem Intellekt auch eine implizite Medientheorie ausmachen.[24] Der materiale Intellekt scheint jedenfalls selbst, als universal menschlicher, einer Graphie oder Schrift im weitesten Sinne zu bedürfen.

Vor diesem Hintergrund gewinnt die berühmte Passage aus *De Anima*, in welcher Aristoteles den *nous* oder *intellectus* (in der deutschen Übersetzung: meist *Geist*, zuweilen auch *Vernunft*) mit einer Wachstafel vergleicht, auf der noch gar nichts geschrieben steht, eine konkrete Bedeutung. Eine deutsche Übersetzung gibt die betreffende Passage (429 a bis 430 a) aus *De Anima* folgendermaßen wieder:

> »dass der Geist der Möglichkeit nach auf irgendeine Art und Weise die denkbaren Dinge ist, der Verwirklichung nach aber keines, bevor er sie denkt; »der Möglichkeit nach« meint wie auf einer Schreibtafel, auf der in Wirklichkeit noch nichts geschrieben ist.«[25]

Die berühmte leere Schreibtafel des Aristoteles ist nicht einfach ein Intellekt als subjektives Vermögen. In der von Averroes' kommentierten lateinischen Passage aus Aristoteles' Abhandlung lesen wir: »Quamadmodum enim tabula nullam picturam habet in actu neque in potential propinqua actui, ita in intellectu materiali non est aliqua formarum intellectarum quas recipit, neque in actu neque in potential propinqua actui.«[26] Wie aus der Wortwahl (intellectu materiali) deutlich wird, hat Averroes, wenn er auf den Vergleich mit der Schreibtafel zurückkommt, den materialen/möglichen Intellekt im Sinn. Er ist es, welcher »der Möglichkeit nach«, wie es bei Aristoteles heißt, alles werden kann und genau in dieser passiven Rezeptivität jeglicher Form der

---

23 Esposito, Roberto (2018): Zwei. Die Maschine der politischen Theologie und der Ort des Denkens, Zürich: diaphanes, S. 213.

24 Das schlägt Augusto Illuminati vor, wenn er Parallelen zum *general intellect* bei Marx herstellt, wodurch der materiale Intellekt zur Gesamtheit der Erzeugnisse einer intellektuellen Öffentlichkeit wird, die in posse allen zugänglich ist. Illuminati, Augusto (2022): Averroè, une traduzione ininterrota, in: Doctor Virtualis. Rivista online di storia della filosofia medievale 17, S. 107–129, hier S. 128–129.

25 Aristoteles (2011): Über die Seele, übersetzt und herausgegeben von Gernot Krapinger, Stuttgart: Reclam, S. 153. Diese Übertragung wird hier der neueren, von Klaus Corcilius besorgten und bei Meiner erschienenen Übersetzung vorgezogen, da Übersetzung und folglich auch Auslegung der Begriffe eine größere Affinität zur italienischen Debatte aufzuweisen scheinen.

26 Averroes (1953): Commentarium magnum in Aristotelis De anima libros (1953), hrsg. von F. Stuart Crawford, Cambridge/Massachusetts: Cambridge UP, S. 430.

Schreibtafel gleiche, die alles Erdenkliche aufzunehmen fähig ist, ein Reservoir der Formen darstellt.[27]

Wenn nun aber die Phantasie zwischen dem im Einzelnen zum *intelellectus agens* werdenden und dem allen gemeinsam zur Verfügung stehenden *intellectus materialis* vermittelnd einspringt, indem sie die Formen beim Erkennen zu aktivieren hilft, so ist sie es, die den Einzelnen mit dem kollektiven Intellekt zusammenschließt: »Die Vernunft ist auf sie angewiesen, da nur durch ihre Phantasmen die reine Transparenz des Intellekts zu einem Denken von etwas werden kann.«[28] Diese Funktion mag auf den ersten Blick an die vermittelnde Rolle erinnern, welche die Einbildungskraft bei Immanuel Kant spielt, indem sie im Schematismus der reinen Vernunft zwischen begrifflichem Inhalt und Anschauung einspringt. Allerdings instauriert die averroistische Philosophie gerade kein transzendentales Subjekt, dessen »Ich denke« jede intellektuelle Handlung begleiten soll. Averroes konzipiert mit seinem geteilten Intellekt vielmehr einen unpersönlichen Raum des Denkens, in dem das eigene Denken (intellectus agens) nicht ohne ein kollektiver Formenreservoir (intellectus materialis) möglich ist. So kann Roberto Esposito Averroes als Ersten innerhalb einer Reihe von Denkern positionieren, die das Dispositiv der Person attackiert hätten, welches die okzidentale Philosophie-Tradition spätestens ab Descartes explizit ausgebildet hat.[29] Der materiale Intellekt lässt sich in diesem Rahmen als Raum des Denkmöglichen verstehen, in dem nicht einer allein denkt, sondern alle denken können. Wobei sie dies nur durch das Zurückgreifen auf das Tun und Denken anderer vermögen: − »e finalmente a pensare non sono piú io«.[30]

Agamben liest Averroes

Es ist die zuletzt genannte Verbindung von Phantasie und Intellekt, an der Agambens systematischste Lektüre von Averroes ansetzen wird. Sie findet sich im zweiten Abschnitt der Abhandlung *Das Wort und das Phantasma*. Die Studie, die sich dem Zu-

---

27 Vgl. Davidson, Herbert A. (1992): Alfarabi, Avicenna and Averroes, on Intellect. Their Cosmologies, Theories of the active Intellect, and Theories of Human Intellect, New York: Oxford University Press, S. 296: »he [Averroes − F.S.] compares the material intellect not to a writing tablet but to the disposition that the tablet has for writing«. Diese Bestimmung aus dem mittleren Kommentar wird im Großen Kommentar verändert: »He insists now that Aristotle compared the material intelltect to the writing tablet and not to the disposition in the tablet« (ebd.).

28 Esposito, Roberto (2018): Zwei. Die Maschine der politischen Theologie und der Ort des Denkens, Zürich: diaphanes, S. 213.

29 Ebd., S. 209−293.

30 Agamben, Giorgio (2022): Quel che ho visto, udito, appreso…, Torino: Einaudi 2022, S. 36. Siehe Anmerkung 4.

sammenhang von Sprache, Bild und Phantasie im mittelalterlichen Denken widmet, wird erstmals 1977 in der Aufsatzsammlung *Stanzen* veröffentlicht. Darin rekonstruiert Agamben die Verflechtung von Wort und Phantasma als wiederkehrende Konfiguration des mittelalterlichen Denkens. Sie ruht für ihn einer bestimmten Praxis des Kommentars auf. Im zweiten Abschnitt der Abhandlung, *Eros im Spiegel*, wird diese Praxis erörtert. Ausgangspunkt ist ein bestimmtes Zitat-Verständnis, das der mittelalterlichen Philosophie bescheinigt wird:

> für das Mittelalter gibt es keine Möglichkeit, einen Text im neuzeitlichen Sinne des Wortes zu zitieren, weil das Werk des *auctor* auch sein Zitat einschließt. Man könnte daher sagen, so paradox dies auch klingen mag, daß die mittelalterlichen Texte als Zitate in den *antiqui auctores* enthalten sind (was unter anderem die Vorliebe des Mittelalters für die Glosse als literarische Form erklärt)«[31]

Die Glosse stellt eine Form des Kommentars dar, der nicht selten interlinear ausfällt, also zwischen den Zeilen eines Prätextes eingetragen wird. Kommentar und Kommentiertes verschmelzen auf diese Weise auf den Seiten eines Codex. Diese Zitatpraxis wird im Laufe der Abhandlung auch der musikalischen Variation über ein Ausgangsthema verglichen (134). Die Variation dient dabei als Beispiel dafür, die Praxis der arabischen Aristoteles-Kommentatoren näher zu charakterisieren, welche die Werke dieses Philosophen glossieren. Das Vorgehen des mittelalterlichen Denkens »bearbeitet ein gegebenes Thema, das es durch kleine Abweichungen reproduziert und umstellt, was bisweilen zu einer völligen Umbildung des Ausgangsmaterials führen kann« (123). Die zur Variation über ein Thema neigende Zitatpraxis der mittelalterlichen Philosophie ist so nicht einfach Kommentierung eines feststehenden Inhalts. Die Praxis des Kommentators schafft den Sinn des Originals ständig neu.[32] Sie führt durch ihre Re-Lektüre die angelegten Verständnispotenziale aus, aus denen sich die »Entwicklungsoffenheit« einer Philosophie ergibt; ein Begriff, den Agamben Ludwig Feuerbach entlehnt.[33]

---

[31] Agamben, Giorgio (2006): Stanzen, Zürich/Berlin: Diaphanes, S. 125. Zahlen in Klammern hinter Zitaten weisen in diesem und den nächsten beiden Abschnitten Seitenangaben aus, die sich auf diese Ausgabe beziehen.

[32] Diese These ließe sich tatsächlich an Averroes diversen Re-Lektüren der Schreibtafel-Vergleichs bei Aristoteles diskutieren. Wie Davidsons Darstellung der *Drei Abhandlungen über die Conjunction* verdeutlicht, liest Averroes darin den Vergleich auf unterschiedliche Weise und überschreibt kommentierend gewissermaßen die eigenen Lektüren, die ihrerseits schon Kommentare darstellen. Davidson, Herbert A. (1992): Alfarabi, Avicenna and Averroes, on Intellect. Their Cosmologies, Theories of the active Intellect, and Theories of Human Intellect, New York: Oxford University Press, S. 272.

[33] Agamben, Giorgio (2009): Signatura Rerum. Zur Methode, Frankfurt: Suhrkamp 2009, S. 7.

So pauschal Agambens Argument über *das* Mittelalter daherkommen mag: Es wird darin eine Idee von Autorschaft entfaltet, der sich Agambens Text und damit die von ihm vollzogene Averroes-Auslegung performativ anzuschließen scheint. *Das Wort und das Phantasma* beginnt selbst mit einem Zitat aus Platons *Philebos*. Dabei soll der Platon-Rekurs zunächst erklärtermaßen der Einschränkung jener bekannten These dienen, dass das Mittelalter diesen schlecht bis nicht gekannt habe.[34] An der Passage 39 a des platonischen Dialogs wird gerade die von Sokrates vorgetragene Erinnerungslehre hervorgehoben. Sokrates spricht hier davon, dass die »mit den Sinneswahrnehmungen verschmelzende Erinnerung und die dabei sich abspielenden inneren Vorgänge (*pathémata*) […] gewissermaßen Reden in unsere Seele zu schreiben« scheinen (123). Zur gleichen Zeit trete aber neben dem Schreiber noch ein anderer »Werkmann« im Menschen auf: »Ein Maler, der nach dem Schreibkünstler die Bilder jener Gespräche in die Seele einzeichnet« (123).

Was bedeutet diese Engführung Platons mit dem mittelalterlichen, doch weit stärker aristotelisch geprägten Denken? Erstens erweitert Agamben damit das aristotelische Bild vom Intellekt als Schreibtafel auf einen Aristoteles' bekannten Prä-Text hin. Zweitens plausibilisiert diese Erweiterung ansatzweise die von Agamben vertretene Grundannahme, dass es sich beim Verhältnis von Bild und Phantasma um ein tradiertes Problem handelt (oder ein wiederaufgenommenes Thema gemäß der Logik des mittelalterlichen Kommentars). Drittens scheint sich dieses Thema sodann bereits bei Aristoteles, der im Mittelalter auch als »Schreiber der Natur« bekannt war[35], als Variation zu erweisen. Viertens kommt bei der zitierten Platon-Passage auch das Bild zu Wort, wodurch auf eine Insuffizienz jeder philosophisch-psychologischen Beanspruchung der berühmten Schreibtafel-Metapher des Aristoteles hingewiesen wird. Wird der Geist in *De Anima* einer Schreibtafel verglichen, auf der noch gar nichts geschrieben stehe, so ist nicht nur auf einer Idee des Geistes als Ort der Schrift, sondern auch des Bildes zu bestehen.[36] Agamben liest das von Sokrates eingeführte Bild des Malers dabei als Allegorie auf die Phantasie.[37] Schon in Platons *Theaitetos* würde das menschliche

---

34   »Platon nimmt im Denken des Mittelalters auf den ersten Blick keinen gleichermaßen bedeutenden Platz ein, doch die so gern wiederholte Behauptung, daß das Mittelalter sein Werk nur wenig, und jedenfalls nicht aus erster Hand, gekannt habe, ist wohl übertrieben« (124).

35   So die Einordnung von Aristoteles im spätbyzantinischen Wörterbuch der *Suda*. Siehe Agamben, Giorgio (2015ª): Die Sache selbst, in: ders., Die Macht des Denkens, Frankfurt am Main: S. Fischer, S. 25.

36   Das Bild der Schreibtafel geistert seinerseits als Variation durch die europäische Kulturgeschichte. Es hat Konjunktur wenigstens bis zu Sigmund Freuds Aufzeichnung über den Wunderblock, welche Jacques Derrida in die aristotelische Tradition zurückgestellt hat. Derrida, Jacques (1971): Freud und der Schauplatz der Schrift, in: Ders.: Die Schrift und die Differenz, Frankfurt am Main: Suhrkamp.

37   »Der Künstler, der im zitierten Passis von Platon der Seele die Abbilder (*eikónas*) der Dinge einzeichnet, ist die Phantasie, und tatsächlich werden diese »Ikonen« wenig später »Phantas-

Gedächtnis mit einer wächsernen Tafel verglichen, auf der sich Abdrücke dessen bildeten, was darin behalten wird. Aristoteles habe die platonische Metaphorik schließlich in eine geschlossene psychologische Theorie überführt, die wiederum seine mittelalterlichen Kommentatoren zu explizieren versuchen (126) – und in deren Auslegung, wie man hinzufügen darf, die Schriftmetaphorik bisweilen Überhand zu nehmen scheint.

Gegenüber dem Behalten der Worte als Schrift im Gedächtnis ist die Phantasie hingegen notwendig, um eine Vorstellung zu haben, welche für die Arbeit der Erinnerung noch grundlegender ist und dem Wiedererkennen überhaupt bildhafte Modelle liefert. So erscheint die Phantasie auch bei Agambens Averroes als Bindeglied zwischen den singulären Bildern der Sinneswahrnehmung und den eingebildeten Vorstellungsinhalten (128). Phantasma und Einbildungskraft sind dementsprechend für die aristotelische Psychologie zentral, insofern die Phantasie eine Kraft darstellt, aus der sich Verstand, Empfindung, Traum und Sehergabe, Gedächtnis wie auch Sprachvermögen speisen (129). Mit diesem letzten Punkt ist bereits ein Verbindungsweg zum Sprachdenken angezeigt.

Die arabische Aristoteles-Auslegung des Mittelalters, wie Agamben sie als Variationen erzeugende Kommentarpraxis rekonstruiert, erarbeitet in Verbindung mit den Phantasmen ihre Lehre der Vorstellungsbilder (*intentiones*). Spätestens mit Avicenna greift sie hierfür zusätzlich auf das Wissen der mittelalterlichen Medizin zurück. Neben dem Hinzukommen einer Theorie des im männlichen Samen vorkommenden Pneuma, das eine gesteigerte Rezeptivität gewährleisten soll, lokalisiert der arabische Arzt und Philosoph Avicenna die Phantasie im Menschen in einer von drei feuchten Höhlen, welche er im Kopf annimmt. Die Phantasie ist dabei zunächst für die *intentiones*, die erinnerten Bilder von singulären Dingen, zuständig. Avicenna unterscheidet fünf aufsteigend geordnete Kräfte: die Phantasie oder den Gemeinsinn, welche die Formen der Sinne empfängt; die Imagination, welche sie festhält; die in Bezug auf das Leben vorstellende und auf die Seele denkende Kraft; die beurteilende Kraft; sowie Gedächtnis und Erinnerung (132). Im aufsteigenden Durchgang durch sie werde das aufgenommene und von der Phantasie bearbeitete Wahrnehmungsbild entblößt, d.i. von seinen stofflichen Akzidenzien entledigt. Das Auge, welches zuvor die Sinneneindrücke erfährt, kommt dabei der Funktion nach einem Spiegel gleich, der das nur Zufällige von der notwendigen Form abstreift und so den Übergang vom Akzidentellen zum Wesen vollzieht.[38]

Hier liegt offenbar eine ganze Erkenntnistheorie im Zeichen des Bildes vor. Sie sei u.a. durch die Kritik Thomas von Aquins an Averroes, dem letzten und einfluss-

---

men« (*phantásmata*) (40a) genannt« (125).

[38] Ebd., S. 135.

reichsten in dieser Reihe arabischer Denker, verloren gegangen. Mit Averroes gelte es hingegen zu sehen,

> daß das Bild für einen arabischen Autor sehr wohl der Ort werden kann, an dem sich der Schauende mit dem Geschauten vereint. Denn wenn aus der Sicht des Mittelalters der Spiegel der Ort schlechthin war, wo *oculus videt se ipsum* und wo ein und dieselbe Person zugleich Sehendes und Gesehenes ist, symbolisiert andererseits die Vereinigung mit dem eigenen Bild in seinem vollkommen blanken Spiegel häufig die Vereinigung mit dem Übersinnlichen – einer mystischen Theorie zufolge, welche die arabischen Autoren nachhaltig beeinflußt hat, aber auch der christlichen Tradition des Mittelalters wohlvertraut ist. (143)

Diese mystische Theorie des Bildes wird in Stanzen mehr aufgerufen als erörtert. Dass sich eine Theorie der Bilder oder intentionalen Spezies bei Averroes finden lässt, bestätigt auch Emmanuele Coccia, der den arabischen Philosophen in seinem Buch Sinnenleben für ihre Rehabilitation ständig bemüht.[39] Dieselbe intentionale Spezies behandelt Agambens Aufsatz *Das »spezielle« Sein*. 2005 in der Sammlung Profanierungen erschienen, widmet sich dieser kurze Text just der Rolle des Spiegels und der spekulativen Erkenntnis im Mittelalter, deren Grundzüge schon in Avicennas medizinischem Diskurs vorgezeichnet liegen.[40] Das Vorstellungsbild oder das Phänomen einer Dingerscheinung wird als Spezies gedacht. Spezies aber sind, wo sie in Subjekten vorkommen, Intentiones (der von Coccia gebrauchte Begriff der intentionalen Spezies lässt beide zusammenfallen). Beide Male handelt es sich um intelligible Formen, die jeweils nur in den unterschiedlichen Medien der Wahrnehmung oder der Fantasie anzusiedeln sind.[41] Die Spekulation geht von wahrgenommenen Spezies-Bildern aus, die nichts anderes als die Beliebigkeit, die Quodlibetalität oder das So-Sein einer bestimmten Erscheinung ausmachen.[42] Sie sind nicht die Universalien allgemeiner in-

---

39   Coccia, Emanuele (2020): Sinnenleben. Eine Philosophie, Berlin: Hanser, S. 17–20.

40   Agamben, Giorgio (2005): Das »spezielle« Sein, in: ders.: Profanierungen, Frankfurt am Main: Suhrkamp, S. 51–56, insbes. S. 54–55.

41   Diese Leseweise folgt derjenigen bei Coccia, Emanuele (2005): La trasparenza delle immagini. Averroè e l'averroismo, Milano: Bruno Mondadori, S. 125: »L'essere speciale o intenzionale di qualcosa non designa alto che l'esistenza mediale di una forma« (»Das spezielle oder intentionalee Sein einer Sache bezeichnet nichts anderes als die mediale Existenz einer Form«). Agambens Nähe zu Coccia, die oben schon betont wurde, reicht bis in die Terminologie: *essere speciale* ist auch der Originaltitel von Agambens Aufsatz aus *Profanierungen.*

42   Siehe dazu auch Coccia, Emanuele (2019): Quodlibet. Logica e fisica dell'essere qualunque, in: Giorgio Agamben. Ontologia e politica, ed. Valeria Bonnacci, Macerata: Quodlibet, S. 123–134; Maier, Anneliese (1963): Das Problem der »species sensibilis in medio« und die neue Naturphilosophie des 14. Jahrhunderts, in: Freiburger Zeitschrift für Philosophie und Theologie 10, S. 3–32.

telligibler Formen, sondern mit Akzidenzien behaftete Bilder, d.h. Ausdruck einer spezifischen ontologischen Differenz, extrahiert aus singulär Seiendem. Mittels der Phantasie nun, die diese Spezies-Bilder zu reproduzieren und zu verändern vermag, finden sie sich in den Einzelwesen zu Intentiones verdichtet, zu Bildern in Subjekten. Auf sie greift etwa auch das Wiedererkennen zurück, wie es im aktiven Intellekt unwillkürlich vollzogen wird. Die Vereinigung mit dem Übersinnlichen kann daher im Spiegel (lat. speculum) vollzogen werden – also buchstäblich spekulativ –, weil die intelligiblen Formen auf ihrer untersten Stufe nichts anderes sind als Extraktionsphänomene aus dem sinnlichen Sein der Dinge, die zu ihrer Wiedervergegenwärtigung der Phantasie bedürfen.[43]

[Bei Averroes wird] der gesamte Erkenntnisprozeß im buchstäblichen Sinne als Spekulation gedacht [...], als Reflexion der Phantasmen von Spiegel zu Spiegel: Spiegel und Wasser sind die Augen und der Sinn, welche die Form des Gegenstandes reflektieren, Spekulation ist aber auch die Phantasie, die sich die Phantasmen bei Abwesenheit des Gegenstandes »einbildet«. Erkennen heißt, sich über einen Spiegel beugen, aus dem die Welt entgegenschlägt, ein Spähen nach Bildern, die zurückgeworfen werden von Widerschein zu Widerschein: und der mittelalterliche Mensch befindet sich immerzu vor einem Spiegel, ob er nun um sich blickt oder sich seiner Einbildung überläßt (136–137)

Aus den im materiellen Intellekt extrahierten Formen setzen sich auch die intelligiblen Formen zusammen, die der agentielle Intellekt wiederum mithilfe von Phantasmen auf neue Spezies richtet. Das Begehren nach Schönem ist der Antrieb dieser zirkulären Maschine, mittels derer der Intellekt in seinen verschiedenen Phasen das Gesehene sich zu eigen macht – und indem er es in Worte kleidet, wie die Dichter es tun, die Menschheit daran teilhaben lässt. Mit dem averroistischen Dichter Guido Cavalcante wird Agamben das Phantasma als »*copula* zwischen dem Individuum und dem einzigen möglichen Verstand [*intellectus possibilis*]« (141), dem materiellen Intellekt betrachten. Die Dichtung bildet so eine Brücke zwischen Phantasmen- bzw. Bildtheorie und Sprachdenken.

---

43 Die Auffassung der Welt als Rätsel-Spiegel, in dem Gott nicht direkt sichtbar ist, geht zurück auf Korinther 1, 13,12 und wird auch in einem im Mittelalter einflussreichen Text wie Augustinus' *De Trinitate* aufgegriffen. Vgl. dazu Largier, Nikolaus (1999): Spiegelungen. Fragmente einer Geschichte der Spekulation, in: Zeitschrift für Germanistik 9.3, S. 616–636, hier S. 616. Für eine reiche Dokumentation der Rolle des Spiegels im Mittelalter siehe Baltrušaitis, Jurgis (1986): Der Spiegel. Entdeckungen, Täuschungen, Phantasien, Gießen: Anabas.

Begehren und Dichtung, Phantasma und Stimme

Unterwegs zur Sprache spielt ein Faktor ins Denken des Bildes hinein, den nach dem Mittelalter erst Jacques Lacan im 20. Jahrhundert wieder mit dem Spiegelbild zu verbinden wusste: das Begehren. Wenn Agamben es ihm gleichtut, dann lässt er seine Lektüre des Averroes nicht nur unter der Hand mit den psychoanalytischen Theorien des Phantasmas konkurrieren, die Ende des 1960er Jahre im Umkreis der Lacan-Schule aus dem Boden schießen[44]: Er folgt damit auch einem philosophisch beschlagenen Liebesdichter und Averroisten in der Tradition des dolce stil nuovo, Guido Cavalcante.[45] Guidos Kanzone *Donna me prega* kleidet sich als Antwort auf die Frage einer der Frauen, die von den mittelalterlichen Liebesdichtern seit den provenzalischen Trobadors traditionell besungen werden. Auf ihre Nachfrage, was die Liebe sei, nennt Guidos komplexes und philosophisch explikatives Lied diese ein Akzidenz. In der zweiten Strophe werden dabei eine Reihe Motive aufgerufen, die von Averroes bzw. aus der in *Stanzen* entfalteten Verbindung aus arabischem Aristotelismus und Medizin bekannt sind: die Liebe erhebt sich vom Ort aus, wo Gedächtnis ist (»dove sta memora«), sie gewinnt Form ganz nach der Weise wie Averroes das Medium der Erkenntnis von Bildern beschreibt: als durchscheinendes Licht (»come/diaffan da lume«). Das Bild der Geliebten, ihre gesehene Form ist für Cavalcanti Gegenstand der Liebesdichtung des *dolce stil nuvovo*, der in der Tradition der erfinderischen Troubadour-Dichtung stehend, neue Formen und Worte für das Liebeserlebnis findet. Hier ist das Bild der Geliebten, ihre zur Intentio werdende Spezies zugleich Anreiz und Ausgangspunkt einer sprachgenerativen Bewegung: »Ven da veduta forma che s'intende,/che prende – nel possibile intelletto,/come in subietto, – loco e dimoranza.« Ort und Bleibe findet das Bild der Geliebten, einmal aufgenommen, im »possibile intelletto«. Über diesen aber drängt es zur Sprache – und provoziert die Gedichte des *dolce stil nuovo*, dessen Poetik Cavalcantis Kanzone metastufig auszusprechen wagt.

Guidos Einspeisung averroistischer Philosopheme in die Liebesdichtung dient Agamben allerdings zu weit mehr, als nur die Bedeutung der Phantasie im mittelalterlichen Denken des materialen Intellekts zu erweisen. »Das Erbe, das die Liebeslyrik des 13. Jahrhunderts der europäischen Kultur vermacht hat« liege nicht allein in der Liebeskonzeption; wichtiger sei »vielmehr der Nexus von Eros und poetischer Spra-

---

44 Laplanche, Jean/Pontalis J.-B. (2023): Urphantasie, Gießen: Psychosozial Verlag. Siehe zum Verhältnis von Sprache und Begehren bei Lacan und der Vorläuferrolle der mittelalterlichen Liebesdichtung dafür Wild, Cornelia (2016): Die Liebe der trobadors, in: von Koppenfels, Martin/Zumbusch, Cornelia (Eds.): Handbuch Literatur und Emotionen, Berlin: De Gruyter, S. 261–274.

45 Cavalcante, Guido (1991): Le Rime – Die Gedichte, Nach einer Interlinearübersetzung von Geraldine Gabor, in deutsche Reime gebracht von Ernst-Jürgen Dreyer, Mainz: Dieterich'sche Verlagsbuchhandlung. Alle italienischen Zitate von Guidos *Donna me prega* in diesem Absatz: ebd., S. 66.

che« (206). Die Beliebigkeit sowie die Liebenswürdigkeit, die Agamben beide aus dem Begriff des quodlibetalen Wahrnehmungsbildes der Spezies herausliest[46], wird in der Dichtung des *Dolce Stil Nuovo,* die von der Betrachtung der Geliebten ihren Ausgangspunkt nimmt, flagrant. Dieser Nexus erweist sich somit als einer zwischen Wort, Begehren und Phantasma: letzteres das als Intentio in subiecto begehrte Bild der Geliebten, für das die Dichter Worte zu finden haben.

Dabei ist genauer zu bestimmen, was poetische Sprache hier umfasst. Denn bei ihr handelt es sich nicht nur um die Sprache der Dichtung. Poetische Sprache ist vom Begehren nach einem Bild aktiviert. In der Formen erfindenden Dichtung des Mittelalters wird daraus ein Begehren nach Sprache.[47] Agamben hat bereits in seinem ersten Buch *L'uomo senza contenuto* (1971) eine Archäologie des griechischen Begriffs *poiesis* vorgelegt. Dessen ursprünglicher Sinn sei der modernen Ästhetik nach Baumgarten abhandengekommen. Kants *Kritik der Urteilskraft* und Hegels *Vorlesungen über die Ästhetik* gingen gerade von betrachtbaren, einem kontemplierenden Subjekt gegenüberstehenden musealisierten Werken aus. Einer solchen Ästhetik steht die Poetik gegenüber – in Form des ursprünglichen Sinnes von *poiesis,* der auf eine »Pro-Duktion in die Anwesenheit« verweist, bei der etwas »vom Nichtsein ins Sein« trete.[48] Dies lässt sich als nicht nur rhetorische Verlebendigung von Vorstellungen durch die Sprache lesen. Es kann auch als sprachgenerativer Akt verstanden werden: als ein Begehren nach Sprache oder nach mehr Sprache. Man kann den Prototyp solcher *poiesis* somit auch – und Agamben scheint dies später zu tun – im adamitischen Akt der Benennung oder des Namen-Gebens vollzogen sehen.[49] Ein Aspekt von *poiesis* besteht offenbar im Schaffen sprachlicher Zeichen unter dem Druck der intentionalen Spezies, Guidos »veduta forma«.

Theorie der Stimme und Kritik der Schrift

Die gesungenen und zur Musik gesetzten Lieder des *dolce stil nuovo* samt der Poetik Guidos, in welche die averroistische Erkenntnistheorie zur originären Schöpfung von Sprachmaterial drängt, stehen hinter Agambens gesamten Konzept der Stimme, das mit einer neuen, nicht platonischen Kritik der Schrift einhergeht. Dies deutet sich bereits in *Stanzen* an. Denn das dort explizierte und oben rekonstruierte Verhältnis von Phantasma und Laut wird von Agamben als Alternative zum Verhältnis von Signifikat und

---

46 Agamben, Giorgio (2003): Die kommende Gemeinschaft, Berlin: Merve, S. 9–25.

47 Wild, Cornelia (2016): Die Liebe der trobadors, in: von Koppenfels, Martin/Zumbusch, Cornelia (Eds.): Handbuch Literatur und Emotionen, Berlin: De Gruyter, S. 261–274.

48 Agamben, Giorgio (2012): Der Mensch ohne Inhalt, Berlin: Suhrkamp, S. 92.

49 Agamben, Giorgio (2023): La voce umana, Macerata: Quodlibet, S. 24–25.

Signifikant in der Linguistik Ferdinand de Saussures empfohlen. Man könnte »den Zeichenbegriff ($\frac{s}{S}$, wobei s der Signifikant und S das Signifikat ist)« auch »in aristotelische Begriffe übersetzen, [wobei er sich] auf diese Weise abbilden ließe: ($\frac{P}{l}$, wobei l für ›Laut‹ und P für ›Phantasma‹ steht)« (199). Nun ist es eine bedeutungsschwere Änderung, statt von einem eng mit der Schrift verbundenem Signifikanten von einem Laut zu sprechen. Wie Jacques Derrida im Ausgang von Saussure gezeigt hat, besteht historisch dahingehend eine enge Beziehung zwischen Schrift und Signifikant, da erst die Schrift die Isolierung unterscheidbarer semiotischer Elemente erlaubt hat, die zum Ausgangspunkt linguistischer Systematisierungen der Sprache werden konnte, bis hin zu ihrer Kodifizierung in Grammatiken und ihrer Formalisierung in der Kommunikations- und Informationstheorie des 20. Jahrhunderts.[50] Die Veränderung des Sausurre'schen Modells steht ganz im Dienst der Aufwertung einer Stimme, die *poiesis* betreibt.

Eine Theorie der Stimme versucht Agamben nach eigenen Aussagen bereits Ende der 1970er Jahre zu schreiben, also zeitlich in enger Nähe zu *Das Wort und das Phantasma.* Das Vorwort zur zweiten Auflage von *Kindheit und Geschichte* (*Infanzia e storia,* 1978 und 2001) weist diesen Text als Resultat eines ursprünglich geplanten Buches über die menschliche Stimme aus.[51] Erst kürzlich und mit einer Verzögerung von 45 Jahren hat Agamben ein solches Buch tatsächlich vorgelegt.[52] Wenn sich angesichts der Stimme eine durchhaltende Argumentationslinie herausschälen lässt, dann besteht sie in der Entgegensetzung der Stimme zu jeglicher Theorie der Sprache, welche letztere im 20. Jahrhundert auf Schrift und Grammatik, auf Code und Programm zu reduzieren bestrebt war.

Eine Reflexion dieses Gegensatzes begegnet erstmals 1969 in dem bis heute nicht ins Deutsche übersetzten Aufsatz *L'Albero dell' linguaggio.*[53] Der Text stellt Verbindungen von Noam Chomskys Idee einer generativen Grammatik zur barocken Vorstellung einer Idealsprache bei Leibniz her. Beide sollen aus einer reinen Kombinatorik von Elementen bestehen, welche eine eingeborene menschliche Rationalität als ihre Disposition voraussetzen. Das *Tertium Comparationis* liegt für Agamben darin, dass beide Male die Geburt der Linguistik als Wissenschaft mit dem Eintritt in einen semiologischen Horizont zusammenfällt (»la nascita della linguistica come scienza coincide con

---

50   Vgl. Derrida, Jacques (1973): Grammatologie, Frankfurt am Main: Suhrkamp, S. 16–48.; siehe
       dazu auch Stetter, Christian (1999): Sprache und Schrift, Frankfurt am Main: Suhrkamp.

51   Agamben, Giorgio (2004): Kindheit und Geschichte. Zerstörung der Erfahrung und Ursprung der
       Geschichte, Frankfurt am Main: Suhrkamp, S. 7–9.

52   Agamben, Giorgio (2023): La voce umana, Macerata: Quodlibet.

53   Agamben, Giorgio (1968): L'albero del Linguaggio, in: Journal of Italien Philosophy 1 (2018),
       S. 2–11 (ursprünglich in: Ulise XXI.IX [1968]).

l'entrata definitiva e senza residui dell linguaggio in un orizzonte semiologico«).[54] Man kann dies als Adaption einer zentralen Einsicht aus Derridas *Grammatologie* erblicken. Ein semiologischer Horizont fasst die Sprache als Ensemble kombinierbarer Elemente auf, welche grammatisch kodifiziert sind und interpretiert sie in dieser Hinsicht als Schrift im weiteren Sinne: als Ensemble diskret unterschiedener Elemente, die sich als solche schon als fixiert und somit als Schrift im weiten Sinne von Derridas Schriftbegriff auffassen lassen.[55]

Hinter dem Begriff des Semiologischen steht außerdem der Rekurs auf eine vom Linguisten Emile Benveniste 1955 vorgebrachte Unterscheidung. Benveniste differenziert zwischen Semiotischem und Semantischem der Sprache. Agamben übernimmt dieses Begriffspaar schon Ende der 1970er Jahre in *Kindheit und Geschichte* und von da an immer wieder, um den Unterschied zwischen den allgemeinen Strukturen der Sprache, welche im 20. Jahrhundert die Form einer Schrift und eines Codes anzunehmen beginnen und dem Sagen-Wollen als Akt der Spontaneität einzelner Sprechender zu beschreiben.[56] Während das Semiotische das sprachliche Rohmaterial samt den gültigen Verknüpfungsregeln umfasst, die Lexik, Grammatik, Orthografie beschreiben und vorgeben (was sich als Bestand eines kodifizierten Schriftsystems ansprechen lässt), so steht all dem das Semantische als Kraft des Ausdrucks und der Motivierung des sprachlichen Rohmaterials gegenüber, die nur im konkreten Diskurs operativ werden kann. Geht es Agamben, wie er oft betont, um das *factum loquendi* oder die nackte Tatsache, dass gesprochen wird, so liegt stets diese Unterscheidung zugrunde.

Gegenstand von Agambens Kritik ist nun nicht so sehr Derrida, der das linguistische Primat der Schrift für die Konstitution einer grammatisch-semiologischen Sprachauffassung 1967 in seiner *Grammatologie* erstmals kritisch offengelegt hat. Es ist viel mehr Noam Chomskys Transformationsgrammatik. Sie erscheint als radikalste Ausformung der strukturalistischen Linguistik, wo sie eine abstrakte logische Maschine (eine »macchina logica«) in den Menschen hineinprojiziert.[57] Dies sei nichts Geringeres als die Realisierung des Traums der Sprache einer rationalistischen Philosophie, welchen

---

54 Ebd., S. 3.

55 Vgl. dazu Attell, Kevin (2015): Giorgio Agamben. Beyond the Threshold of Deconstruction, New York: Fordham UP, S. 37: »But for Agamben, in viewing *différance* as the unsurpassable limit and (non)origin of signification, and thus foreclosing the possibility of neutralizing or circumventing the metaphysics that is founded on this logic, Derrida is confined to the Oedipal understanding of the enigma, an understanding of language fundamentally as code«.

56 Agamben, Giorgio (2004): Kindheit und Geschichte. Zerstörung der Erfahrung und Ursprung der Geschichte, Frankfurt am Main: Suhrkamp, S. 78–82; Agamben, Giorgio (2023): La voce umana, Macerata: Quodlibet, S. 21–23. Vgl. Stetter, Christian (1999): Sprache und Schrift, Frankfurt am Main: Suhrkamp, S. 7. Stetter sieht diesen Gegensatz bereits bei Wilhelm von Humboldt artikuliert an als jenen zwischen lebendigem Wort der Rede und grammatischem Zeichen.

57 Agamben, Giorgio (1968): L'albero del Linguaggio, in: Journal of Italien Philosophy 1 (2018), S. 2–11, hier S. 10.

Agamben zu Leibniz' Idee eines Sprachbaums historisch zurückdatiert. Geträumt werde von einem Ensemble kombinierbarer Elemente, die Kombinationsregeln unterliegen und der logischen Zusammensetzung der Welt entsprechen. Es ist dabei wohl nicht irrelevant, dass bei Leibniz der Intellekt als genauso angeboren behandelt wird, wie das Sprachvermögen in der Generativen Grammatik.[58] In beiden Fällen wird ein Logos, der auch pragmatisch im Oszillationsverhältnis zwischen Denken und Welt gedacht werden könnte, zu einer menschlichen Universalie erklärt. Dem setzt Agamben 1968 schon die Etymologie des Logos entgegen, die »l'atto di raccogliere, di mantenere e portare qualcosa« umfasst[59] – den Akt des Sammelns, des Behaltens und des Tragens von etwas. Es sind gerade diese Bedeutungen, die man auch im Begriff des averroistischen Intellekts eingetragen sehen kann. Das Inter-leggere intentionaler Spezies über den Intellekt erlaubt sprachgenerative Poiesis.[60]

Agambens politische Philosophie nimmt – auch – von diesem Sprachproblem ihren Ausgang, denn die Theorie der Stimme, die mit dem konkreten Austausch im Diskurs verbunden wird, verweist stets auf eine Gemeinschaft der Sprechenden.

> Die Stimme hat sich nie in die Sprache eingeschrieben, und das Gramma – Derridas Denken hat es rechtzeitig gezeigt – ist nichts anderes als die Form der Voraussetzung seiner selbst und der Potenz. Der Raum zwischen Stimme und Logos ist ein leerer Raum, eine Grenze im Kantischen Sinne. Nur weil der Mensch in die Sprache geworfen ist, ohne von einer Stimme in sie eingeführt worden zu sein, nur weil er sich im experimentum linguae aufs Spiel setzt – ohne eine »Grammatik«, in dieser Leere und Aphonie –, werden für ihn so etwas wie ein éthos und eine Gemeinschaft möglich[61]

---

58   Dazu Trabant, Jürgen (2012): Weltansichten. Wilhelm von Humboldts Sprachprojekt, München: C.H. Beck, S. 263

59   Agamben, Giorgio (1968): L'albero del Linguaggio, in: Journal of Italien Philosophy 1 (2018), S. 2–11, hier S. 10.

60   Vergleichbares hat Dieter Mersch in seiner Kritik der Sprechakttheorie vorgebracht. Mersch klagt ein, dass sowohl die vor allem bereits konstituierte Performanzregeln bereitstellenden Spielarten der Sprechakttheorie als auch Derridas Dekonstruktion es versäumten, den Akt der Differenzsetzung als »Möglichkeit des radikal Neuen« zu begreifen. Dieser als katachrestisch markierte Moment verweise vielmehr auf eine Ekstase – Mersch assoziiert Heidegger *Ek-sistenz* als Moment der Stiftung –, welches außerhalb der Sprache anzusiedeln sei und einen Neuanfang markiere. Heideggerianisch reformuliert: Es kann neue Sprechakte, neue Worte, neue Sprachformen geben, weil es ein nicht schon in Sprache aufgehendes In-der-Welt-Sein gibt. Mersch, Dieter (2004): Performativität und Ereignis. Überlegungen zur Revision des Performanz-Konzeptes der Sprache, in: Fohrmann, Jürgen (Ed.): Rhetorik. Figuration und Performanz, Stuttgart/ Weimar: J. B. Metzler, S. 526–528.

61   Agamben, Giorgio (2001): Kindheit und Geschichte. Zerstörung der Erfahrung und Ursprung der Geschichte, Frankfurt am Main: Suhrkamp, S. 15.

Daraus, dass es eben keine angeborene Grammatik und keine abstrakte Sprachmaschine oder »macchina logica« im Menschen gibt, die über Elemente und Kombinationsregeln verfügt, entspringt die Notwendigkeit des Einzelnen, sich sprechend immer wieder auf andere hin zu überschreiten.

Man kann so ersehen, warum Agamben sich im *Homo-sacer*-Projekt permanent Einschübe zu Sprachphilosophie und Dichtung erlaubt. Die Theorie der Stimme, über Guido auf averroistischer Grundlage gewonnen, ist das Fundament eines Politikverständnisses, das sich dem engen Zusammenhang von Sprechen und Handeln verpflichtet weiß.

Forma-di-Vita und möglicher Intellekt

Die averroistische Beeinflussung von Agambens Denken lässt sich so noch an einem letzten Konzept ablesen: am Begriff der Lebensform. Schon das Exposé des *Homo-sacer*-Projekts *Forma-di-Vita* (1991) führt diesen Schlüsselbegriff im Titel.[62] Agamben definiert die Lebensform dabei als ein Leben, »dem es in seiner Lebensweise um das Leben selbst geht«.[63] Wie die Forschung nicht übersehen hat, ist diese Formulierung ein deutlicher Tribut an Heideggers Definition des Daseins.[64] Allerdings ist Heideggers Dasein in *Sein und Zeit* von den Anderen, die als Mitdasein firmieren, terminologisch klar unterschieden. Im Exposé des *Homo-sacer*-Projekts und dann abermals in dessen letztem Teil *L'uso dei corpi* (2014) wird hingegen ein kollektives Moment der Lebensform hervorgekehrt. Hier behauptet sich der averroistische gegen den heideggerianischen Einfluss.

Das *Lebensform*-Exposé definiert das Denken als ein »Band, das die Lebensformen in einen unauflöslichen Zusammenhang setzt.«[65] Hier klingt die mittelalterliche Konjunktion des Einzelnen mit dem kollektiven Intellekt im Prozess des Denkens via aktivem Intellekt an. Damit ist eine Distanz zu Heideggers Dasein ausgemacht, dem die

---

62 Agamben, Giorgio (2000): Lebensform, in: ders.: Mittel ohne Zweck, Zürich/Berlin: Diaphanes, S. 13–20.

63 Ebd., S. 13.

64 Heidegger, Martin (1993): Sein und Zeit, 17. Auflage, Tübingen: Niemeyer, S. 12: »Das Dasein ist ein Seiendes, das nicht nur unter anderem Seienden vorkommt. Es ist vielmehr dadurch ontisch ausgezeichnet, daß es diesem Seienden in seinem Sein *um* dieses Sein selbst geht«. Man kann sich fragen, ob (und wenn ja: mit welchen fatalen Konsequenzen) Heideggers Daseinsanalyse in eine politische Theorie überführbar wäre. Siehe hierzu Geulen, Eva (2009): Agambens Politik der Nicht-Beziehung, in: Sabeth Buchmann/Helmut Traxler/Stephen Geene (Eds.): Avantgarde. Film. Biopolitik, Wien, S. 58–68.

65 Agamben, Giorgio (2000): Lebensform, in: ders.: Mittel ohne Zweck, Zürich/Berlin: Diaphanes, S. 17.

anderen in Gerede und Diktatur des Man gegenüberstehen. Unter Rekurs auf die Passage *De Anima* 429 a – b des Aristoteles wird Denken als Akt begriffen »in jedem Gedachten die Erfahrung einer reinen Potenz des Denkens zu machen«[66]. Diese Erfahrung sei »immer Erfahrung einer gemeinsamen Potenz«.[67] Diese gemeinsame Potenz spricht Agamben auch als »Intellektualität« an[68] und erweist sie so als averroistische Erbschaft, die aber erneut komplexer vermittelt ist. Wie Agamben zu einer averroistisch inspirierten Theorie der Stimme über Guido gelangt, so zur Lebensform über Dante Alighieri.

In den philologischen Arbeiten von Maria Corti findet sich die averroistische Beeinflussung Dantes gut aufgearbeitet.[69] Im dritten Abschnitt des ersten Buches von Dantes *Monarchia* findet sich ein überdeutlicher Rekurs auf die Intellekt-Theorie des Aristoteles, die unverhohlen Anleihen bei Averroes macht. Als äußerste Kraft des Menschen (*vis ultima in homine*) bezeichnet Dante dort »das erfassende Sein mittels des möglichen Intellekts« (*esse apprehensivum per intellectum possibilem*).[70] Nun stellt der vermeintliche Monopsychismus Averroes' nicht einfach eine Negation des Denkens des Einzelnen dar, sondern hebt diesen in einen gemeinschaftlichen Intellekt auf. Dies versteht schon Dante und setzt daher in *De Monarchia* eine Vielheit (*multitudinem*) an, in welcher sich der tätige Intellekt realisiere.

> Und weil dieses Vermögen weder durch einen einzigen Menschen noch durch eine der oben unterschiedenen, besonderen Gemeinschaften auf einmal gänzlich verwirklicht werden kann, ist es notwendig, daß es in der menschlichen Gattung eine Vielheit gibt, durch welche dieses ganze Vermögen verwirklicht wird.[71]

Was seinen Rekurs auf die *multitudo* angeht, ruht Dantes Einsicht ganz ausdrücklich der Aristoteles-Deutung des arabischen Philosophen auf.[72] »Dante hat Averroes dahin verstanden: Das Menschengeschlecht als Ganzes verwirklicht die Möglichkeiten, die in der möglichen Vernunft ruhen«.[73] Das gilt auch für Agambens Lebensform, die immer

---

[66]   Ebd., S. 18.

[67]   Ebd.

[68]   Ebd., S. 19.

[69]   Corti, Maria (2007): Dante and Islamic Culture, in: Dante Studies 125, S. 57–75.

[70]   Alighieri, Dante (1989): Monarchia, Einleitung, Übersetzung und Kommentar von Ruedi Imbach und Christoph Flüeler, Stuttgart: Reclam, S. 69.

[71]   Ebd., S. 69 (»Et quia potentia ista per unum hominem seu per aliquam particularium comunitatum superius distinctarum tota simul in actum reduce non potest, necesse est multitudinem esse in humano genere, per quam quidem tota potential hec actuetur«; ebd., S. 68).

[72]   Ebd., S. 69: »Und dieser Lehre stimmt Averroes im Kommentar zum *Buch über die Seele* bei« (*Et huic sentantie concordat Averrois in comento super hiis que* De Anima).

[73]   Flasch, Kurt (2006): Meister Eckhart. Die Geburt der »Deutschen Mystik« aus dem Geist der arabischen Philosophie, München: C.H. Beck, S. 54.

schon eine Zusammenlebensform ist. Sie bezieht sich nicht allein auf das Denken als abstrahierenden Akt, den ein einziger Denker oder ein einziger Sprechender vollzieht. Dies wäre genau jene Sprachreflexion im 20. Jahrhundert, die – sei's in Form generativer Grammatiken, sei's in Gestalt davon inspirierter *language genes* – Sprachfähigkeit zu einer gattungsspezifischen anthropologischen Differenz erklärt. Ihr zufolge sondert sich der Mensch um den Preis von anderen Lebewesen ab, dass die Sprache ihm als biologische Disposition inhäriert. Das *Lebensform*-Exposé fasst seinen zentralen Begriff dagegen als »Innigkeit dieses unteilbaren Lebens« auf, das bereits »in der Materialität der körperliche Vorgänge und der gewohnten Lebensweisen« stecke: »nicht weniger als in der Theorie, dort und nur dort ist Denken.«[74] Das Menschliche bestimmt sich so nicht über eine biologische Substanz oder Mitgift, sondern durch seine kollektiv vorgenommene Selbstbestimmung in Denken und Handeln.

Spezies, oder Horizonte des Intellekts: Ausblick mit Averroes

Ein Aufsatz, der im Zusammenhang von Averroes' materialem Intellekt so oft von »Entwicklungsoffenheit« sprach, muss zum Schluss einen Ausblick auf die Entwicklungsmöglichkeiten seiner Überlegungen eröffnen.

Agamben selbst deutet in *Das »spezielle« Sein* nur kurz an, dass sich damit auf Wahrnehmungsbilder bezogene Phänomene wie Narzissmus und Verliebtheit – nicht nur innerhalb der kulturellen Semantik des Mittelalters – deuten lassen.[75] Eine Theoriekonkurrenz zu Theorien des Imaginären wie der Phänomenologie, aber auch der Psychoanalyse wurde schon angedeutet. Angesichts des Siegeszugs digitaler Bildmedien und der von ihnen entfesselten Sozialdynamiken sind Theorien des bildgebundenen Narzissmus heute wieder brandaktuell.[76] Es wäre auszuloten, was Averroes' Begriff intentionaler Spezies hier beitragen kann. Dafür wäre auch das Verhältnis von Spezies und Spektakel zu klären. Agambens häufiger Rekurs auf Guy Debords *Gesellschaft des Spektakels* könnte sich hier als mehr erweisen denn nur als ein idiosynkratisches Festhalten an der situationistischen Kulturkritik.[77]

---

74 Agamben, Giorgio (2000): Lebensform, in: ders.: Mittel ohne Zweck, Zürich/Berlin: Diaphanes, S. 20.

75 Agamben, Giorgio (2015): Das »spezielle« Sein, in: ders., Profanierungen, Frankfurt am Main: Suhrkamp, S. 55–56.

76 Als Quelle von Populismus und Ressentiments wurde der Narzissmus etwa kürzlich wieder ins Spiel gebracht bei Fleury, Cynthia (2023): Hier liegt Bitterkeit begraben. Über Ressentiments und ihre Heilung, Berlin: Suhrkamp.

77 Geulen, Eva (2004): Giorgio Agamben zur Einführung, Hamburg: Junius, S. 111.

Ist in der jüngeren Zeit über die Disziplinen-Grenzen hinweg ein neuerwachtes Interesse an der Phänomenologie zu beobachten[78], so scheint der averroistische Intellekt samt den Rollen, die Spezies und Intention darin spielen, sich überdies als Korrespondenzpartner, aber auch Kritik phänomenologischer Intentionalität zu empfehlen.[79] Agambens eigener Umgang mit Spezies-Bildern in seinen kleineren Arbeiten zu den Bildkünsten kann selbst schon als teils averroistisch inspirierte, post-phänomenologische, post-psychoanalytische Lektüre zeitgenössischer Bildphänomene der neuen Medien gelesen werden.[80] In eine vergleichbare Richtung hat Emanuele Coccia in den letzten Jahren Averroes auch für seine Theorie des Sinnenlebens fruchtbar zu machen versucht. Diese fügt sich – vielleicht zu sehr? – in eine im Zuge des *New Materialsm* und Neuen Realismus stehende Kritik des *linguistic turn* ein, insofern mit dem Spezies-Bild einer nicht einfach völlig in der Sprache aufzuhebenden Erkenntnisform große Aufmerksamkeit zuteilwird.[81] Ob ein neuer Materialismus allerdings wirklich so ausschließlich mit Bildern, so entschieden ohne Sprache auskommt, bleibt zu diskutieren. Überhaupt wäre auch die Rolle, die ein »alter«, aus der mittelalterlichen Philosophie sich speisender Materialismus einnimmt, zu erwägen. Agambens Averroes-Rezeption bietet hier erste Ansatzpunkte.

Nicht zuletzt könnte der von einer kollektiven Lebensform, einer *multitudo* von Sprechenden unablösbare averroistische Intellekt zu einem vielleicht nicht unwichtigen Ansprechpartner in der jüngst an Fahrt gewonnenen Auseinandersetzung mit den bild- und textgenerativen Verfahren sogenannter künstlicher Intelligenzen werden. ChatGPT (GPT-4: im Moment der Niederschrift dieses Textes in aller Munde) und andere generieren über künstliche neuronale Netze (KNN) und maschinelles Lernen (ML) Texte und Bilder, die wie von Menschen geschaffen wirken.[82] Den aktuellen Sprachprozessoren wurde dabei wiederholt attestiert, dass sich ihre Kombinationsprozesse vor allem aus akkumulierten Trainingsdaten ergeben als auch dass sie Kohärenz und inhaltliche Motiviertheit der

---

78   Sneis, Jørgen (2018): Phänomenologie und Textinterpretation. Studien zur Theoriegeschichte und Methodik der Literaturwissenschaft, Berlin/Boston: De Gruyter; Schnell, Alexander (2019): Was ist Phänomenologie?, Frankfurt am Main: Klostermann; Schnell, Alexander (2021): Der frühe Derrida und die Phänomenologie. Eine Vorlesung, Frankfurt am Main: Vittorio Klostermann; 2019 stand ein von Anatol Heller und Robert Loth organisierter Workshop an der Humboldt-Universität zu Berlin unter dem Titel *Literatur und Phänomenologie.*

79   Schon Husserls Begriff des intentionalen Gegenstandsbewusstseins verweist auf mittelalterliche Philosophie zurück: vgl. Perler, Dominik (2020): Theorien der Intentionalität im Mittelalter, 3., unveränderte Auflage, Frankfurt am Main: Vittorio Klostermann.

80   Vgl. insbesondere die kleineren Texte in Agamben, Giorgio (2010): Nacktheiten, Frankfurt am Main: S. Fischer 2010; Agamben, Giorgio (2005): Profanierungen, Frankfurt am Main: Suhrkamp.

81   Coccia, Emanuele (2020): Sinnenleben. Eine Philosophie, München: Hanser.

82   Vgl. Bajohr, Hannes (2019): Schreibenlassen. Texte zur Literatur im Digitalen, Berlin: August; Mersch, Dieter (2019): Kreativität und Künstliche Intelligenz. Einige Bemerkungen zu einer Kritik künstlicher Intelligenz, in: Zeitschrift für Medienwissenschaft 19.3.

generierten Texte nicht gewährleisten können[83]. Dieses Problem scheint das Verhältnis von Semiologie und Semantik, Schrift und Stimme nach Agamben zu berühren. Ob eine AI-Kritik wirklich ohne maschinenexterne Wirklichkeitserwägungen wie die lebensweltliche Situiertheit und Verkörperung auskommen kann (so Hubert L. Dreyfus' klassische Kritik früher maschineller Intelligenz) ist dabei noch keineswegs gesprochen.[84] Die sich auf Averroes berufende Idee, dass Bild und Wort letztlich nur im Medium eines kollektiven Intellekts und vermittels einer konstitutiven Sprecherstimme überhaupt sinnstiftend und tatsächlich neue Möglichkeiten generierend miteinander verbunden werden können – dass nur dieser Akt zwischen individuellem agentiellem und kollektivem materialem Intellekt mit der Phantasie als Medium im emphatischen Sinne Denken und Sprechen bestimmt – könnte hier vielleicht nicht die schlechtesten Debatteneinwürfe liefern. Daneben erlaubt der Rückgang auf einen historisch frühen Begriff des *intellectus* auch die kulturgeschichtliche Frage nach der Genealogie von Begriffen wie ›Intelligenz‹ zu adressieren samt den historischen Neubesetzungen und Begriffsverschiebungen, wobei der Fall AI nur den jüngsten Moment bezeichnet. [85]

Auf mittelalterlichen Bilddarstellungen des Averroes wurden dem Philosophen oft die Augen ausgekratzt.[86] Vielleicht kann man von diesen speziellen Sehapparaten heute neuen Gebrauch machen.

---

[83] Bender, Emily M./Gebru, Timnit/McMillan-Major, Angelina et al (2021): On the Dangers of Linguistic Parrots: Can Language Models be too big?, in: FAccT '21: Proceedings of the 2021 ACM Conference on Fairness, Accountability, and Transparency, S. 616: »Text generated by an LM is not grounded in communicative intent, any model of the world, or any model of the reader's state of mind. It can't have been, because the training data never included sharing thoughts with a listener, nor does the machine have the ability to do that«.

[84] Dreyfus, Hubert L. (1985): Was Computer nicht können. Die Grenzen künstlicher Intelligenz, Königstein/Taunus: Athenäum; ders. (1992): What Computers still can't do. A Critique of artificial Reason, Massachussetts: MIT Press. Vgl. zu einer jüngeren Kritik an Dreyfus, die vor allem über Hans Blumenbergs Argument läuft, dass bereits die Rhetorik, damit aber die menschliche Rede überhaupt artifizielle Züge aufweise: Weatherby, Leif (2022): Intermittent Legitimacy: Hans Blumenberg and AI, in: New German Critique 145.

[85] Eine disziplinenübergreifende Genealogie des Intelligenzbegriffs, die wissenschaftsgeschichtlich hochrelevant wäre, liegt meines Wissens nicht vor. Die gängigen Begriffsgeschichten in Psychologie, Kognitionswissenschaft oder AI-Forschung (siehe nur exemplarisch Danziger, Kurt (1997): Naming the Mind. How Psychology found its Language, London: Sage; Sternberg, Robert J. (1990): Metaphors of Mind. Conceptions of the Nature of Intelligence, Cambridge: Cambridge UP) weisen in ihren äußerst selektiven historischen Parcours kaum je vor die Neuzeit zurück, wobei die dann herangezogenen Referenzen wie John Locke oder David Hume durchaus noch unter dem phantomhaften Einfluss der ihnen vorausliegenden Philosophiegeschichte stehen.

[86] Vgl. Brenet, Jean-Baptiste (2015): Averroès, L'Inquiétant, Paris: Les belles Lettres., S. 35–39 (die Abbildungen: S. 36, S. 38).

Literaturverzeichnis

Agamben, Giorgio (1968): L'albero del Linguaggio, in: Journal of Italien Philosophy 1 (2018), S. 2–11 (ursprünglich in: Ulise XXI.IX [1968]).

Agamben, Giorgio (1996): Categorie Italiane. Studi di Poetica, Venedig: Marsilio.

Agamben, Giorgio (1998): Bartleby oder die Kontingenz, Berlin: Merve.

Agamben, Giorgio (2000): Lebensform, in: Ders.: Mittel ohne Zweck, Zürich/Berlin: Diaphanes, S. 13–20.

Agamben, Giorgio (2001): Idee der Prosa, Frankfurt am Main: Suhrkamp.

Agamben, Giorgio (2003): Die kommende Gemeinschaft, Berlin: Merve.

Agamben, Giorgio (2005): Das »spezielle« Sein, in: Ders.: Profanierungen, Frankfurt am Main: Suhrkamp, S. 51–56.

Agamben, Giorgio (2006): Stanzen, Zürich/Berlin: Diaphanes.

Agamben, Giorgio (2009): Signatura Rerum. Zur Methode, Frankfurt: Suhrkamp.

Agamben, Giorgio (2010): Nacktheiten, Frankfurt am Main: S. Fischer.

Agamben, Giorgio (2018): Intelletto D'amore, in: Agamben, Giorgio/Brenet, Jean-Baptiste: Intellect d'amour, Lagrasse: Editions Verdier, S. 13–34.

Agamben, Giorgio (2021): Der Gebrauch der Körper, Frankfurt am Main: S. Fischer.

Agamben, Giorgio (2022): Quel che ho visto, udito, appreso…, Torino: Einaudi.

Alighieri, Dante (1989): Monarchia, Einleitung, Übersetzung und Kommentar von Ruedi Imbach und Christoph Flüeler, Stuttgart: Reclam.

Aristoteles (2011): Über die Seele, übersetzt und herausgegeben von Gernot Krapinger, Stuttgart: Reclam.

Attell, Kevin (2015): Giorgio Agamben. Beyond the Threshold of Deconstruction, New York: Fordham UP.

Averroes (1869): Drei Abhandlungen über die Conjunction des separaten Intellects mit dem Menschen, herausgegeben, übersetzt und erläutert von J. Herz, Berlin: H.G. Herman.

Bajohr, Hannes (2019): Schreibenlassen. Texte zur Literatur im Digitalen, Berlin: August.

Baltrušaitis, Jurgis (1986): Der Spiegel. Entdeckungen, Täuschungen, Phantasien, Gießen: Anabas.

Bender, Emily M./Gebru, Timnit/McMillan-Major, Angelina et al (2021): On the Dangers of Linguistic Parrots: Can Language Models be too big?, in: FAccT '21: Proceedings of the 2021 ACM Conference on Fairness, Accountability, and Transparency.

Bloch, Ernst (1963): Avicenna und die Aristotelische Linke, Frankfurt am Main: Suhrkamp.

Blumenberg, Hans (2018): Husserl – ein Averroist?, in: Ders., Phänomenologische Schriften 1981–1988, ed. von Nicola Zambon, Berlin: Suhrkamp 2018.

Brenet, Jean-Baptiste (2015): Averroès, L'Inquiétant, Paris: Les belles Lettres.

Cavalcante, Guido (1991): Le Rime – Die Gedichte, Nach einer Interlinearübersetzung von Geraldine Gabor, in deutsche Reime gebracht von Ernst-Jürgen Dreyer, Mainz: Dieterich'sche Verlagsbuchhandlung.

Coccia, Emanuele (2005): La trasparenza delle immagini. Averroè e l'averroismo, Milano: Bruno Mondadori.

Coccia, Emanuele (2019): Quodlibet. Logica e fisica dell'essere qualunque, in: Giorgio Agamben. Ontologia e politica, ed. Valeria Bonnacci, Macerata: Quodlibet, S. 123–134.

Coccia, Emanuele (2020): Sinnenleben. Eine Philosophie, München: Hanser.

Corti, Maria (2007): Dante and Islamic Culture, in: Dante Studies 125, S. 57–75.

Danziger, Kurt (1997): Naming the Mind. How Psychology found its Language, London: Sage.

Davidson, Herbert A. (1992): Alfarabi, Avicenna and Averroes, on Intellect. Their Cosmologies, Theories of the active Intellect, and Theories of Human Intellect, New York: Oxford University Press.

de Libera, Alain (1991): Penser au Moyen Âge, Paris: Editions de Seuil.

Derrida, Jacques (1971): Freud und der Schauplatz der Schrift, in: Ders.: Die Schrift und die Differenz, Frankfurt am Main: Suhrkamp.

Derrida, Jacques (1974): Grammatologie, Frankfurt am Main: Suhrkamp.

Dreyfus, Hubert L. (1985): Was Computer nicht können. Die Grenzen künstlicher Intelligenz, Königstein/Taunus: Athenäum.

Dreyfus, Hubert L. (1992): What Computers still can't do. A Critique of artificial Reason, Massachussetts: MIT Press.

Esposito, Roberto (2018): Zwei. Die Maschine der politischen Theologie und der Ort des Denkens, Zürich: diaphanes.

Flasch, Kurt (2006): Meister Eckhart. Die Geburt der ›Deutschen Mystik‹ aus dem Geist der arabischen Philosophie, München: C.H. Beck.

Fleury, Cynthia (2023): Hier liegt Bitterkeit begraben. Über Ressentiments und ihre Heilung, Berlin: Suhrkamp.

Geulen, Eva (2004): Giorgio Agamben zur Einführung, Hamburg: Junius.

Geulen, Eva (2009): Agambens Politik der Nicht-Beziehung, in: Sabeth Buchmann/Helmut Traxler/Stephen Geene (Eds.): Avantgarde. Film. Biopolitik, Wien, S. 58–68.

Hasse, Dag Nikolaus (1999): Das Lehrstück von den vier Intellekten in der Scholastik: Von den arabischen Quellen bis zu Albertus Magnus, in: Récherches des théologie et philosophie mediévale 66.2, S. 22–28.

Illuminati, Augusto (2002): L'intelligentia di Averroè, in: Belfagor, 57.1, S. 103–108.

Illuminati, Augusto (2022): Averroè, une traduzione ininterrota, in: Doctor Virtualis. Rivista online di storia della filosofia medievale 17, S. 107–129.

Kotsko, Adam/Salzani, Carlo Salzani (Eds.) (2017): Agamben's Philosophical Lineage, Edinburgh: Edinburgh UP.

Laplanche, Jean/Pontalis J.-B. (2023): Urphantasie, Gießen: Psychosozial Verlag.

Largier, Nikolaus (1999): Spiegelungen. Fragmente einer Geschichte der Spekulation, in: Zeitschrift für Germanistik 9.3, S. 616–636.

Maier, Anneliese (1963): Das Problem der ›species sensibilis in medio‹ und die neue Naturphilosophie des 14. Jahrhunderts, in: Freiburger Zeitschrift für Philosophie und Theologie 10, S. 3–32.

Mersch, Dieter (2004): Performativität und Ereignis. Überlegungen zur Revision des Performanz-Konzeptes der Sprache, in: Fohrmann, Jürgen (Ed.): Rhetorik. Figuration und Performanz, Stuttgart/Weimar: J. B. Metzler.

Mersch, Dieter (2019): Kreativität und Künstliche Intelligenz. Einige Bemerkungen zu einer Kritik künstlicher Intelligenz, in: Zeitschrift für Medienwissenschaft 19.3.

Perler, Dominik (2020): Theorien der Intentionalität im Mittelalter, 3., unveränderte Auflage, Frankfurt am Main: Vittorio Klostermann.

Schnell, Alexander (2019): Was ist Phänomenologie?, Frankfurt am Main: Vittorio Klostermann.

Schnell, Alexander (2021): Der frühe Derrida und die Phänomenologie. Eine Vorlesung, Frankfurt am Main: Vittorio Klostermann.

Sneis, Jørgen (2018): Phänomenologie und Textinterpretation. Studien zur Theoriegeschichte und Methodik der Literaturwissenschaft, Berlin/Boston: De Gruyter.

Sternberg, Robert J. (1990): Metaphors of Mind. Conceptions of the Nature of Intelligence, Cambridge: Cambridge UP.

Stetter, Christian (1999): Sprache und Schrift, Frankfurt am Main: Suhrkamp.

Trabant, Jürgen (2012): Weltansichten. Wilhelm von Humboldts Sprachprojekt, München: C. H. Beck.

Weatherby, Leif (2022): Intermittent Legitimacy: Hans Blumenberg and AI, in: New German Critique 145, S. 11–39.

Wild, Cornelia (2016): Die Liebe der trobadors, in: von Koppenfels, Martin/Zumbusch, Cornelia (Eds.): Handbuch Literatur und Emotionen, Berlin: De Gruyter, S. 261–274.

Winkelmann-Liebert, Holger (2005): Die Intellektlehre des Averroës, in: Der Islam. Zeitschrift für Geschichte und Kultur des islamischen Orients 82, S. 273–290.

Maximilian Priebe

Edgar Morin – Kosmologe der Komplexität

Porträt eines transdisziplinären Intellektuellen

ABSTRACT: The following article is a portrait of the French sociologist, philosopher, Systems thinkers and public intellectual Edgar Morin. It aims to present the life and works of Edgar Morin to a German-speaking audience. Introductory in nature, it does not claim to offer more than a concise, contemporary, and, where needed, critical summary of Edgar Morin's main theoretical tenets. It proceeds by offering, first, a brief overview of Morin's biography and a loose sketch of his position in the landscape of French 20th century philosophy. Based on a close reading of Edgar Morin's chief theoretical oeuvre, La Méthode, it subsequently reconstructs his thought in four steps, paying attention to a) to the context of Morin's specific intellectual concerns and his new cosmological »method«, b) to his theory of nature, c) to his theory of society, and d) finally to his ethics. The profile which should emerge from this procedure is one of an intellectual who is grappling with a wide-spanning, holistic thinking; whose working style is transdisciplinary and directed against academic specialisation; and whose philosophical concerns centre around the normative expectations of classical humanism. Edgar Morin is a thinker who invites us to think with him through matters of the contemporary world, and his viewpoints are here discussed and critically evaluated with particular reference to the relevance of his thought for the ecological discourse, and for the current challenges of ›knowledge societies.‹

KEYWORDS: Edgar Morin; Systems Theory; Ecology; Knowledge Society; Cybernetic Hegelianism; Philosophy of Nature; French 20th Century-Thought

Edgar Morin ist seit den 50er Jahren des 20. Jahrhunderts eine der beständigsten Stimmen in den französischen Geistes- und Sozialwissenschaften. Mit einer konsistenten Werkgeschichte, die vom Ende des zweiten Weltkrieges bis in die Zeit der Covidkrise und des Ukrainekrieges reicht, kondensieren sich im Denken dieses vielseitigen Intellektuellen nicht nur mehrere Generationen frankophoner Philosophiediskurse, sondern auch ein beträchtliches Stück europäische Zeitgeschichte. Der französischen, spanisch- und portugiesischsprachigen Öffentlichkeit durch eine Vielzahl medialer Bezüge und Sekundärliteratur bekannt, ist Morins Stellung im deutschen Sprachraum bis heute nur marginal. Dabei nimmt sein Werk eine Schlüsselposition in einer Reihe von Debatten über Ökologie, Mensch-Maschinen-Interaktion, Massenkultur und neuzeitlicher Subjektivität ein, deren Aktualität global unbestritten sind. So fungieren die kybernetisch und systemtheoretisch aktualisierten Positionen von Edgar Morin beispielsweise als Bezugspunkte von so unterschiedlichen Denkern wie Niklas Luhmann, Roland Barthes, oder den zeitgenössischen Theoretiker:innen des Anthropozäns.[1] Daneben hat Morin die sozial- und kulturtheoretischen Ansätze zum Verständnis von Massenmedien, Stars, Krisen und einem post-cartesianischen Naturbegriff in Frankreich entscheidend mitgeprägt.[2] Im Folgenden soll deshalb das Werk Edgar Morins anhand einiger Hauptaspekte – Methodologie, Naturtheorie, Gesellschaftstheorie und Ethik – vorgestellt und kontextualisiert werden, um nicht zuletzt auch eine Rezeption seiner bereits ins Deutsche übersetzen Werke für ein Fachpublikum anzuregen.

I. Biographischer Überblick

Edgar Morin wurde 1921 in Paris unter dem Namen Edgar Nahoum als Sohn jüdischer Einwanderer aus Thessaloniki geboren. Nach seinem Abschluss am Lycée Rollin studierte er an der Sorbonne Philosophie und Jura (ein Studienfeld, welches damals auch

---

1   Roland Barthes und Edgar Morin haben gemeinsam ihre wissenschaftlichen Karrieren unter der Leitung des Soziologen George Friedmann im *Centre d'études de communication de masse* begonnen; vgl. den diesbezüglichen Hinweis in Kauppi (1990): *Tel Quel: La constitution sociale d'une avant-garde.* Helsinki: Societa Scientiarum Fennica, S. 93. Sie sind danach, wie Edgar Morins Biograph Emmanuel Lemineux (2009) herausstellt, ununterbrochen befreundet geblieben, vgl. *Edgar Morin. L'indiscipliné,* Paris: Seuil, S. 309–336. Niklas Luhmann (1984) zitiert Edgar Morin an prominenten Stellen seines Hauptwerks: vgl. *Soziale Systeme. Grundriß einer allgemeinen Theorie.* Frankfurt am Main: Suhrkamp, S. 44. Für einen Vergleich zwischen den Theorien Luhmanns und Morins, siehe Curvello/ Skroferneker (2008): A comunicação e as organizações como sistemas complexos: uma análise a partir das perspectivas de Niklas Luhmann e Edgar Morin. In: *E-Compós,* n° 11/3. Die Zusammenhänge zwischen dem Denken Morins und den Debatten im Feld der Ökologie und im Anthropozän-Diskurs sind untergründiger. Erstere schließen über den Systembegriff und die Kybernetik an die Quellen Morin'scher Theorien an, beispielsweise an Gregory Bateson; letztere aktualisieren, wie beispielsweise Peter Haff (2014) in seinem Konzept der »Technosphäre« (Humans and technology in the Anthropocene: Six rules. In: *The Anthropocene Review,* 1/2, 2014, S. 127) implizit Edgar Morins Konzept der »Noosphäre«, welches dieser (1991) in *La méthode 4. Les idées* (Paris: Seuil) wiederum den Texten Teilhard de Chardins, Édouard Le Roys, und Vladimir Vernadskys entlehnt, ohne diese Quellen eingehend zu diskutieren; vgl. Vernadsky (1945): The Biosphere and the Noosphere. In: *American Scientist,* 33/1, S. 1–12.

2   Vgl., in Bezug auf seine Werke zur Populärkultur, Morin (1956): *Le cinéma ou l'homme imginaire. Essai d'anthropologie sociologique.* Paris: Les Éditions de Minuit; sowie Morin (1957): *Les stars.* Paris : Editions du Seuil, 1957. Auf Deutsch erschienen sind Teile seines Werkes im Verlag Turia + Kant, so u.a. der erste Band seines Hauptwerkes: *Die Methode. Die Natur der Natur,* herausgegeben von Wolfgang Hofkirchner (2010) und übersetzt und mit einem Nachwort versehen von Rainer E. Zimmermann, Wien: Turia & Kant. Im Folgenden werden die Werke Morins aus Gründen der Übersichtlichkeit und Vollständigkeit jedoch nach Ersterscheinungsdatum und in der französischen Originalausgabe zitiert; die Übersetzungen wurden vom Verfasser des Artikels angefertigt.

Soziologie und Psychologie umfasste) und war ebenfalls an der École des Sciences Politiques eingeschrieben, womit er einem bereits sehr transdisziplinären Studienprogramm folgte.[3] Nach dem Einmarsch der Wehrmacht in Paris flüchtet die Familie Nahoum nach Südfrankreich, um der Deportation zu entgehen. Edgar änderte seinen Nachnamen, setzte zunächst sein Studium in Toulouse fort und arbeitete kurzzeitig als wissenschaftlicher Assistent für Julien Benda in Carcassonne.[4] Im Jahr 1943 brach er sein Studium ab und schloss sich der kommunistischen Widerstandsbewegung an. Das Kriegsende verbrachte er in Deutschland als Offizier der *Forces Françaises Libres*, wo er von 1945 bis 1947 als Leiter des Propagandabüros der französischen Militärverwaltung in Südwestdeutschland arbeitete. Diese Erfahrung bot schließlich auch die Grundlage für sein erstes Buch, *L'an zéro de l'Allemagne*.[5] Während dieser Zeit machte Edgar Morin zunächst eine politische Karriere in der Kommunistischen Partei Frankreichs, entfremdete sich der Partei gegenüber jedoch aufgrund seiner Desillusionierung über deren Haltung gegenüber dem Stalinismus. 1951 wurde er aus der Partei ausgeschlossen.[6] Morin wandte sich zunächst Versuchen in der Poesie und den schönen Künsten zu, fand letztlich aber besseren Anschluss an die sich zu dieser Zeit in Frankreich etablierenden Sozialforschung.[7] Ohne jemals eine Doktorarbeit verfasst zu haben, nur mit Lizenzen in Geschichte, Geografie und Recht, wurde er 1950 mit der Unterstützung von Maurice Merleau-Ponty, Pierre George und Vladimir Jankélévitch in die soziologische Sektion des *Centre National de la rechérche scientifique* (CNRS) aufgenommen.[8]

Edgar Morins Weg durch das Universitätssystem ist von erstaunlichen Wendungen geprägt. Seine erste strikt akademische Veröffentlichung, noch vor seinem Eintritt in das CNRS, war eine ethnologische und anthropologische Untersuchung zum Problem des Todes, der – nunmehr unterstützt von Georges Friedmann – 1956 und 1957 soziologische Untersuchungen über das Kino und die Welt der Stars folgten.[9] In dieser Zeit gründete er mit Roland Barthes, Jean Duvignaud und Colette Audry die Zeitschrift *Arguments*, die belegt, dass Morin trotz seines Parteiausschlusses das Interesse am Marxismus nicht verloren hatte. Zu dieser Zeit rezipiert er das Werk heterodoxer

---

3 Morins Philosophielehrer am Lycée war der Historiker und Anthropologe Jean-Pierre Vernant, später Lehrstuhlinhaber am Collège de France für vergleichende Religionswissenschaft, vgl. Lemineux: *L'indiscipliné*, S. 260.

4 Vgl. Lemineux: *L'indiscipliné*, S. 113–123.

5 Zur Einordnung dieses aus einer deutschen Perspektive hochinteressanten Werkes, vgl. Martine Floch (2021): L'An zéro de l'œuvre d'Edgar Morin. In: *Matériaux pour l'histoire de notre temps*, 137–138/3, 2021, S. 129–137.

6 Vgl. Lemineux: *L'indiscipliné*, S. 269–301.

7 Vgl. Morin/ Wolton (2011): Grand entretien. In: *Hermès*, 60/2, S. 241–243.

8 Vgl. Lemineux: *L'indiscipliné*, S. 301–309.

9 Supra: Note 2; vgl. auch Edgar Morin (1948): *L'Homme et la Mort*. Paris, Éditions Corrêa.

Marxisten aus dem deutschen Sprachraum, darunter Herbert Marcuse, Georg Lukács und Karl Korsch. In diesen Jahren werden von ihm schließlich auch die *Revue française de sociologie* und *Communications* mitgegründet.[10] Barthes und Morin inspirieren sich seit den 60er Jahren gegenseitig. So bezieht sich Roland Barthes in seinem letzten Essay *La chambre claire* noch auf Morins Frühwerk über den Tod.[11] Im Anschluss an Morins Hinwendung zur Welt der Zeichen und Erzählungen kommt es zu einer Kontroverse mit Pierre Bourdieu über die Massenkultur.[12] Eine erste wirklich transdisziplinäre Studie, die Soziologie und Ethnologie miteinander verbindet, führt Morin 1967 in die Bretagne, wo er sich mit der Beziehung zwischen Modernität, Zeitwahrnehmung und sozialer Entwicklung im ländlichen Raum beschäftigt.[13] Ein Jahr später folgt anlässlich der Studentenrevolte die mit Claude Lefort und Cornelius Castoriadis herausgegebene zeitdiagnostische Analyse: *Mai 68, La Brèche.*[14] In dieser Zeit erleidet Morin eine schwere Krankheit und wendet sich verstärkt den Themen Körperlichkeit, Natur und Biologie zu. Forschungstätigkeiten und Reisen führen ihn in die Vereinigten Staaten, was ihn mit der Bürgerrechtsbewegung und der kalifornischen ›Counter-Culture‹ in Kontakt bringt.[15] Nach seiner Rückkehr nach Frankreich orientiert er sich noch stärker transdisziplinär. Er schließt sich Forschern an, die an einem Dialog zwischen Wissenschaft und Politik interessiert sind: der ›Gruppe der 10‹, in der sich auch Michel Serres, Henri Atlan und André Leroi-Gourhan befinden.[16] Der entscheidende Schritt in der Herausbildung seines Denkens über ›Komplexität‹ – ein Schritt, der ebenfalls 1969 stattfindet – ist jedoch eine Einladung als zeitweiliges Mitglied des *Salk Institutes,* ein biomedizinisches Labor in Kalifornien, interdisziplinärer Schmelztiegel und Bindeglied zwischen der damaligen französischen und amerikanischen Forschungslandschaft. Das *Salk Institute* ist der Ort, an dem Bruno Latour einige Jahre später mit der Anwendung soziologischer Forschung auf die Naturwissenschaften experimentieren wird, Ort, an dem Morin den Biologen Jacques Monod, den amerikanischen Lacan-Interpreten Anthony Wilden und nicht zuletzt eine der zentralen Figuren der amerikanischen systemtheoretischen Debatten, den Anthropologen und Kybernetiker Gregory Bateson, den Ehemann der Anthropologin Margaret Mead, kennenlernt.[17] Er entdeckt dort

---

10   Vgl. Lemineux: *L'indiscipliné,* S. 309–370.

11   Vgl. Barthes (1980): *La chambre claire. Note sur la photographie.* Paris: Gallimard, S. 113.

12   Vgl. Morin/ Wolton: Grand entretien, S. 248–250.

13   Vgl. Morin (1967): *Commune en France. La métamorphose de Plodémet.* Paris: Fayard.

14   In ihr analysiert Edgar Morin u.a. die soziologischen und zeitgeschichtlichen Bedingungen der studentischen Organisation, vgl. Morin (1968): La communeauté étudiante. In: Morin/ Lefort/ Castoriadis (2008): *Mai 68. La brèche: suivi de Vingt ans après.* Paris: Fayard, S. 13–41.

15   Später aufgezeichnet in Morin (1970): *Journal de Californie.* Paris: Editions du Seuil.

16   Vgl. Lemineux: *L'indiscipliné,* S. 468–469.

17   Zur besseren Einordnung der Forschungskultur dieses Ortes empfiehlt sich die kurze Einführung Jonas Salks zu Bruno Latour und Steve Woolgar (1979): *Laboratory life. The construction of*

ebenfalls die Schriften von Ludwig von Bertalanffy, Norbert Wiener und Claude Shannon; und trifft den Mathematiker Heinz von Foerster.[18] Nach seiner Rückkehr nach Frankreich vertieft Morin diese Erforschung des wissenschaftlichen und philosophischen Diskurses; er studiert Physik und die Mathematik der Thermodynamik, trifft Ilya Prigogine, René Thom und Jean-Pierre Dupuy.[19] Nach dieser äußerst intensiven Forschungsphase ist nicht nur Morins Position als Forschungsdirektor am CNRS gefestigt, sondern er ist nun auch in der intellektuellen Landschaft verwurzelt, die Frankreich nach der 68er-Revolution prägen wird; ein Zeitgeist, den Morin in einer transdisziplinären Art des Schreibens und Denkens zum Ausdruck bringt.[20] Für diesen Neuanfang steht sein Buch *Le Paradigme Perdu*, der Start einer Schaffensperiode, die mit *La Méthode* und dem »Komplexen Denken« (*pensée complexe*) ihren Höhepunkt findet.[21]

II. Eine enzyklopädische Methode

Über sich selbst sagt Morin, »die Hauptbesessenheit [*obession principale*] seines Werkes beträfe die conditio humana.«[22] Dies ist nicht auf den ersten Blick ersichtlich. Betrachtet man *La Méthode*, so fallen zunächst allerlei naturwissenschaftlich-technische Termini auf, wohingegen ein klassisch humanistisches Vokabular, das eine solche Selbstbeschreibungen vermuten ließe, eigentlich abwesend ist. Bei genauerem Hinsehen lässt sich jedoch feststellen, dass Morins Wechsel von den Geistes- zu den Naturwissenschaften Anfang der 1970er Jahre in der Tat von einem tiefgreifenden Interesse am Menschen geprägt war. So beklagt Morin in *Le Paradigme Perdu* die Armut einer Beschreibung des Menschen, die nur auf seine soziale Einbettung schaut und nicht auch auf seine bio-physische Konstitution. In seinem Essay *Pour une Crisologie* (›Für eine Wissenschaft der Krise‹) versucht Morin schließlich zum ersten Mal, ein kybernetisches Vokabular auf eine Erklärung des klassischen Topos des Humanisten, auf die ›Krise des zeitgenössischen Bewusstseins‹, anzuwenden. Dieser Versuch führt Morin zu einer Charakterisierung moderner Gesellschaften anhand einer systemtheoretischen Rhetorik, wie man sie in Deutschland am ehesten von Niklas Luhmann kennen würden: »Moderne soziale Systeme sind als solche schwach integriert [...] und die Beziehungen zwischen Individuen, Gruppen, Klassen, Parteien, Ethnien schwanken

---

    scientific facts. Princeton: Princeton University Press, S. 11–14.

18   Vgl. Lemineux: *L'indiscipliné*, S. 473–480.

19   Vgl. Lemineux: *L'indiscipliné*, S. 480–500.

20   Vgl. Morin (1973): *Le paradigme perdu. La nature humaine.* Paris: Points.

21   Vgl. Morin (1990): *Introduction à la pensée complexe.* Paris: Points.

22   Morin (2001): *La Méthode 5: L'humanité de l'humanité.* Paris: Seuil, S. 13.

auf unterschiedliche Weise zwischen komplementären und antagonistischen Aktivitäten.«[23]

Tatsächlich bietet dieser kleine Text, der genau ein Jahr vor Publikation des ersten Bandes von *La Méthode* erschien, bereits eine Verdichtung der meisten Themen, die Morin in den folgenden Büchern behandelt, und in denen sozial- und naturwissenschaftliche Fragen in Beziehung zueinander gesetzt werden. In seiner Einleitung zum Hauptwerk im Jahr 1977 findet diese Ausrichtung schließlich ihre programmatische Artikulation. Hier betont Morin unter Rückgriff auf die Unmöglichkeit, in der Quantenmechanik den Beobachter vom beobachteten System zu trennen, dass die Naturwissenschaften auf der einen Seite nicht vergessen dürfen, wie jede ›objektive‹ Erkenntnis der Natur auf der subjektiven Situierung des Forschers in einem Kontext beruht, wiederum die Geisteswissenschaften ihrerseits aber auch nicht vergessen dürften, dass ihre Forschungsgegenstände mit biologischen und physikalischen Tatsachen zu tun haben.[24] Morin kommt zu dem Schluss, dass es an der Zeit ist, die Haltung eines neuen »enzyklopädischen Geistes« einzunehmen, die die bloße Anhäufung und Aufzählung von Wissensobjekten zugunsten eines »verflochtenen« Denkens aufgibt, das in der Lage ist, Wissenseinheiten aus verschiedenen Bereichen miteinander in Beziehung zu bringen, sie in Bewegung zu versetzen und in zirkuläre Argumentationsstrukturen zu verwandeln: »Es geht darum, zu *enzyklopädieren*, das heißt zu lernen, die disjunkten Gesichtspunkte des Wissens in einem aktiven Kreislauf zu artikulieren.«[25] Was sich dann für Morin aus diesem enzyklopädischen Projekt ergibt, sind zunächst einige Leitfragen:

> [...] Ich habe natürlich nicht versucht, die Anthropologie auf die Biologie zu reduzieren, noch wollte ich eine ›Synthese‹ des Wissens up to date erstellen. Ich wollte zeigen, dass die empirische Naht [soudure empirique], die seit 1960 über die Ethologie der höheren Primaten und die hominine Vorgeschichte zwischen Tier und Mensch, Natur und Kultur gezogen werden konnte, es erforderlich macht, den Menschen als ein dreifaches Konzept aus Individuum, Spezies und Gesellschaft zu begreifen, bei dem kein Begriff auf einen anderen reduziert oder einem anderen untergeordnet werden kann. Dies erforderte in meinen Augen ein komplexes Erklärungsprinzip und eine Theorie der Selbst-

---

23   Morin (1976): Pour une crisologie. In : *Communications* 25/1, S. 154.

24   Die Quellen, auf die sich Morin mit Bezug auf die Quantenphysik bezieht, bleiben über sein Werk hinweg gleich. Er orientiert sich vor allem an Bernard d'Espagnat (1965): *Conceptions de la physique contemporaine. Les interprétations de la mécanique quantique et de la mesure.* Paris: Hermann; und an Werner Heisenberg (1969): *Der Teil und das Ganze: Gespräche im Umkreis der Atomphysik.* München: Piper.

25   »Il s'agit d'en-cyclo-péder, c'est-à-dire d'apprendre à articuler les points de vue disjoints du savoir en un cycle actif.« Morin (1977): *La Méthode 1. La nature de la nature.* Paris: Seuil, S. 19.

organisation [auto-organisation]. Eine solche Perspektive wirft neue, noch grundlegendere und radikalere Probleme auf, denen man sich nicht entziehen kann:
- Was bedeutet das radikale Auto der Selbstorganisation [auto-organisation]?
- Was ist Organisation?
- Was ist Komplexität?[26]

Es sind diese Leitfragen, denen Morin in den sechs Bänden seines Hauptwerks folgt. Die Behandlung reicht von der Kosmologie, der Metaphysik der Natur und der Integration lebender Phänomene in das physikalische Universum über das Phänomen des Lebens und den Ursprung des menschlichen Geistes im Gehirn bis hin zur »noologischen« Struktur des Wissens des Menschen über die Welt. Erst in den letzten beiden Bänden, *La Société de la Société* und *L'Éthique: L'Humanité de L'Humanité* – welche sich im Vergleich zu der etwas mehr als tausendseitigen Behandlung der Natur- und Lebensphänomene als recht kurz erweisen! – befasst sich Morin mit der Struktur der Gesellschaft und den sozialen Phänomenen. Dieses enzyklopädische Projekt von *La Méthode* liest sich daher eher wie der Versuch, eine Kosmologie zu entwickeln, wie Morin auch freimütig beteuert: »Die Frage der Kosmogenese ist […] die Schlüsselfrage der Genese der Methode.«[27] Wer Morin durch sein Werk folgen will, muss sich also bemühen, sich mit der komplexen Beziehung zwischen der Erklärung der Natur und der ihr zugrunde liegenden Gesellschaftstheorie auseinanderzusetzen. Dies soll im Folgenden getan werden.

In dieser Hinsicht kann Morins ›humanistische‹ Selbstbeschreibung als Leitfaden dienen, denn bei seinem Streifzug durch die Grundstrukturen des Kosmos ist seine Aufmerksamkeit stets auf die Auswirkungen gerichtet, die die ›Natur der Dinge‹ auf unser eigenes Selbstverständnis hat – oder haben sollte. Darüber hinaus macht Morin nie einen Hehl daraus, dass er nicht als Physiker, sondern als ein Geisteswissenschaftler spricht, der es sich zur Aufgabe gemacht hat, zerstreutes Wissen neu zusammenzufassen; und der seine ›Methode‹ nicht als formale Methodologie, sondern vielmehr als »eine forschende Anleitung für den Weg des Denkens«[28] versteht. Es handelt es sich also, trotz der Priorität, die einem ganzheitlichen Ansatz des Kosmos eingeräumt wird, grundsätzlich um einen humanistischen Ansatz, und zwar, wie wir später noch besonders sehen werden, nicht nur in Bezug auf die Methode, sondern auch in Bezug auf den theoretischen Inhalt.

---

26 Morin: *La Méthode 1*, S. 10.
27 Morin: *La Méthode 1*, S. 45.
28 Morin (1986): *La Méthode 3. La connaissance de la connaissance.* Paris: Seuil, S. 26–27.

III. Eine Erklärung der Natur

Was ist also laut Morin die Natur der Dinge, was steht am ›Ursprung‹ des Kosmos? In seiner Antwort stellt Morin die klassische westliche Metaphysik auf den Kopf, die selbst in ihrer modernen, von der aristotelischen Ontologie der Substanz befreiten Variante noch vom Primat einer Entwicklungslinie ausgeht, die von einem ›einfachen Grundelement‹ zum ›komplexen Ganzen‹ führt. Denken wir dabei an die Geschichtsphilosophie der Aufklärung, in der ›komplexe‹, arbeitsteilige Gesellschaften in verschiedenen Stadien aus primitiven Gesellschaften hervorgehen; an Darwins Evolutionsbiologie, in der komplexe Biosysteme aus ›einfachen‹ Einzellern entstehen, oder an die moderne Physik, in der sich aus ›einfachen‹ Atomen komplexe Moleküle und noch komplexere Aggregate bilden. Genau gegen diese intuitive Annahme setzt Morin den Dreh- und Angelpunkt seiner Theorie: nämlich die Idee, dass »der Kosmos sich organisiert, indem er zerfällt.«[29] Für Morin ist diese Vorstellung einer zerfallenden Grundenergie eingebettet in eine Kosmogonie, die alle Mikrostrukturen durch eine grundlegende Komplexität begründet, ja sogar in die Idee, dass das Phänomen der Komplexität niemals als Endpunkt eines Entwicklungsprozesses, sondern als Beginn jeder Einheit gedacht werden muss: »Das Atom ist komplexer als das Molekül.«[30] Das, was grundlegend ist, ist komplexer als das, was sich daraus aufbaut. Komplexität ist kein Aggregatskonzept, sondern ein Grundkonzept. Morin nennt diese Grundannahme die Idee eines »Chaosmos«,[31] und es ist diese Annahme, die in den verschiedenen Zusammenhängen und in vielen von Morin angeführten Beispielen immer wieder auftaucht.

In diesem Sinne kann man Morin durchaus als Chaostheoretiker beschreiben. Für ihn entspringen alle stabilen Strukturen, wie die symmetrischen Fraktale, die sich spontan bilden, aus Kraftzentren der Unordnung und Turbulenz. Und Morin bezieht sich in der Tat auf die Physiker, die die Chaostheorie später mathematisch präzisieren. Ihm geht es jedoch nicht darum, die Unberechenbarkeit des Chaos formalisierbar zu machen, sondern vielmehr darum, die Idee eines chaotischen, ungeordneten und damit paradoxerweise ordnenden »Strudels«[32] als kosmisches Grundprinzip zu etablieren. Dabei veranschaulicht Morin den Ursprung von Ordnungsstrukturen in einer chaotische Kosmogenese auch durch explizit religiöse Vorstellungswelten:

---

29   Morin: *La Méthode 1*, S. 45.

30   Morin: *La Méthode 1*, S. 150.

31   Morin: *La Méthode 1*, S. 57. Dieser Ausdruck taucht allerdings auch schon auf bei Gilles Deleuze (1968): Différence et Répétition. Paris: Presses universitaires de France, S. 80., und davor bei James Joyce (2020 [1939]): Finnegans Wake. London: Alma Classics, Buch I, Kapitel 5. Auf beide Okkurenzen referiert Morin nicht explizit.

32   »D'un tourbillon« – Morin: *La méthode 1*, S. 41.

Die archaische Idee des Schöpfergottes Elohim wird in keiner Weise in der Idee von Adonai, dem Gott-Herrn, oder von JHVH, dem Gott-Gesetzgeber, ausgedrückt. Der Singular Plural von Elohim beschreibt eine *unitas multiplex* von Genien, die in ihrer Gesamtheit eine Antriebskraft [*un Générateur*] bilden. Man kann sich diese Genien materialistisch als treibende Energie vorstellen [...]. So vereint die Idee von Elohim die Idee des genetischen Wirbels, die Idee der schöpferischen Kraft und die Idee des organisatorischen Prozesses und übersetzt sie in sich selbst, ohne sie zu unterscheiden. Wie sich der vor-sonnenartige Wirbel nach vollendeter Genese in eine organisatorische Ordnung verwandelt, aus der die scheinbar universellen Gesetze der Natur hervorgehen, so macht Elohim – der thermodynamische Wirbel – [...] Platz für den Gott und Urheber des Gesetzes JHVH. JHVH ist kein Sonnengott, sondern ein kybernetischer Gott. JHVH schreibt das Gesetz ein, d.h. er setzt ein Informationsdispositiv zur Steuerung und Kontrolle der anthropo-sozialen Maschine ein. Er wird zum Programmgott. Das *I-Ging* oder Buch der Wandlungen der archaischen chinesischen Magier bringt das beispielhafteste Bild dieser Identität des Genetischen und des Generischen; Ying-Yang.[33]

Diese Passage ist trotz ihrer opaken Bildsprache aufschlussreich, da sich hier bereits alle Grundlagen abzeichnen, auf denen Morin seine Kosmologie aufbaut: zum einen die Idee von antagonistischen Kräften, die einander entgegenwirken und durch ihre Interaktion eine paradoxe Stabilität schaffen, und zum anderen die Auffassung, dass die Ausbreitung komplexer Strukturen auf eine Quelle zurückzuführen ist, die selbst viel komplexer ist als die von ihr ausgehenden Strukturen. Im ordnenden Zerfall einer ursprünglichen »kosmischen Katastrophe«[34] breitet sich Komplexität durch das Universum aus und führt dazu, dass auf der Grundlage einer tiefsten souveränen Unruhequelle verschiedene Ebenen des Realen entstehen können, die eine höhere strukturelle Ordnung, aber eine geringere Grundkomplexität aufweisen. Komplexität, Chaos und Entropie fungieren also auf einer metaphysischen Ebene als verschlungene kosmische Grundkraft, auf deren Basis weniger komplexe, weniger chaotische, enthalpische (neg-entropische) Ordnungen entstehen können, die wiederum höhere Ebenen der Realität hervorbringen.[35]

Morins Gesellschaftstheorie ist eine Ableitung dieser Kosmologie. Um diese zu erreichen, rekonstruiert Morin zunächst die Entstehung selbststabilisierender Strukturen in der anorganischen und organischen Welt, führt die Konzepte des stabilen Zustands (*steady state*) und der Homöostase ein, und beschreibt, wie sich offene Strukturen in einem fließenden Gleichgewicht mit ihrer Umwelt stabilisieren und wie die Generativität physikalischer Strukturen das Konzept eines ›geschlossenen Kreislaufs‹ vor-

---

33 Morin: *La Méthode 1,* S. 228–229.
34 Vgl. für mehr Details Morin: *La méthode 1,* S. 33–42.
35 Vgl. Morin: *La Méthode 1,* S. 225–231.

aussetzt, der durch Zirkulationsprozesse Energie aus der Umwelt aufnehmen, speichern und schließlich wieder in das Objekt oder den Organismus einspeisen kann, so dass dieser sich selbst regeneriert. In einer provokanten Neuinterpretation von Norbert Wieners Kybernetik, die mit dem Konzept der unbelebten Maschine die Idee eines teleologischen Zwecks wieder in die Beschreibung natürlicher Prozesse eingeführt hatte, bezeichnet Morin dieses Konzept eines geschlossenen Kreises, der sich selbst zersetzt und dadurch regeneriert, als »Maschine«.[36] Ebenso zentral ist für ihn der Abschluss dieser metaphysischen Rekonstruktion durch die Neudefinition und Wiedereinführung von Claude Shannons Informationsbegriff, den Morin – ganz im Sinne seiner Grundannahme einer Urkomplexität – bereits in der Grundstruktur des Lebens als Effekt eines Zufallswirbels ausmacht und zum spezifischen Merkmal aller Lebewesen erhebt: »Es gibt, [...] keine extra-biologische Information. Information ist immer mit negentropisch organisierten Wesen verbunden [...] und mit metabiotischen Wesen, die sich von Leben ernähren.«[37] Auf der Grundlage einer informationsbasierten Selbststrukturierung können sich schließlich zerebrale Ordnungen bilden, die es dem Menschen, wie auch anderen Lebewesen, ermöglichen, Fähigkeiten zur Anpassung an die Umwelt zu erwerben, die zur Bildung der ersten genuin intersubjektiven Prozesse führen und auf diese Weise jede Untersuchung von ›Wissen‹ mit dem Phänomen ›Leben‹ verknüpfen:

> Die Selbstpoiesis und das Subjekt hängen von der kognitiven Dimension der Rechenfähigkeit [*computation*] ab, die wiederum von der Selbstpoiesis [*l'auto-poièse*] des Subjekts abhängt. [...]. Sein, Tun, Erkennen sind im Bereich des Lebens ursprünglich undifferenziert, und selbst wenn sie differenziert werden, bleiben sie untrennbar. [...] Leben organisiert sich anhand von Erkenntnis [*connaissance*] selbst. Leben ist nur durch Erkennen lebensfähig und lebenswert. Geboren werden heißt erkennen.[38]

Morin zufolge ist der grundlegende Wandel in der Natur zur Erklärung des Sozialen jedoch nicht so sehr die Entwicklung und Selbstorganisation von zerebralen Lebewesen, sondern die Entwicklung der Sprache, die Morin unter Rückgriff auf seinen eigenen Begriff der ›Maschine‹ ebenso wie unter Bezugnahme auf Saussures strukturelle Semiotik und Chomskys Linguistik als »Doppelgelenkmaschine« [machine à double-articulation] definiert:

---

36 Morin: *La Méthode 1*, S. 156–173.
37 Morin: *La Méthode 1*, S. 316.
38 »Naitre, c'est connaitre.« – Morin: *La Méthode 3*, S. 47–48. Morin entlehnt den Begriff der Autopoeisis, wie es seinerseits Luhmann tut, den Werken Humberto Maturanas und Francisco Varelas; vgl. deren Studie, die drei Jahre nach Ersterscheinen von *La méthode* erscheint; Maturana undVarela (1980): *Autopoiesis and Cognition. The Realization of the Living*. Dordrecht: Reidel.

In der primatischen Evolution vollziehen sich mit dem Homo sapiens zwei Schlüssel-mutationen einer eigentlich maschinellen Entwicklung [...]. Die erste ist charakteristisch für archaische Gesellschaften. Die Kultur taucht auf. Als generativer Speicher, der die Regeln der sozialen Organisation bewahrt, ist sie die reproduktive Quelle von Wissen, Know-how und Verhaltensprogrammen; d.h. die begriffliche Sprache ermöglicht eine prinzipiell unbegrenzte Kommunikation zwischen Individuen, die Mitglieder derselben Gesellschaft sind. Nun ist diese Sprache – und das ist unbemerkt geblieben, weil sie unsichtbar und scheinbar immateriell ist – eine echte Maschine, die natürlich nur funktioniert, wenn es einen Sprecher gibt. [...] Tatsächlich produziert die Sprachmaschine Worte, Äußerungen, Sinn, die ihrerseits in die anthropo-soziale Praxis eingreifen und dort Handlungen und Leistungen hervorrufen. Diese Sprachmaschine verbindet zwei schöpferische Eigenschaften: die nahezu unbegrenzte Schaffung (*poiesis*) von Äußerungen und die nahezu unbegrenzte Übertragung/Reproduktion von Botschaften. Sie ist sowohl eine repetitive als auch eine poietische Maschine. Daher kann man sagen, die große Revolution der Hominisation sei nicht nur die Kultur, sondern auch die Bildung dieser Maschine-Sprache, welche sich durch ihre hochkomplexe Organisation (einer doppelt phonetisch/semantischen Artikulation) vollständig mit der anthropo-sozialen Maschine und all ihren Kommunikations- und Organisationsprozessen verzahnt, [...] und für deren weiteren Entwicklungen notwendig wird.[39]

So gelangt Morin mittels einer kosmologischen Erklärung zu einer Theorie, mit der er soziale und kulturelle Phänomene erklärend in den größeren Kontext des Universums einbetten kann. Es ist daher nicht überraschend, dass Morins Gesellschaftstheorie eine Theorie der Emergenz ist. Es sei aber daran erinnert, dass Morins Ansatz geradezu konträr zu den meisten aus der Philosophie bekannten Emergenztheorien angelegt ist: es sind bei ihm eben nicht komplexere Eigenschaften, die aus einfacheren Strukturen hervorgehen, sondern vielmehr einfachere Strukturen, die aus komplexeren Strukturen hervorgehen.[40] In diesem Sinne kann das Individuum komplexer sein als die Gesellschaft. Und dennoch gibt es eine stufenweise Entwicklung, die von ›unten‹ nach ›oben‹ verläuft. Dieses Aufsteigen wird immer durch die basale Komplexität der zugrunde-liegenden Ebene ermöglicht: von einem Individuum zu einer Familie, von der Familie zu einem Dorf, und so weiter. Man kann sagen, dass Morin eine Art umgekehrte Dialektik betreibt, in dem Sinne, dass er die Entwicklung von Synthesen aus Gegen-

---

39   Morin: *La Méthode 1*, S. 167.

40   Aus der logischen Erwägung heraus, dass in Morins zugrundeliegender *Konstitutions*ebene die weiteren Entfaltungsmöglichkeiten der aus ihnen entstehenden *Derivations*ebenen schon immer ontologisch *angelegt* sein müssen, würde es sogar Sinn machen, seine Theorie eher als eine ›Emanations‹- oder als eine ›Supervenienztheorie‹ zu bezeichnen. Vgl. Beckermann Ansgar (1992): Supervenience, Emergence, and Reduction. In: Posner (ed.): *Emergence or Reduction? Essays on the Prospects of Nonreductive Physicalism.* Berlin: De Gruyter, S. 94–119.

sätzen nachzeichnet. Und dies passt gut zu der biographischen Notiz, nach der Morins philosophische Neugier aus seiner Lektüre der Werke Hegels entstand, dessen Grundansätze sich überall in Morins Werk wiederfinden:

> [...] jeder Mensch trägt, wie der singuläre Punkt eines Hologramms, den Kosmos in sich. Man könnte auch sagen, dass jedes Individuum, selbst jenes, welches am meisten auf schier banales, organisches Leben reduziert wird, in sich selbst einen Kosmos bildet. [...]. Individuelle Einheit erzeugt eine Dualität und knüpft eine Vielheit. Das Eine trägt in sich tatsächlich Andersartigkeit, [...], Negativität, Antagonismen. Wie Hegel sagte, ist Identität die Vereinigung von Identität und Nichtidentität.[41]

IV. Eine Theorie der Gesellschaft

Diese Ansicht ist ein guter Ausgangspunkt, um Morin's Gesellschaftstheorie näher zu skizzieren. Sie ermöglicht es Morin, die Besonderheiten eines sozialen Phänomens als ein ›für sich‹ (*pour soi*) zu behalten, auch wenn dieses Phänomen nur das Produkt eines grundlegenderen Prozesses ist. So führt Morin niemals die Existenz von Überstrukturen wie dem Staat oder der Spezies als Grund an, um den Handlungsspielraum von Entitäten auf niedrigeren Ebenen zu verneinen – wie es deterministische Sozialtheorien oft tun. In diesem Sinne bewahrt Morins Soziologie sorgfältig eine Theorie des Subjekts. Seine Emergenztheorie besteht nämlich gerade darin, dass er die Konzeption der Gesellschaft aus der Konzeption des Individuums entwickelt:

> Was Gesellschaften von Organismen unterscheidet, ist nicht die Arbeitsteilung, die Spezialisierung, die Hierarchie oder die Informationsvermittlung, die es bei den einen wie bei den anderen gibt, sondern die Komplexität der Individuen. Eine Gesellschaft braucht hochentwickelte Individuen.[42]

Obwohl für Morin also das Individuum als methodologische Einheit auf der Mesoebene zwischen Makrostrukturen wie der Gesellschaft und Mikrostrukturen wie der Biologie seines Gehirns angesiedelt ist und potenziell unter erstere subsumiert oder auf letztere reduziert werden kann, bedeutet dies nicht, dass das Individuum als vollständig von einer dieser Ebenen *bestimmt* angesehen werden sollte: »Subjekt-Sein heißt, sich nicht nur zum Zwecke der Erkenntnis, sondern auch zum Zwecke der Handlung in das Zentrum der je eigenen Welt zu stellen.«[43] Morin schreibt dem Individuum hier eine

---

41   Morin: *La Méthode 5*, S. 104. Zu Morins Hegellektüre, siehe Lemieux: *L'indiscipliné*, S. 152–153.
42   Morin: *La Méthode 5*, S. 184.
43   Morin: *La Méthode 5*, S. 78.

Sphäre der Freiheit (»Autonomie-Abhängigkeit«[44]) zu, die durch die biologisch-untergeordnete und die sozial-übergeordnete Ebene sowohl ermöglicht als auch eingeschränkt wird. Das Individuum wird als Träger unabhängiger Handlungen betrachtet, es bildet autonome soziale Beziehungen, es ist die Grundlage für die Reproduktion der Art, indem es Familienverbände und spontane soziale Strukturen auf der Mesoebene schafft, und es kann nun seinerseits auf die Gesellschaft zurückwirken, die ihrerseits nur durch die Vielzahl individueller Handlungen in ihrer Komplexität ermöglicht wird:

> Innerhalb jeder Gesellschaft ist jedes Individuum sowohl ein egozentrisches Subjekt als auch ein Moment/Element eines soziozentrischen Ganzen. [...]. Das Individuum ist in der Gesellschaft, die in dem Individuum ist. [...]. Individuen produzieren die Gesellschaft, die die Individuen produziert; die geistige Entstehung von Individuen bedingt die Organisation der Gesellschaft; während die Emergenz eines jeden individuellen Geistes wiederum von eben jener sozialen Organisation abhängig ist.[45]

Diese Theorie des Subjekts impliziert ontologische, aber ebenso epistemologische und normative Annahmen. Schauen wir zunächst in Morins Sozialontologie. Wir haben gesehen, dass für Morin alles, was sozial existiert, entweder auf zugrunde liegende ontologische Strukturen (Emotionen, Gehirn, Körper) zurückgeführt oder in höheren ontologischen Strukturen (Familie, Gemeinschaft, Gesellschaft, Spezies) aufgelöst werden kann, seine Autonomie und Existenz aber gerade aufgrund seiner ontologischen »Einbettung« [*encastrement*] in angrenzende Strukturen behält. Wie wir bereits in Bezug auf die Rolle, die die Sprache für Morins Evolutionstheorie spielt, angedeutet haben, ist diese *Unabhängigkeit-von-der-Abhängigkeit* [*indépendence-co-dépendence*] im Fall der Kultur, die von Morin als die ontologisch tiefste Quelle jeder Entwicklung des Individuums identifiziert wird, besonders deutlich zu erkennen:

> Kultur ist die wichtigste Emergenz, die der menschlichen Gesellschaft eigen ist. Jede Kultur konzentriert in sich ein doppeltes Kapital: einerseits ein kognitives und technisches Kapital (Praktiken, Wissen, Know-how, Regeln); andererseits ein mythologisches und rituelles Kapital (Überzeugungen, Normen, [...]). Es ist ein Gedächtnis- und Organisationskapital, wie es das genetische Erbe für das Individuum ist. Die Kultur verfügt wie das genetische Erbe über eine eigene Sprache [...], die das Erinnern, die Kommunikation und die Weitergabe dieses Kapitals von Individuum zu Individuum und von Generation zu Generation ermöglicht. [...]. Die Kultur gibt Form und Norm vor.

---

44   Morin: *La Méthode 5*, S. 321.

45   Im Original ist die Verschränkung umgedreht : »Des individus produisent la société qui produit les individus ; l'émergence sociale dépend de l'organisation mentale des individus, mais l'émergence mentale dépend de l'organisation sociale.« Morin: *La méthode 5*, S. 190–191.

Von Geburt an beginnt der Einzelne, das kulturelle Erbe zu integrieren, das seine Bildung, seine Orientierung und seine Entwicklung als soziales Wesen sicherstellt. [...]. So unterwirft und ermächtigt die Kultur das Individuum zugleich. Kultur ist in ihrem Prinzip die generative/regenerative Quelle der Komplexität menschlicher Gesellschaften. Sie integriert die Individuen in die gesellschaftliche Komplexität und bedingt die Entwicklung ihrer jeweiligen individuellen Komplexität.[46]

Dieser Fokus auf die Generierung und Re-Generierung sozialer Beziehungen durch die Kraft der Kultur offenbart, dass Morins Sozialontologie, wie auch seine Kosmologie im Allgemeinen, radikal relational ist: alles, was existiert, existiert nur auf der Grundlage seiner Beziehungen zu anderen Entitäten, die sich ihrerseits durch ihre Beziehungen definieren.[47] Aber woher kommen diese Relationen, und woher kommen die Entitäten selbst, die miteinander verbunden werden können? Morins Kosmologie hat uns bereits gezeigt, dass er sich jeder Metaphysik widersetzt, die ahistorische Substanzen postuliert, und dass er sich ontologischen Fragen eher durch Prinzipien der Onto*genese* als durch Prinzipien der Hypo*stase* nähert, also eher durch das Bild des ewigen Strudels als durch das eines ewigen Seins. So lokalisiert Morin sowohl den Ursprung der Beziehung als auch den Ursprung der verbundenen Entität in der Kategorie des »Ereignisses«:

[...] die Identität der Spezies reinkarniert sich durch die unterschiedlichen oder sogar divergierenden Geschichten der Individuen. Weder die Spezies verleiht dem Individuum Existenz, noch das Individuum der Spezies: Sie verleihen sich gegenseitig Existenz durch Neubeginn, Wiederholung, Reproduktion. [...]. Wir befinden uns in einer Art analogem oder mimetischem Wieder-Spiel [*re-jeu*] dessen, was bereits gespielt wurde. [...]. Der ontogenetische Prozess kann als Wiederholung des bereits Erlebten aufgefasst werden, als Reproduktion eines Organismus nach dem Vorbild des erzeugenden Organismus, der seinerseits ein Abbild war, etc. [...]. Unser mentales Erinnern und das generative Wiedererinnern sind beide Produzenten eines Doppels [*d'un double*], aber im ersten Fall ist dieses Doppelte imaginär, im zweiten Fall ist es wiederum ein Akt, ein Produkt, ein reales Wesen. Im einen wie im anderen Fall ist das Eingeschriebene nicht eine ›Tatsache‹, sondern vielmehr ist dessen Repräsentation – sein Bild, sein Modell – ein Zeichen, eine ›Stenografie‹, eine Markierung, die an das Ereignis erinnert. Unser Gehirngedächtnis speichert keine Wahrnehmungen, sondern engrammiert Zeichen, die mit anderen Gedächtniseinträgen in Verbindung stehen und an andere Ereignisse erinnern. [...] Diese Erinnerung ist eine imaginäre Wiederauferstehung [...] des erinnerten Ereignisses [...].[48]

---

46   Morin: *La Méthode 5*, S. 189.
47   Vgl. Morin: *La Méthode 5*, S. 238–239.
48   Morin: *La Méthode 1*, S. 329–330.

Nicht nur die individuelle Identität, sondern Morins gesamte soziale Ontologie besteht somit aus den Grundkategorien ›Ereignis‹ und ›Beziehung‹. Aus diesen Entitäten, die durch Wirbel-Regeneratoren [tourbillons-régénérateurs] (oder »Auto-Öko-Reorganisatoren«[49], wie Morin sie auch nennt) selbstreproduzierend sind, ergibt sich das Netzwerk sozialer Strukturen, die sich gegenseitig ihre Existenz verdanken und die in verschiedene Analysekategorien (Mikro-, Meso-, Makroebene) eingeordnet werden können. So ist Morins Emergenztheorie der Gesellschaft auch eine Rückkopplungstheorie: soziale Einheiten gehen aus den ihnen zugrunde liegenden Strukturen hervor und bilden ihrerseits die Basis, auf der andere, höhere Strukturen entstehen können; sie sind aber auch untereinander verbunden. Ein Ereignis auf einer Ebene wird daher zwangsläufig Auswirkungen auf Ereignisse auf darunter oder darüber liegenden Ebenen haben. Morin, der sehr wohl gesehen hat, dass der logische Kern einer ›reinen‹ Emergenztheorie nicht ohne die Hilfe anderer Prämissen die ontologische Autonomie oder Stabilität eines isolierten Dings erklären kann, hat daher sein Konzept des Emergenzphänomens von Anfang an auf diese nuancierte Weise definiert: nämlich nicht als ein einfaches Epiphänomen, sondern als einen rückwirkenden Effekt, der in eine rekursive Schleife [boucle] mit der Struktur eingebunden ist, die ihn hervorgebracht hat. Es zeigt sich also, dass, obwohl die Kategorie der rückwirkenden Emergenz analytisch in zwei Elemente zerlegt werden kann, es für Morin sinnvoll ist, Emergenz und Rückwirkung in diesem Bild der Rekursivität zu synthetisieren. Dies verstärkt auch Morins grundlegende Tendenz, seine Ontologie als ein »Netzwerk«[50] von Ereignissen in zirkulierenden Schleifen zu begreifen, in dem das Ganze grundsätzlich im Teil enthalten ist und alle Teile zusammen das Ganze bilden. Es ist ganz im Sinne Blaise Pascals, der Morin, neben Hegel, wie kein anderer Denker geprägt hat:

> Da also alle Dinge verursacht und verursachend, erhalten und erhaltend, vermittelt und vermittelnd sind und alle durch ein natürliches und unmerkliches Band miteinander in Verbindung stehen, welches die entferntesten und verschiedensten verbindet, halte ich es für unmöglich, die Teile zu kennen, ohne das Ganze zu kennen, ebenso wie das Ganze zu kennen, ohne die Teile zu kennen.[51]

Schließlich ist es also diese Verbindung der Teile in einem Ganzen und des Ganzen in einem Teil (welche Morin »hologrammatisches Prinzip« nennt) noch mehr als die ›reine‹ Emergenz, die der autonomen Existenz jeder sozialen Einheit zugrunde liegt: denn die Emergenz des Individuums aus der Biologie und die Emergenz der Gesell-

---

49	Morin: Pour une crisologie, S. 155.
50	So zumindest die Interpretation Éric Letonturiers, vgl. Letonturier (2011): Réseau, Communication et Complexité. In: *Hermès*, 60/2, S. 106.
51	Pascal (1977 [1670]): *Pensées*, Paris: Gallimard, Fragment 185, S. 159.

schaften aus der Masse der Individuen erklären allein nicht, warum biologische, subjektive und soziale Einheiten als autonome Akteure betrachtet werden müssen. Erst die wechselseitigen Auswirkungen und Rückkopplungen der Ebenen in einer Schleife stabilisieren sie in ihrer Autonomie und ermöglichen »die Rückkopplung der auf der höheren Ebene erworbenen Emergenzen auf die niedrigeren Ebenen«[52] und umgekehrt:

> So produziert sich die Gesellschaft selbst aus der biologischen Reproduktion, die sich wiederum selbst nach soziologischer Norm reproduziert. Hier wird die Komplexität der gesellschaftlichen Selbstorganisation verständlich: Sie hat sich durch ihre Beziehung zu den beiden anderen Selbstorganisationen der menschlichen Trinität [Individuum & Spezies] selbst hervorgebracht und regeneriert. Die drei trinitarischen Instanzen – Individuum, Spezies, Gesellschaft – sind untrennbar miteinander verzahnt wie drei voneinander abhängige Räder einer trinitarischen Polyorganisation, und sie generieren sich gegenseitig. Das soziale Band ist nicht das Produkt eines mythischen Vertrags oder eines rein physischen Zwangs. Es ist das Produkt der trinitarischen Schleife.[53]

Allerdings kann die Zirkulation der Auswirkungen von Ereignissen durch verschiedene Sphären des biologischen und sozialen Seins dessen Existenz auch genauso destabilisieren, wie es sie prinzipiell ontologisch stabilisiert. Wenn zum Beispiel das Ereignis einer politischen Entscheidung, sagen wir, einen Krieg oder eine Wirtschaftskrise hervorbringt, kann diese emergierte soziale Sphäre, die die Politik ist und die normalerweise durch ihre ontologische Autonomie andere Sphären intra-stabilisiert, andere Sphären auch gefährden: und zwar im Falle des Krieges oder einer Umweltkatastrophe bis zum Äußersten: bis zur biologischen Grundstruktur. Der Einfluss der Kybernetik auf Morins Denken zeigt sich sehr deutlich in diesem ständigen Beharren auf *feedback loops*.[54] Fast könnte man Edgar Morins »komplexes Denken« auch als ›hegelianische Kybernetik‹ oder als ›kybernetischen Hegelianismus‹ bezeichnen.[55]

---

52 Morin: *La Méthode 5*, S. 216.
53 »[…] le produit de la boucle trinitaire«, Morin: *La méthode 5*, S. 194–195.
54 Vgl. die ursprüngliche Formulierung der kybernetischen Grundidee in Rosenblueth/ Wiener/ Bigelow (1943): Behavior, Purpose and Teleology. In: *Philosophy of Science* 10/1, S. 21.
55 Diese Interpretation gewinnt zumindest ideengeschichtlich an Schärfe, wenn man in Betracht zieht, dass Morin selbst die Kybernetik Norbert Wieners als eine Art (hegelianische) Konter-Revolution der Teleologie gegen den reinen Behaviorismus sah: »Wiener's Rehabilitation des Zwecks konnte als eine epistemologische Revolution gegenüber dem Behaviorismus (Piaget) angesehen werden. Mehr noch, sie lässt uns verstehen, dass die Geistes- und Sozialwissenschaften sich an die Idee des Zwecks klammerten (Comte, Marx, Tönnies usw.), nicht weil sie im Vergleich zu den Naturwissenschaften rückständig waren, sondern weil die Ausrottung jeglichen Zwecks ihren Gegenstand unverständlich machte. […]. Der Fortschritt der Wissenschaften vom Leben und vom Menschen kann und darf nicht in der Reduktion des Seins auf

Wir haben bereits erwähnt, dass Morins Theorie des Subjekts nicht nur seine grundlegenden ontologischen Annahmen offenlegt, sondern auch epistemologische und normative Konsequenzen hat. Denn indem Morin die subjektive Freiheit in eine Sphäre zwischen verschiedenen gesellschaftlichen Maßstäben einordnet, vermeidet er einerseits die notorische Debatte zwischen einem methodologischen Holismus und einem methodologischen Individualismus und eröffnet andererseits die Möglichkeit einer soziologisch begründeten Individualethik. Fokussieren wir uns zunächst auf die methodologische Ebene, um dann auf ihre normativen Konsequenzen eingehen zu können.

Die Überwindung eines Schismas zwischen Holismus und Individualismus ergibt sich bereits aus Morins Dialektik selbst, da ein solcher Ansatz natürlich in der Lage ist, diese beiden Positionen einfach in eine noch umfassendere Darstellung zu integrieren. So verweist Morin einerseits gegen einen einseitigen Holismus auf konkrete historische Ereignisse, bei denen die spezifischen Entscheidungen der Individuen, ihre Emotionen oder ihr Charakter einen entscheidenden Einfluss auf die Entwicklung der historischen Prozesse hatten. Eines von Morins Lieblingsbeispielen in diesem Zusammenhang ist die dreifache Kombination aus Wetterfaktoren, Informationen der Geheimdienste und konkreten Entscheidungen einer kleinen Anzahl von Militärs und Politikern, die es Stalin im Winter 1941/42 ermöglichte, die von Hitler gestartete Offensive nicht nur zu stoppen, sondern die Wehrmacht in den folgenden Jahren sogar vernichtend zu schlagen.[56]

Gegen einen einfachen Individualismus auf der anderen Seite betont Morin die Vielzahl struktureller Gegebenheiten, die das menschliche Verhalten bedingen und vorstrukturieren und die es aus einer soziologischen Perspektive oft irrelevant machen, ob eine bestimmte soziale Handlung vom Individuum x oder vom Individuum y ausgeführt wurde. Hier bezieht sich Morin nicht nur aktiv auf Marx' Konzept des »generischen Menschen«, sondern auch auf die Tatsache, dass viele soziale Prozesse und sogar individuelle Leidenschaften und Irrationalitäten durch biologische Prädispositionen erklärt werden können und einfach als Aggregat für die soziologische Erklärung ohne Kenntnis bestimmter individueller Details vorausgesetzt werden können:

> Der Begriff ›generisch‹ geht hier über den Begriff ›genetisch‹ hinaus und schließt ihn ein. Er bezieht sich auf die generative und regenerative Quelle des Menschen, diesseits und jenseits von Spezialisierungen, Abgrenzungen und Unterteilungen. Das gleiche

---

Verhalten (behavior) und dann in der Reduktion des Verhaltens auf eine äußere Kausalität erfolgen.« Morin: *La Méthode 1*, 267.

56   Morin: *La Méthode 5*, S. 240.

Erbgut der Art ist allen Menschen gemeinsam und gewährleistet alle [...] Merkmale der Einheit [...].[57]

Dies ermöglicht es laut Morin, Gesellschaften, Gemeinschaften, Gruppen, soziale Interaktionen und Prozesse als Aggregate zu betrachten und zu untersuchen, ohne diese Aggregate jedes Mal in ihre einzelnen Teile zerlegen zu müssen.[58] Im Vergleich zu konkreten, in Raum und Zeit begrenzten Fallstudien wird somit auch umfassenden soziologischen Verallgemeinerungen eine gewisse Allgemeingültigkeit zugesprochen:

> Das Leben und [...] die Gesellschaft sind ungeheure Konstruktionen von Ereignissen, sie sind [...] Paläste, die aus Strudeln von Ereignissen gemacht sind. Aus all dem entstehen die Ordnung des Lebens und [...] die biologischen Gesetze. Und tatsächlich kann man von [...] demografischen, ökologischen [und] [...] behavioralen Gesetzen sprechen. Die menschlichen Gesellschaften wiederum, die ebenfalls von der Textur her ereignisorientiert sind, gehorchen nicht nur soziologischen Gesetzen, sondern bringen erneut Gesetze hervor, denen sie gehrochen müssen. So sehen wir, wie sich etwas Bemerkenswertes herauskristallisiert: Generative Information erzeugt ›nur‹ Ereignis, aber verwandelt es in Ordnung und Organisation, ohne dass es aufhört, Ereignis zu sein.[59]

Individuen und konkrete Zufälle können demnach die spezifische Form, die die soziale Ordnung annimmt, maßgeblich beeinflussen und müssen eingehend untersucht werden, wenn diese spezifische Form aus Forschungssicht relevant ist. Indem Morin nun die Behauptung sowohl individualistischer als auch holistischer Ansätze, sie könnten das Ganze des Sozialen allein erklären, zurückweist und stattdessen beide Ansätze miteinander koppelt, verortet er sich aber als Denker, der die sozialen Gesetze als historisch kontingent und gleichzeitig als gültig anerkennt:

> Obwohl die Geschichte ihre Determinationen und ihre Logik hat, ist sie auch irrational, weil sie Lärm und Wut, Unordnung und Zerstörung mit sich bringt. Wir müssen Marx und Shakespeare zusammenbringen. In der Tat haben die griechischen Tragiker, die Elisabethaner und insbesondere Shakespeare gezeigt, dass die Tragödien der Macht nichts anderes als Tragödien der menschlichen Leidenschaft, der Unbewusstheit und der Maßlosigkeit sind.[60]

---

57 Morin: *La Méthode 5*, S. 63.
58 Vgl. Morin (2007): *Sociologie.* Paris: Fayard, 8–12.
59 Morin: *La Méthode 1*, S. 333.
60 Morin: *La Méthode 5*, S. 257.

Dies ist ein ehrgeiziges epistemologisches Programm. Auf der einen Seite wird hier der Anspruch von Prognosefähigkeit hinter den Anspruch einer ›erklärenden Beschreibung‹ eines Phänomens zurückgestellt, auf der anderen Seite behält sich das ›komplexe Denken‹ einen antirelativistischen, naturalistischen Realismus vor, der einen fundamentalen Erkenntnisanspruch auf die Grundprinzipien des Kosmos formuliert. Natürlich hängt genau dieser Anspruch nun davon ab, was Morin eigentlich darunter versteht, etwas zu ›erklären‹. Dies bedeutet für ihn eben nicht, die Bedingungen zu spezifizieren, unter denen man die Bewegung eines Objekts vorhersagen kann. Im Gegenteil, ›erklären‹ bedeutet, für Morin, die Prinzipien kennen zu lernen, die ein Phänomen beherrschen. Und erneut ist Morin's Hauptprinzip im Begriff der »Schleife« zusammengefasst:

> Die Idee der Schleife [*boucle*] trägt in sich das Prinzip einer weder atomistischen noch holistischen Erkenntnis [...]. Sie bedeutet, dass man nur von einer kognitiven Praxis ausgehen kann [...], welche unfruchtbare Begriffe, wenn sie disjunkt oder nur antagonistisch sind, produktiv zusammenwirken lässt. Sie bedeutet, dass jede Erklärung, anstatt reduktionistisch zu sein [...], durch ein rekursives [...] Spiel [...] gehen muss. Die Schleife tritt an die Stelle des hohlen, souveränen Begriffes [*maître-mot*] [...] sie ist eine notwendige Vermittlung, sie ist die Einladung zu einem generativen Denken. [...]. Unterhalb der Schleife gibt es keine Essenz, keine Substanz, nicht einmal das Reale: Das Reale entsteht durch die Schleife der Interaktionen, die Organisation produzieren [...]. So findet eine große Veränderung der Basis statt. Es gibt keine Ausgangsentität für Wissen mehr [...]. Es gibt ein zirkuläres Spiel, das diese Entitäten hervorbringt, die wie Momente einer Produktion erscheinen.[61]

Morin ist sich durchaus bewusst, dass ein solcher Erklärungsansatz, welcher mechanisch-kausale Elemente durch abstrakte Formprinzipien ersetzt, von klassisch-neuzeitlichen Erkenntnistheorien frontal attackiert werden kann. Andererseits ist es gerade dieses klassische Paradigma eines kausalen Mechanismus, das den Hauptgegenstand von Morins Kritik bildet: Seine Artikulation des ›komplexen Denkens‹ ist in diesem Sinne genau der Versuch, ein wissenschaftliches Paradigma zu formulieren, das den reduktionistischen Erklärungsanspruch cartesisch verstandener Naturwissenschaften zurückweisen kann, ohne in einen esoterischen Holismus einerseits oder in eine aristotelische Doktrin von der Ursache von Form und Wirkung andererseits zurückzufallen. Inwieweit dieser Versuch eines neuen erkenntnistheoretischen Paradigmas überzeugend und in der Praxis erfolgreich sein kann, ist eine spannende und relevante Frage, die von der gegenwärtigen Wissenschaftstheorie noch

---

61 Morin: *La Méthode 1*, S. 381–382.

nicht eingehend behandelt wurde.[62] Hier fehlt allerdings der Platz, um Morins Argumente einer eingehenden philosophischen Analyse zu unterziehen.

V. Eine hologrammatische Ethik der Komplexität

Eine der wichtigsten Auswirkungen seiner Gesellschaftstheorie und seines ›prinzipiellen‹ Erklärungsstils besteht nun darin, dass Morin die Begriffe, die er zur beschreibenden Erklärung sozialer und natürlicher Phänomene verwendet, in eine »teleonomische«[63] Theorie der Normen übersetzen kann, denen die Individuen in ihrem individuellen Leben, bei ihrer Bewertung sozialer Phänomene und bei ihren Versuchen, die Gesellschaft zu organisieren, folgen sollten. Dieser Zusammenhang ist offensichtlich. Wenn es beispielsweise stimmt, dass nur eine funktionierende Feedback-Schleife das Leben eines Lebewesens erhält, und wenn Lebewesen sich selbst erhalten wollen, dann folgt daraus, dass wir auch versuchen sollten, uns in funktionierenden Schleifen zu organisieren. Dies impliziert bestimmte politische und ethische Denkrichtungen. In ihnen überwindet Morin einige der Prämissen, die in der Neuzeit zu dem notorischen Problem geführt haben, wie sich das Werturteil dessen, was sein sollte, aus dem empirischen Urteil dessen, was ist, ableiten lässt. Es ist eine Richtung, die effektiv zu einer klassisch antiken Auffassung der Einheit von Normativem und Faktischem zurückführt, und so visiert es Morin selbst auch an: »Die Physis verweist zusammen mit dem Kosmos auf die Griechen zurück.«[64] Dies macht einige von Morins Argumenten über die Gesellschaft zu sowohl normativ-präskriptiven als auch empirisch-deskriptiven Ansatzpunkten.

Im sozialen Kontext, und im normativen Sinne, fungiert Komplexität so nämlich nicht nur als evolutionäre Beschreibung eines sozialen Stadiums, sondern als Ideal. Eine Gesellschaft erscheint unter der Perspektive des Morin'schen Theoriegebäudes als gut, wenn sie Komplexität zulässt, ohne von dieser Komplexität selbst erdrosselt zu werden.

62　Kurz nach Erscheinen der ersten gesellschaftstheoretischen Arbeiten Morins nehmen einige Rezensenten diese philosophischen Fragen in der Tat auch auf, vgl. Matarasso (1975): Edgar Morin ou le nouvel éloge de la folie. In: *Annales. Histoire, Sciences Sociales*, 30/1, S. 177–185; Koch (1987): Kosmos and Hodos. A Biassed Reading of Edgar Morin's ›La méthode‹ In: *Revue européenne des sciences sociales*, 75/25, S. 73–93; oder auch noch Banywesize (2007): Edgar Morin et le réenchantement des sociétés humaines. In: *Sociétés*, 98/4, 23–39. In den letzten Jahrzehnten dominiert allerdings weniger ein wissenschaftstheoretisches, sondern eher ein anwendungsorientiertes Interesse an den Arbeiten Morins, z.B. in der Ökologie, in den Kommunikationswissenschaften oder auch in den Feldern von Organisation und Management, siehe Schmitt (2021): Si Edgar Morin m'était conté : désordre, dialogique et complexité. In: *Projectics*, 30/3, S. 71–85.

63　Morin: *La Méthode 1*, S. 263.

64　Morin: *La Méthode 1*, S. 356.

Denn eine komplexe Gesellschaft zeichnet sich für Morin schlichtweg durch eine größere – und damit wünschenswertere – Vielfalt an Institutionen und eine geringere Regulierung von Handlungsnormen aus und gibt den Individuen dadurch effektiv mehr Spielraum bei der Gestaltung ihrer Lebensweise. Dies wiederum führt, so sein Argument, zu einer größeren Vielfalt an kulturellen Praktiken, die sich in das menschliche Verhalten einschreiben, dieses regenerieren können, und so der Erhaltung und Entwicklung der Spezies zugutekommen. Diese Einführung des Konzepts der sozialen Komplexität als grundlegendes politisches Ideal findet in der Mitte des fünften Teils von *La Méthode* statt, wo Morin zwischen Gesellschaften mit ›hoher‹ und ›niedriger‹ Komplexität unterscheidet:

> Gesellschaften, die dazu tendieren, [...] die Autorität des staatlichen Zentrums so weit wie möglich und in allen Bereichen durchzusetzen, sind von geringer Komplexität. Gesellschaften mit hoher Komplexität begünstigen dagegen die Pluralität des Polyzentrismus und die Spontaneität der Dezentralität. [...]. Der Fortschritt der Wissenschaften ist nicht nur mit disziplinären Spezialisierungen verbunden, sondern auch mit Überschreitungen von Spezialisierungen, mit der Aufstellung allgemeiner Theorien und mit polydisziplinären Zusammenschlüssen. Niedrige soziale Komplexität führt jedoch zu einer Disjunktion von Spezialisierung, Polykompetenz und allgemeinen Kompetenzen. Hohe Komplexität fordert ihre Verbindung. [...]. Und auf jeden Fall führt niedrige Komplexität einfacher zur Ausbeutung der Gesellschaft durch ein Machtzentrum [...]. Die hohe Komplexität lässt Antagonismus und Konkurrenz zu [...], sie toleriert Unordnung und Ungewissheit, während sie sich gleichzeitig als fähig erweist, auf Zufälle zu reagieren. Sie verteilt ihre Emergenzen rückwirkend auf alle Individuen, die wiederum die Möglichkeit haben, ihre Kontrolleure zu kontrollieren. Das bedeutet, dass hohe Komplexität individuelle Autonomie und Bürgersinn beinhaltet [...].[65]

Diese Unterscheidung mag im Lichte der Entwicklungen des 20. Jahrhunderts zunächst recht widersprüchlich erscheinen: Sind die Gesellschaft der Sowjetunion oder die heutige chinesische Staatswirtschaft ›weniger komplex‹, schlichtweg, weil sie Myriaden von sozialen Interaktionen stärker durch einen zentralen Kontrollmechanismus statt durch spontane Allokation laufen lassen? Das erscheint erst einmal nicht der Fall. Aber der Einwand lässt sich umgehen, wenn man sich vergegenwärtigt, dass Morin, wie oben erwähnt, das Konzept der sozialen Komplexität gerade nicht für eine empirische Epochendiagnose moderner Gesellschaften verwendet – denn für ihn ist Komplexität eben grundsätzlich ein Grundmerkmal *aller* Phänomene der Realität und kann daher nicht als *differentia specifica* zur Beschreibung eines ›fortgeschritteneren‹

---

65   Morin: *La Méthode 5*, S. 215–220.

gesellschaftlichen Zustands dienen. In letzterem Fall bezeichnet Komplexität, wenn sie von Morin als Attribut und nicht als Prinzip der sozialen Evolution verwendet wird, vielmehr ein normatives Ideal, das es zu erreichen gilt: eine erfolgreiche soziale Homöostase, die sich in nicht-autoritär verwalteten Gesellschaften besser einstellt als in beherrschten Gesellschaften. Auf dieser Grundlage ist es nicht verwunderlich, dass Morins Gedankengang letztlich in ein Argument für Pluralismus und eine ›offene Gesellschaft‹ mündet, wie man es von Vertretern des klassischen Liberalismus kennt:

> Hohe gesellschaftliche Komplexität fördert individuelle Autonomie: Sie begrenzt die Ausbeutung, schränkt die Unterwerfung ein, ermöglicht körperliche, geistige und seelische Freiheit und, wenn es eine Demokratie gibt, auch freie politische Entscheidungen. Diese hohe Komplexität hängt mit der Entwicklung der Kommunikation, des wirtschaftlichen und ideellen Austauschs und dem Spiel der Gegensätze zwischen Interessen, Leidenschaften und Meinungen zusammen. Daher wächst der Bereich der menschlichen Freiheit mit der Zunahme der individuellen Wahlmöglichkeiten.[66]

Morin ist keineswegs blind für mögliche Kritik an dieser Argumentation und betont die Gefahr, dass sich die Entwicklung hin zur Komplexität derart verabsolutieren kann, dass sie genau jene Rückkopplungsprozesse zwischen Individuum und Gesellschaft unterbricht und erstickt, die selbst als einzige die Lebensfähigkeit ihrer eigenen Komplexität über einen langen Zeitraum hinweg aufrechterhalten. Dies erinnert durchaus an die dialektischen Argumente von Marx und Schumpeter, nach denen es gerade der Erfolg eines wirtschaftlich liberalen Systems sein könne, der seine eigene Basis untergräbt.[67] Einige Elemente dieser (Selbst-)Kritik nähern sich so auch einem Bewusstsein für die epistemische Dimension dessen, was Georg Simmel zu Beginn des 20. Jahrhunderts als die »Tragödie der Kultur«[68] bezeichnet hatte – die Idee, nach der es gerade die Überfülle an kollektiver Kultur sein kann, die das Wissen und das Urteilsvermögen des Einzelnen erstickt:

> Es ist bekannt, […] dass sich die gegenwärtigen Entwicklungen dem menschlichen Denken und der menschlichen Weisheit entziehen. Unser Verstand ist mit der unerträglichen Komplexität der Welt überfordert. […] Geistige, emotionale und kulturelle Unterentwicklungen werden durch die wirtschaftliche Entwicklung selbst produziert. Fortschritte in der Information und im Wissen werden von einem Anstieg der Unwis-

---

66   Morin: *La Méthode 5*, S. 316.
67   Vgl. Schumpeter (1942): *Capitalism, socialism and democracy*. London: Routledge, S. 53–58.
68   Zur Einordnung dieser Denkfigur, die Morin an keiner Stelle zitiert, siehe Ritzer (2007): Georg Simmel (1858–1918), *Der Begriff und die Tragödie der Kultur* (1911). In: *KulturPoetik.*, 7/2, S. 259–270.

senheit begleitet, der auf die Zersplitterung und Kompartimentierung des Wissens zurückzuführen ist. Die Emanzipation des Einzelnen und die Bereicherung seines Privatlebens werden oft durch Atomisierung ausgeglichen [...]. Der positiv rückgekoppelte Prozess des beschleunigten Wachstums kann nur zu einem zerstörerischen Ausbruch oder zu einer Metamorphose führen. Das Problem, vor dem die Menschheit steht, ist sowohl fundamental als auch global. Nun ist das Denken, das nur das Stückwerk, das Fragmentarische, das Dekontextualisierte [...] wahrnimmt, zu jeder umfassenden und grundlegenden Konzeption unfähig.[69]

Es scheint jedoch, dass Morin, ähnlich wie Durkheim, mehr an der Frage des sozialen Zusammenhalts in fragmentierten Gesellschaften interessiert ist, und an der Interdependenz von Freiheit und Zwang, die sich aus diesen Umständen ergibt. Auf eine besondere Dialektik zwischen Wissen und Kultur, wie sie beispielsweise in Simmels Denken zu finden ist, geht Morin auch in seiner Analyse der »Noosphäre« nicht ein.[70] Stattdessen geht es – um Gerechtigkeit:

Können wir uns ein soziales Optimum vorstellen, das sowohl mehr Gemeinschaft als auch mehr Autonomie, mehr Einheit und mehr Vielfalt bietet? Was würde ein Maximum an Emergenzen (Freiheit, Kreativität) hervorbringen und ein Minimum an Einschränkungen auferlegen: O ⊃ Max E/Min C? Tatsächlich kann keine Gesellschaft alle Zwänge beseitigen [...]. Wir können nur sagen, dass die ›gute‹ Gesellschaft diejenige ist, die hohe Komplexität erzeugt und regeneriert. [...] Die Gefahren einer solchen Gesellschaft: Hohe Komplexität bringt [...] Freiheiten und Toleranzen mit sich, aber Freiheiten [...] begünstigen Antagonismen und Störungen, und ab einer bestimmten Schwelle führen Störungen [...] zu Rückschritten oder zerstören die erworbene Komplexität. Das einzige Gegenmittel zur extremen Fragilität hoher Komplexität ist das erlebte Gefühl der Solidarität, also der Gemeinschaft, zwischen den Mitgliedern einer Gesellschaft.[71]

An sich ermöglicht es diese durkheimsche Beobachtung von Morin, nach der soziale Komplexität nur dann selbsterhaltend sein kann, wenn sie sich solidarisch selbst regeneriert, eine philosophische Frage nach den Bedingungen individueller Freiheit in komplexen Gesellschaften gerade in Bezug auf Wissensorganisation aufzuwerfen. Denn Morin verortet die Schwierigkeit sozialer Komplexität nicht darin, dass sie immer

---

69 Morin: *La Méthode 5*, S. 281–283.

70 So fehlt die Frage, ob Wissenssysteme beispielsweise unter ihrer eigenen Größe kollabieren können, in den Diskussionen über die Wissenssoziologie im vierten Teil von Morins Méthode, *Les idées*, vollkommen.

71 Morin: *La Méthode 5*, 254–255.

gesteigert werden, sondern dass sie auf einem konstanten Niveau anpassungsfähig und stabil bleiben soll. Konsequenterweise sollte diese Anforderung dann auch für die Struktur von Wissen gelten. Morin selbst weist deutlich darauf hin, dass das ›Ersticken‹ von Wissen durch Wissen ein sehr reales Problem in der modernen Welt ist:

> Als ich meine Lektüre wieder aufnahm [...], ergaben sich aus diesen Lektüren neue Lektüren [...]. Die Lektüreliste wuchs noch schneller als die Liste der bereits überflogenen Bücher. Ich machte weiter, bis ich, überwältigt und erstickend, die intellektuell willkürliche, aber biologisch notwendige Entscheidung traf, mit der Bibliographie aufzuhören und mit dem Schreiben zu beginnen [...]. Ich musste bei dieser Arbeit beides erleben:
> - die bibliografische Tragödie, die in jedem Bereich, auch wenn dieser begrenzt ist, durch die exponentielle Zunahme an Wissen und Referenzen verschärft wird;
> - die Tragödie der Reflexion, die ein Jahrhundert hervorruft, in welchem die sozialen Umstände ein Hindernis für die Reflexion über Wissen darstellen
> - die Tragödie der Komplexität, die auf zwei Ebenen angesiedelt ist: der Ebene des Wissensgegenstands und der Ebene der Erkenntnisarbeit.
>
> [...]. Auf der Arbeitsebene erkennt das komplexe Denken sowohl die Unmöglichkeit als auch die Notwendigkeit einer Totalisierung, einer Vereinigung, einer Synthese. Sie muss daher auf tragische Weise nach Totalität, Einheit und Synthese streben und gleichzeitig *gegen* den Anspruch auf diese Totalität, auf diese Einheit, auf diese Synthese kämpfen, im vollen und unwiderruflichen Bewusstsein der Unvollständigkeit allen Wissens, allen Denkens und jedes Werkes. Diese dreifache Tragödie betrifft nicht nur Studenten, [...], Forscher, Akademiker; es ist die Tragödie von allem: es ist die Tragödie des modernen Wissens. [...]. Unvollständigkeit ist heute das Herzstück des modernen Bewusstseins.[72]

Auf einer persönlichen Ebene wird dieses Problem von Morin reflektiert; auf der Ebene seiner Gesellschaftstheorie ist es dahingegen abwesend. Diesen blinden Fleck kann man dem ansonsten an Themenvielfalt nicht armen Theoriegebäude Morins vorwerfen. Denn das, was Morin über den Zusammenhang zwischen Freiheit und hoher Komplexität sagt, gilt aufgrund seiner analogen Ähnlichkeit auch eindeutig für das Problem des Wissens in zeitgenössischer Informationsgesellschaften. Und für diese Widersprüchlichkeit ist Morin durchaus sehr sensibel.

---

[72] Morin: *La Méthode 3*, S. 28–29.

So rekonstruiert er, dass die Anpassungsfähigkeit komplexer Gesellschaften auf der einen Seite davon abhängt, dass ihre Arbeitsteilung sich immer weiter differenziert und so zu einem Zustand ständigen Wachstums führt; welches diese Differenzierungsprozesse letztendlich selbst stabilisiert.[73] Innerhalb dieses epistemischen Wachstums gibt es zweifellos Anhäufungen und Verdichtungen von Wissen, die gar in einzelnen Persönlichkeiten verankert sind.[74] Aber diese Wissensanhäufungen können jederzeit zerfallen. So benennt Morin klar, dass »der Zerfall archaischer Kulturen […] zum Verschwinden eines großen Teils des angesammelten Wissens«[75] beigetragen hat. Dies führt Morin zu einem besonders ausgeprägten Bewusstsein für die Fragilität der Gegenwart, und für die Möglichkeit ihres Niedergangs: »Viele erworbene Kenntnisse, Gedanken […] degenerieren, wenn sie nicht ständig regeneriert werden. Tatsächlich gibt es in der Geschichte einen enormen Verlust an erworbenem Wissen.«[76] Morin zieht daraus den Schluss, dass die Errungenschaften der Vergangenheit niemals sicher sind, sondern dass sie immer verteidigt, verstanden und erneuert werden müssen: »Wir befinden uns im Zeitalter der endgültigen Krise des linearen und notwendigen Fortschritts […]. Es besteht die Möglichkeit eines solchen Fortschritts, aber er kann nicht irreversibel sein, und jeder Fortschritt erfordert eine ständige Erneuerung.«[77] Dies wäre eine Erneuerungsbewegung bereits bestehender Rückkopplungsmechanismen zwischen Mensch, Gesellschaft und Spezies, wie sie Morin typischerweise in einer Demokratie verortet:

> Demokratie ist die kontinuierliche Erneuerung einer Rückkopplungsschleife: Bürger produzieren Demokratie, die wiederum Bürger hervorbringt. Demokratie basiert sowohl auf dem Konsens der Bürger, die ihre Spielregeln akzeptieren, als auch auf dem Konflikt von Interessen und Ideen. Die Spielregeln ermöglichen die Konfrontation von Ideen durch Wahlen und nicht durch die Anwendung von Gewalt. Demokratie stellt die Vereinigung von Einheit und Uneinigkeit dar; sie ernährt sich endemisch von Konflikten, die ihr ihre besondere Vitalität verleihen. Demokratie lebt in der Pluralität […] und muss diese Pluralität aufrechterhalten, um sich selbst zu erhalten.[78]

Somit erfordert die Aufrechterhaltung der Gesellschaft für Morin ein aktives Bewusstsein des Einzelnen. Und wiederum verfällt Morin hier nicht einem determinis-

---

73   Morin: *La Méthode 5*, S. 224.

74   Von diesem Standpunkt aus ließe sich ein Dialog mit der Wissenstheorie Jürgen Renns beginnen, vgl. Jürgen Renn (2020): *The evolution of knowledge. Rethinking science for the Anthropocene.* Princeton: Princeton University Press.

75   Morin: *La Méthode 5*, S. 251.

76   Morin: *La Méthode 5*, S. 252.

77   Morin: *La Méthode 5*, S. 253.

78   Morin: *La Méthode 5*, S. 225.

tischen Soziologismus, sondern stellt konkrete Erwartungen an das Individuum: »Das Faktum bleibt, dass das menschliche Individuum das Zentrum des Bewusstseins [...] für die Gesellschaft ist.«[79] Und so führt seine Soziologie stets zu einem Verständnis des Singulären und des Einzelnen zurück.

Genau hier aber könnte man Morins Hypothese, nach der immer eine konsistente Subsumption der gesellschaftlichen Entwicklung in der individuellen Persönlichkeit angenommen werden kann, kritisch hinterfragen. Für Morin besteht diese Annahme allein aufgrund seiner Ontologie: »So wie jeder Punkt eines Hologramms die Informationen des Ganzen enthält, von dem er Teil ist, so ist auch die Welt als Ganzes immer in jedem Einzelnen vorhanden.«[80] Hier tritt nun der blinde Fleck von Morins Theoriegebäude allerdings wieder hervor. Denn diese Verbindung zwischen der subjektiven Sphäre und der objektiven Sphäre des Sozialen könnte ja gerade von der Dialektik zwischen Wachstum und Komplexität im Bereich des individuellen Wissens und der ›Unabgeschlossenheit‹ eines jeden Werkes destabilisiert werden. Statt dies anzuerkennen, entwickelt Morin aber auf der Annahme des stabilen ›hologrammatischen‹ Zusammenhangs zwischen Individuum und Gesellschaft eine normative Theorie der Lebensführung. Auf Grundlage der vermeintlichen Korrespondenz zwischen Individuum und Spezies legt diese nahe, dass das Subjekt sein Leben nach den Prinzipien organisieren muss, für die seine Spezies es ausgestattet hat.

Und in dieser Frage der »Endzwecke« [*finalités*] zeigt sich Morin erneut überraschend klassisch. Er schreibt dem Leben einen eigenen Wert und eine eigene Gesetzlichkeit zu, die er in ›natürlichen‹ Aktivitäten wie Kunst, Literatur, Liebe oder Freundschaft sieht. Es ist die de-spiritualisierte Technik, nicht die Kumulation der Komplexität, mit der Morin zufolge das moderne Subjekt immer im Widerspruch stehen wird, weil diese – Morin folgt ganz der These Webers – die Welt einfach entzaubert, entgeistigt und einer rein sachlichen Herrschaft unterwirft, die dem Individuum keine Antwort auf die Frage bietet, *wofür* es lebt. Damit sich der moderne Mensch diesem Widerspruch stellen kann, muss er, so Morin, die besondere Rolle der Poesie erkennen, die dem Leben einen intrinsischen Wert zuschreibt. In dieser »poetologischen« Ethik wird die *Moderne* – und nicht die Komplexität – zum Hauptgegner erfolgreicher Subjektivität: »Die Prosa unserer Zivilisation, das Primat des Ökonomischen, die Invasion der zeitgesteuerten Zeit auf Kosten der natürlichen Zeit, [...] all dies regt durch Gegenwirkung den poetischen Widerstand an.«[81]

Denn »je mehr Prosa in das Leben eindringt, desto mehr reagiert die Poesie. [...]. Poetisch zu leben bedeutet, um des Lebens willen zu leben. [...]. Während der prosaische Staat immer Ziele hat, die ihm äußerlich sind, ist der poetische Staat [...] immer

---

79   Morin: *La Méthode 5*, S. 232.
80   Morin: *La Méthode 5*, S. 266.
81   Morin: *La Méthode 5*, S. 162.

sein eigener Zweck.«[82] Eine stilistische Kritik der Moderne und eine poetologische Konzeption des ›guten Lebens‹ gehen also bei Morin Hand in Hand und bieten das mikropolitische Spannungsfeld, in dem Widerstand, Abweichung und Innovation die Gesellschaft als Ganzes verändern können: »Alle Entwicklung ist die Frucht der erfolgreichen Abweichung, die das System, in dem sie entstanden ist, transformiert.«[83]

Wir könnten daher insgesamt sagen, dass Morins Gesellschaftstheorie ebenso wie seine Forderung nach ›komplexem Denken‹ zu einer individuellen Lebensethik führen, die vom Subjekt fordert, die Gesamtheit seiner Umwelt zu verstehen, zu verbinden, zu verflechten und schließlich aktive Subversionen gegen etablierte Praktiken zu wagen – nicht zuletzt auch, um diese zu regenerieren und so Handlungsweisen eines möglichen zukünftigen Lebens zu ermöglichen. In diesem Projekt offenbart sich Morin letztendlich als der Humanist, als der er sich beschreibt.

Bibliographie

Banywesize, Emmanuel (2007): Edgar Morin et le réenchantement des sociétés humaines. In: *Sociétés*, 98/4, S. 23–39.

Barthes, Roland (1980): *La chambre claire. Note sur la photographie.* Paris: Gallimard.

Beckermann, Ansgar (1992): Supervenience, Emergence, and Reduction. In: Posner Roland: *Emergence or Reduction? Essays on the Prospects of Nonreductive Physicalism.* Berlin: De Gruyter, S. 94–119.

Curvello, João J. A/ Skroferneker, Cleusa M. A (2008): A comunicação e as organizações como sistemas complexos: uma análise a partir das perspectivas de Niklas Luhmann e Edgar Morin. In: *E-Compós*, 11/3.

Deleuze, Gilles (1968): Différence et Répétition. Paris: Presses universitaires de France.

Floch, Martine (2021): L'An zéro de l'œuvre d'Edgar Morin. In: *Matériaux pour l'histoire de notre temps*, 137–138/3, S. 129–137.

Joyce, James (2020 [1939]): Finnegans wake. London: Alma Classics (Evergreen series).

Latour, Bruno/ Woolgar, Steve (1979): *Laboratory life. The construction of scientific facts.* Princeton: Princeton University Press.

Letonturier, Éric (2011): Réseau, Communication et Complexité. In: *Hermès*, 60/2, S. 105–110.

Luhmann, Niklas (1984): *Soziale Systeme. Grundriß einer allgemeinen Theorie.* Frankfurt am Main: Suhrkamp.

Matarasso, Michel (1975): Edgar Morin ou le nouvel éloge de la folie. In : *Annales. Histoire, Sciences Sociales*, 30/1, S. 177–185.

Morin, Edgar (1948): *L'Homme et la Mort.* Paris: Éditions Corrêa.

Morin, Edgar (1956): *Le cinéma ou l'homme imaginaire. Essai d'anthropologie sociologique*, Paris: Les Éditions de Minuit.

---

82 Morin: *La Méthode 5*, S. 162.
83 Morin: *La Méthode 5*, S. 245.

Morin, Edgar (1957): *Les stars*. Paris: Editions du Seuil.

Morin, Edgar (1967): *Commune en France. La métamorphose de Plodémet*, Paris, Fayard.

Morin, Edgar (1968): La communauté étudiante. In : Morin, Edgar/ Lefort, Claude/ Castoriadis, Cornelius (2008): *Mai 68. La brèche : suivi de Vingt ans après*. Paris: Fayard, S. 13–41.

Morin, Edgar (1970): *Journal de Californie*. Paris: Editions du Seuil.

Morin, Edgar (1973): *Le paradigme perdu. La nature humaine*. Paris: Points.

Morin, Edgar (1976): Pour une crisologie. In: *Communications*, 25/1, 1976, S. 149–163.

Morin, Edgar (1977): *La Méthode 1. La nature de la nature*, Paris: Seuil.

Morin Edgar (1986): *La Méthode 3. La connaissance de la connaissance*. Paris: Seuil.

Morin, Edgar (1990): *Introduction à la pensée complexe*. Paris: Points.

Morin, Edgar (1991): *La Méthode 4. Les idées, Leur habitat, leur vie, leurs moeurs, leur organisation*. Paris: Seuil.

Morin, Edgar (2001): *La Méthode 5. L'humanité de l'humanité*, Paris: Seuil.

Morin, Edgar (2007): *Sociologie*. Paris: Fayard.

Morin, Edgar/ Wolton Dominique (2011): Grand entretien. In: *Hermès*, 60/2, S. 241–254.

Haff, Peter (2014): Humans and technology in the Anthropocene: Six rules. In: *The Anthropocene Review*, 1/2.

Lemieux, Emmanuel (2009): *Edgar Morin. L'indiscipliné*, Paris: Seuil.

Kauppi, Niilo (1990): *Tel Quel. La constitution sociale d'une avant-garde*. Helsinki: Societa Scientiarum Fennica.

Koch, Walter A (1987): Kosmos and Hodos. A Biassed Reading of Edgar Morin's ›La méthode‹. In: *Revue européenne des sciences sociales*, 75/25, S. 73–93.

Renn, Jürgen (2020): *The evolution of knowledge. Rethinking science for the Anthropocene*, Princeton: Princeton University Press.

Rosenblueth, Arturo/ Wiener, Norbert/ Bigelow, Julian: Behavior, Purpose and Teleology. In: *Philosophy of Science*, 10/1, S. 18–24.

Ritzer, Monika (2007): Georg Simmel (1858–1918), *Der Begriff und die Tragödie der Kultur* (1911). In: *KulturPoetik.*, 7/2, 2007, S. 259–270.

Pascal, Blaise (1977 [1760]: *Pensées*. Paris: Gallimard.

Schmitt, Christophe (2021): Si Edgar Morin m'était conté: désordre, dialogique et complexité. In: *Projectics / Proyéctica / Projectique*, 30/3, S. 71–85.

Schumpeter, Joseph (2010 [1942]: *Capitalism, socialism and democracy*, London: Routledge.

Vernadsky, Vladimir (1945): The Biosphere and the Noosphere. In: *American Scientist*, 33/1, S. 1–12.

Astrid M. Fellner & Jonas Nesselhauf

»Populäre Kulturen / Popular Cultures«

Tagungsbericht zur 8. Jahrestagung der Kulturwissenschaftlichen Gesellschaft (KWG),
27.9.–30.09.2023, Universität des Saarlandes

Unter dem Titel »Populäre Kulturen / Popular Cultures« hatte die inzwischen achte Jahrestagung der KWG mit 44 Panels und über 150 Vorträgen die kulturwissenschaftliche Auseinandersetzung mit dem ›Popularen‹ und ›Populären‹ zum Ziel. Bezieht sich ersteres etymologisch auf ›volkstümliche‹ Artefakte und Bräuche,[1] wird zweiteres häufig quantitativ (»well liked by many people«) und/oder qualitativ (»inferior kind of work«) verstanden:[2] ›Populär‹ ist, was vielen Menschen gefällt, und was auf breites Interesse stößt, macht sich dementsprechend (ideologisch) ›verdächtig‹.[3] So lässt sich das Populäre zwar kulturhistorisch als Ergebnis der (zunehmend globalisierten) Massen- und Unterhaltungskultur auf die gesellschaftlichen und ökonomischen Umbrüche des 19. und 20. Jahrhunderts zurückführen,[4] doch wurden bspw. Erzeugnisse einer (vermeintlichen) ›Trivialliteratur‹ von den frühen geistes- und kulturwissenschaftlichen Forschungen (noch) weitgehend ignoriert.[5] Erst mit dem kritischen Bewusstsein der anglo-amerikanischen »Cultural Studies« der 1960er Jahre kam die programmatische Forderung, die ›Lücke‹ zwischen ›Hoch-‹ und ›Populärkultur‹ zu schließen (»close the gap«[6]) und Science-Fiction oder Pornographie, Comics oder Schemaliteratur, Popmusik oder Fernsehserien ebenso und mit gleicher Berechtigung in das universitäre Curriculum aufzunehmen.

---

1 Vgl. dazu etwa Thomas Hecken: »Einleitung.« In: ders. (Hrsg.): *Theorien der Populärkultur. Dreißig Positionen von Schiller bis zu den Cultural Studies.* Bielefeld 2007, S. 7–10, hier S. 7.

2 Beide Zitate stammen von Raymond Williams: *Keywords. A Vocabulary of Culture and Society.* London 1988, S. 237.

3 Vgl. exemplarisch Max Horkheimer und Theodor W. Adorno: *Dialektik der Aufklärung. Philosophische Fragmente.* Frankfurt am Main 1988, S. 168f.

4 Vgl. dazu Dominic Strinati: *An Introduction to Theories of Popular Culture. Second Edition.* London 2004, S. 5f.

5 Vgl. überblickend Peter Nusser: *Trivialliteratur.* Stuttgart 1991, S. 10f.

6 Vgl. natürlich Leslie Fiedler: »Cross the Border – Close the Gap.« In: ders.: *Collected Essays, Volume II.* New York 1971, S. 461–485.

Mit dem »Cultural Turn« und der Rezeption von Theorien des »Camp«[7] oder »Trash«[8] ist die reflektierte Beschäftigung mit dem ›Populären‹ auch in den deutschsprachigen Kulturwissenschaften heute längst keine Be- oder gar Absonderheit, sondern Normalität: Theorie und Geschichte, Narration und Ästhetik, Produktion, Distribution und Rezeption von ›populären‹ Artefakten werden mit den jeweiligen inter- und transdisziplinären Fragestellungen und Methoden völlig selbstverständlich von den Kultur-, Medien-, Kunst- und Literaturwissenschaften sowie auch den empirischen Sozialwissenschaften er- und beforscht.

Aber auch speziell innerhalb der »Cultural Studies«/Kulturwissenschaften ist die Beschäftigung mit dem ›Populären‹ von seinem Gegenstand her nicht nur interdisziplinär geprägt, sondern hochgradig international:[9] So lassen sich Mangas und Bollywood-Filme ohne das ›westliche‹ Äquivalent von Comics und der ›Traumfabrik‹ Hollywood nicht verstehen, sind jedoch ganz eigen(ständig)e Phänomene, und wirken längst interdiskursiv auf die westlichen Populärkulturen zurück. Gleichzeitig wächst die Bedeutung des ›Populären‹ nicht nur von Jahr zu Jahr, sondern findet etwa in der individuellen wie kollektiven Performativität (Cosplay, Live Action Rollenspiele etc.) und dem digitalen Raum (mit Social Media Apps wie Instagram oder TikTok, Echtzeit-Multiplayer-Spielen usw.) neue Bereiche, die von der kulturwissenschaftlichen Forschung erschlossen werden müssen.

(1) Aufbau der Konferenz

Mit diesem Themenbereich setzt die von Astrid. M. Fellner (erste Vorsitzende der KWG) und Jonas Nesselhauf (Leitung der KWG-Geschäftsstelle) organisierte Konferenz an der Universität des Saarlandes die Tradition der letzten Jahrestagungen fort, nach »B/Ordering Cultures« (Frankfurt/Oder, 2020)[10] und »Posthumanismus/Transhumanismus« (Graz, 2022)[11] den Schwerpunkt auf ein aktuelles und gesellschaftlich

---

7   Vgl. vor allem Susan Sontag: »Notes on Camp.« In: dies.: *»Against Interpretation« and Other Essays.* New York 1990, S. 275–292.

8   Vgl. etwa Keyvan Sarkhosh: »Trash, Boom, Bang: Ein Forschungsüberblick.« In: Jonas Nesselhauf und Markus Schleich (Hrsg.): *Banal, trivial, phänomenal. Spielarten des Trash.* Darmstadt 2017, S. 11–42.

9   Vgl. bspw. Astrid M. Fellner, Tetiana Ostapchuk und Bärbel Schlimbach (Hrsg.): *(Pop-)Cultures on the Move. Transnational Identifications and Cultural Exchange Between East and West.* Saarbrücken 2018.

10   Vgl. den Tagungsbericht von Maria Klessmann et al.: »Grenzen und Ordnungen aus kulturwissenschaftlicher Perspektive.« In: *Kulturwissenschaftliche Zeitschrift* 5.2 (2020), S. 1–5.

11   Vgl. den Tagungsbericht von Marietta Schmutz: »Posthumanismus. Transhumanismus. Jenseits des Menschen?« In: *Kulturwissenschaftliche Zeitschrift* 8.1 (2023), S. 138–143.

relevantes Thema zu legen, das aber zugleich substantiell an die Grundlagen des eigenen Fachs geht. So hat sich in den vergangenen Jahrzehnten unter Begriffen wie »Popular Culture Studies« oder »Pop(ulär)kulturforschung« die Beschäftigung zunächst zunehmend systematisiert und institutionalisiert: Mit der Gründung von Fachgesellschaften oder Zeitschriften, mit Lehrstühlen oder Studiengängen (vor allem in Nordamerika), mit Forschungsclustern,[12] Konferenzen oder Handbüchern[13] haben sich internationale Schwerpunkte herausgebildet, an denen sich die fünf Achsen der Jahrestagung orientierten:

(a) *Populäre Kultur(en) und Kulturtheorie:* Ein erstes Cluster mit sieben Panels verbindet Fragen des ›Populären‹ mit ›klassischen‹ Ansätzen der Kulturtheorie und trägt damit einem fruchtbaren Forschungsbereich der »Cultural Studies« entsprechende Rechnung.[14] So setzte sich bspw. ein von Bernhard Stricker (Dresden) und Martin Urschel (Mainz) organisiertes Panel mit Ludwig Wittgenstein, ein Workshop von Britta Lange (Berlin) und Carolyn Iselt (Berlin) mit Theodor W. Adorno auseinander. Ein von Karel Šima (Prag) geleitetes Panel widmete sich wiederum dezidiert der Institutionengeschichte der Popkulturforschung im östlichen Europa: Vortragende aus Serbien, Slowenien und Tschechien diskutierten vergleichend die sich nach 1989 neu ergebenden Möglichkeiten der Teilnahme und Teilhabe an den anglo-amerikanischen »Cultural Studies«, nachdem die sozial- und kulturwissenschaftliche Forschung jahrzehntelang stark in der sowjetischen Tradition der »kulturologia« stand.

(b) *Medien des Populären:* Sechs weitere Panels konnten sich medienspezifischen Untersuchungen zu Comics, illustrierten Zeitschriften, Popmusik und Film, aber auch Düften oder rezenten Phänomenen von Sprachtechnologie und -ideologie zuwenden. So fragten Lis Hansen (Hildesheim) und Dirk Hohnsträter (Hildesheim) in ihrem Schwerpunkt zu olfaktorischen Ästhetiken nach den materiellen, atmosphärischen, körperbezogenen, praxeologischen, sozialen und genderspezifischen Dimensionen von Gerüchen und Düften, deren Darstellung in literarischen Texten und Einsatz im Influencermarketing. Ein von Rita Vallentin (Frankfurt a. O.) und Miriam Lind (Mainz) organisiertes Doppelpanel nahm in gleich mehreren Vorträgen ebenso die gegenwärtigen Diskussionen zum sprachreflexiven und geschlechtersensiblen »Gendern« zum Anlass kritischer Perspektiven auf die diskursive ›Macht‹ des Sprechens, und beleuchtete neue »Missionarslinguistiken« im Kontext von Künstlicher Intelligenz aus

---

[12] Der gegenwärtige Sonderforschungsbereich »Transformationen des Populären« (SFB 1472) an der Universität Siegen knüpft an die dort seit den 1980er Jahren bestehenden medienwissenschaftlichen Schwerpunkte an.

[13] Vgl. für die deutschsprachige Forschung v.a. Hans-Otto Hügel (Hrsg.): *Handbuch Populäre Kultur. Begriffe, Theorien und Diskussionen.* Stuttgart 2003 sowie Thomas Hecken und Marcus S. Kleiner (Hrsg.): *Handbuch Popkultur.* Stuttgart 2017.

[14] Vgl. zuletzt etwa Lee Barron: *Social Theory in Popular Culture.* New York 2017 oder John Storey: *Cultural Theory and Popular Culture. An Introduction. Ninth Edition.* New York 2021.

medienlinguistischer Sicht. Ergänzt wurde dieser thematische Fokus am 28. September durch eine ausgesprochen gut besuchte Keynote von Stefan Krankenhagen (Hildesheim) im Musiksaal der Universität, die sich – anknüpfend an sein erst kürzlich erschienenes Buch[15] – mit dem Material und der Materialität des Populären beschäftigte.

(c) *Narrationen und Ästhetiken des Populären:* Darüber hinaus befassten sich sieben Panels mit den klassischen Traditionen und rezenten Möglichkeiten des ›populären‹ Erzählens, gerade auch im Hinblick auf neue mediale Entwicklungen und Technologien wie Games, Social Media oder NFTs. So diskutierten bspw. Moritz Baßler (Münster), Thomas Hecken (Siegen) und Stefan Krankenhagen (Hildesheim) über die Potentiale und Limitierungen einer Ästhetik des Populären, während das von Annette Keck (München) und Roxanne Phillips (Essen) organisierte Panel den »komischen Kasuistiken« nachging, und die von Judith Rauscher (Köln) und Maria Sulimma (Freiburg) eingeladenen Vortragenden aktuelle Forschungsansätze der »Green Popular Culture Studies« beleuchten konnten. Besonderen Anklang bei den Teilnehmer:innen fand das von Amalia Barboza (Linz) organisierte Panel »Die Stummheit der Materialien«, das im UNESCO-Weltkulturerbe Völklinger Hütte stattfand, und in den dortigen Ateliers der Hochschule für Bildende Künste Saar einen Austausch zwischen Künstler:innen und Kulturwissenschaftler:innen in Form von *lecture performances* ermöglichte.

(d) *Themen und Genres des Populären:* Gleich 16 Panels setzten sich mit der Verarbeitung von gesellschaftlich hoch aktuellen Themen in und durch die Pop(ulär)kultur auseinander – von der globalen Corona-Pandemie und Klima-Aktivismus über Queerness und Figurationen weiblicher Herrschaft bis hin zu Krieg und (De)Kolonialisierung – oder nahmen spezifisch ›populäre‹ Genres wie den Western oder den Märchenfilm in den Blick.[16] Aber auch ein Doppelpanel zu den »Popular Border Cultures« oder Vorträge zu populären Imaginationen des Posthumanen in Fernsehserie und Videospiel, zur medienvergleichenden Darstellung von ›Abfallräumen‹ oder zum Monarchischen in der populären Kultur ergänzten diesen Themenschwerpunkt um fruchtbare Perspektiven.

(e) *Globalität des Populären:* Eine weitere Dimension der »Popular Culture Studies« fokussiert sich auf die Globalität des Populären im reziproken Verhältnis zu den jeweiligen kulturellen Traditionen:[17] Der klaren Dominanz europäischer und nord-

---

15   Stefan Krankenhagen: *All these Things. Eine andere Geschichte der Popkultur.* Berlin 2021.

16   Vgl. dazu exemplarisch Sarah E. Daly (Hrsg.): *Theories of Crime through Popular Culture.* Cham 2021, Erica B. Edwards und Jennifer Esposito: *Intersectional Analysis as a Method to Analyze Popular Culture. Clarity in the Matrix.* New York 2019, Katie Milestone und Anneke Meyer: *Gender and Popular Culture. Second Edition.* Cambridge 2020 sowie Adrienne Trier-Bieniek: *Feminist Theory and Pop Culture.* Rotterdam 2015.

17   Vgl. etwa Toby Miller (Hrsg.): *The Routledge Companion to Global Popular Culture.* New York 2015 oder Kōichi Iwabuchi, Chris Berry und Eva Tsai (Hrsg.): *Routledge Handbook of East Asian Popular Culture.* New York 2016.

amerikanischer Formate stehen regionale, stark individuelle Erscheinungsformen in Musik oder Street Art, Film oder Tanz gegenüber, wobei sich ebenso fruchtbare Verbindungen und Rückwirkungen in alle Richtungen finden lassen.[18] Dies wurde auch in den sieben Panels der Tagung deutlich, deren Vortragende u.a. aus Chile, Frankreich, Großbritannien, Indien, Kanada, Marokko, Neuseeland oder den USA kamen, und die visuellen Kulturen in Südasien, koreanische oder lateinamerikanische Popkulturen oder methodische Fragen der Interkulturalität oder der Übersetzbarkeit diskutierten. So beschäftigten sich nicht nur die Themen der Panels und Vorträge mit sehr unterschiedlichen Regionen und Ländern, sondern auch insgesamt 42% der Teilnehmenden selbst reisten aus dem Ausland nach Saarbrücken an oder waren von dort aus digital zur Konferenz zugeschaltet.

(f) *Studierendensektion:* Über die Internationalität der Vortragenden hinaus konnte das Tagungsthema auch zahlreiche junge Wissenschaftler:innen ansprechen: Etwa 40% der Teilnehmenden waren Post-Docs, etwa 30% Promovierende – und ohnehin macht ja die Statusgruppe der Studierenden und Promovierenden innerhalb der KWG-Mitglieder gut ein Drittel aus. Und so war auch die Studierendensektion der Kulturwissenschaftlichen Gesellschaft auf der Jahrestagung mit zwei Panels vertreten: Am 28. September fand ein Workshop zum Thema »TikTok – cringe or crucial? Eine interaktive Annäherung an ein populäres soziales Medium« statt, am folgenden Tag ein studentisches Vernetzungstreffen. Dabei konnte die Teilnahme von interessierten Studierenden auch dieses Jahr erneut gefördert und Reise- und Übernachtungskosten durch die KWG übernommen werden.

(2) Mitgliederversammlung

Neben den Sektionstreffen, dem Austausch und der Vernetzung der KWG-Mitglieder, ist auch die Mitgliederversammlung ein fester Bestandteil einer jeden Jahrestagung. So lud der Vorstand am 29. September in den Musiksaal der Universität, um über die Aktivitäten des vergangenen Jahres zu berichten, den Finanz- und Geschäftsbericht vorzustellen, über den Verlagswechsel der *Kulturwissenschaftlichen Zeitschrift* zu informieren, und gemeinsam mit den Mitgliedern neue Vorhaben zu erarbeiten. Dazu zählten dieses Mal u.a. die Förderung des wissenschaftlichen Austausches und der Vernetzung durch einen neuen Druckkostenzuschuss für die KWG-Schriftenreihe im Transcript Verlag sowie ein erstes »Scholars at Risk«-Programm zur finanziellen und ideellen Unterstützung von kulturwissenschaftlichen Forschenden, deren Arbeit bspw.

---

18   Vgl. Ann Brooks: *Popular Culture. Global Intercultural Perspectives.* London 2014.

aufgrund von Krieg, Gewalt oder Vertreibung erschwert oder gar verunmöglicht wurde.

Daran anknüpfen soll auch die nächste Jahrestagung an der Leucorea Universität in der Lutherstadt Wittenberg vom 10. bis 12. Oktober 2024: Mit der Kulturwissenschaftlichen Gesellschaft im zehnten Jahr ihres Bestehens sind die Sektionen und Mitglieder aufgerufen, die weitere Zukunft in Workshops und Paneldiskussionen aktiv mitzugestalten.

(3) Rahmenprogramm

Wie bei jeder KWG-Jahrestagung stellt das Rahmenprogramm eine wichtige Schnittstelle zwischen dem wissenschaftlichen Teil, den Panels und Vorträgen einerseits, und der ästhetischen Praxis wie auch der Sichtbarkeit und Vermittlung an eine interessierte Öffentlichkeit andererseits dar. So konnten zwei Künstler:innen aus Los Angeles zur feierlichen Eröffnung der Konferenz am 27. September in der Aula der Universität des Saarlandes gewonnen werden: Basierend auf dem realen Fall von Tyisha Miller (1979–1998) imaginiert die engagierte Performance »Dreamscape« von Natali Micciche und John »Faahz« Merchant in einer (Ver-)Mischung aus Beatboxing, gesprochenem Wort und Tanz das Innenleben und den Tod der jungen afroamerikanischen Myeisha Mills, die im Dezember 1998 von vier Beamten des Riverside Police Department erschossen wurde, als sie bewusstlos in einem Auto lag. Anhand von Zitaten aus dem tatsächlichen Autopsiebericht und den erschreckenden klinischen Details der zwölf Schusswunden erinnert sich Myeisha an die 19 Jahre ihres Lebens, ihr Aufwachsen, ihre Hobbies oder ihre Freude am Sport. Im Anschluss an die Performance stellten sich die beiden Schauspieler:innen einer Fragerunde, bei der es zu einem regen Austausch über Polizeigewalt und institutionalisierten Rassismus in den USA kam, aber auch die Möglichkeiten von Performancekunst als ästhetisches Medium der kritischen Reflexion und der interkulturellen Vermittlung besprochen werden konnten.

Im Anschluss an die Mitgliederversammlung fanden dann am 29. September im Saarbrücker Osthafen gleich zwei breit sichtbare Events statt: Zunächst eröffnete John »Faahz« Merchant den Abend mit einer Performance aus wort- und klangstarkem Beatboxing sowie vor allem aber auch interaktiven Mitmach-Aktionen für das zahlreich anwesende Publikum, das über gemeinschaftliche Laut- und Vokalübungen an die Kunstform herangeführt wurde und in Erläuterungen kulturhistorische wie auch biographische Hintergründe über den Musikstil und dessen politisch-gesellschaftliche Bedeutung in den USA erfahren konnte. Daran schloss sich eine Podiumsdiskussion zum Thema »Popkultur im Saarland: Kulturräume auf dem Weg aus der Peripherie ins Zentrum« an: Dabei diskutierten der Oberbürgermeister der Stadt Saarbrücken, Uwe Conradt, der Intendant des Saarländischen Rundfunks, Martin Grasmück, das Vorstandsmitglied des PopRats Saarland e.V. und früherer Generaldirektor des UNESCO Weltkulturerbes Völklinger Hütte, Meinrad Maria Grewenig, sowie Nil Berber, Abteilungsleiterin im Ministerium für Bildung und Kultur Saarland und Kathy Zorn von der Kulturgut Ost GmbH.

Das Organisationsteam bedankt sich bei der Deutschen Forschungsgemeinschaft (DFG) für die Förderung der Reisekosten für promovierte ausländische Teilnehmer:innen sowie beim Internationalisierungsausschuss der Universität des Saarlandes, beim Deutsch Amerikanischen Institut (DAI) Saarland und der US-amerikanischen Botschaft für die finanzielle Unterstützung des Rahmenprogramms.

Das vollständige Programmheft, das Abstractbook sowie Fotos und Informationen zum Rahmenprogramm finden sich auf der Konferenzseite unter https://kwg-ev.org/populaere-kulturen-2023.